THE SEDUCER'S DIARY ■ ANDRAS NAGY

A simple love story that by degrees turns dark and complex,
as the protagonist sets out to prove – or not – the existence
of God by deliberately embarking on a course of seduction.
Loosely based on the autobiographical writings of the
Danish philosopher Kierkegaard, this is Nagy's
best-received play so far.

UNSENT LETTERS ■ ANDOR SZILAGYI

A man and a woman – Angelus and Angelina – meet at
a railway station, fall in love and part, thinking they'll never
meet again. But the play shows them meeting again and
again, though always in a different time. Funny, enigmatic
and poignant, *Unsent Letters* plays with the idea of the many
missed opportunities in life.

MULLER'S DANCERS ■ AKOS NEMETH

Müller has deserted the dance company he founded, and
his dancers' careers and private lives fall apart without him.
Explaining the metaphor at its heart, the play's first director
commented; 'For forty years we [in Hungary] had been held
tightly by the hand – and it was comfortable. Now they let
go, and we all feel confused . . . '

EVERYWOMAN ■ PETER KARPATI

This modern retelling of the medieval Everyman story, set
in Budapest today, covers the last day in the life of a
middle-aged woman who learns she has cancer. Her
attempts to arrange everything before she dies serve to
reveal her whole history . . .

D1475064

Other volumes in the International Collection

HUNGARIAN PLAYS

NEW DRAMA FROM HUNGARY

THE SEDUCER'S DIARY ANDRAS NAGY
English version by Julian Garner

UNSENT LETTERS ANDOR SZILAGYI
Translated by Ildikó Patthy

MULLER'S DANCERS AKOS NEMETH
English version by Daniel Mornin

EVERYWOMAN PETER KARPATI
English version by Jack Bradley

Selected and introduced by

László Upor

THE INTERNATIONAL COLLECTION

NICK HERN BOOKS
London
in association with

Hungarian Plays first published in Great Britain in 1996 as an original paperback by Nick Hern Books Limited, 14 Larden Road, London W3 7ST

The Seducer's Diary © 1996 Andras Nagy
English version © 1996 Julian Garner
Unsent Letters © 1996 Andor Szilagyi
Translation © Ildikó Patthy
Muller's Dances © 1996 Akos Nemeth
English version © 1996 Daniel Mornin
Everywoman © 1996 Peter Karpati
English version © 1996 Jack Bradley

Introduction © 1996 Laszlo Upor

The authors of the original plays and of the English versions have asserted their moral rights

Typeset by Country Setting, Woodchurch, Kent TN26 3TB
Printed and bound in Great Britain by Athenaeum Press Ltd.,
Gateshead, Tyne & Wear

A CIP catalogue record for this book is available from the British Library

ISBN 1 85459 244 0

Contents

Acknowledgements

Thanks for financial support to

The Hungarian National Cultural Fund
The British Council in Hungary
The Milan Füst Foundation for Translations
The Budapest City Council
The József Eötvös Foundation
ARTISJUS Agency for Plays
Hungarian Theatre Institute

From the many people whose work was a great contribution to
this book the editor is specially grateful for their personal help to
Viveca Abrahams (representative of the British Council at the time)
and Tibor Solténszky (Brouhaha Hungary)

L.U.

Introduction

In spite of the fact that there was once a 'golden' age, when Ferenc Molnár was a regular resident on Broadway stages, while his fellow expatriate Hungarians were equally at home running large parts of Hollywood and the British film industry, Hungary has never been a theatrical powerhouse.

And, despite a current annual sale of five million tickets for theatre, opera and ballet in Hungary, this land of ten million Magyars cannot be said to boast a fertile culture of new home-grown drama: those people who choose to spend their nights out in darkened auditoriums staring at brightly lit stages do not necessarily want to see the products of their contemporary Hungarian writers' imaginations.

But, it is pointless both to recall past splendours or to lament their absence at the present. The aim of publishing a collection of contemporary Hungarian plays in translation is to demonstrate what Hungary *does* have rather than to talk of what we once had, or what we now lack. This volume attempts to provide a wide-ranging introduction to what is being written and performed in the Hungarian theatre *now*.

The Social Background

The common experience of the people (or, more precisely, the *peoples*) in this region today is that the collapse of political barriers have not solved social problems. Indeed, some problems have become even more intractable. Inequalities among people and differences in their opportunities have widened tremendously. In this age of free enterprise, while some enjoy the benefits of economic boom, many others have found themselves much less secure, and more open to exploitation. Where once the central ideology provided something against which to struggle, there is now, as the Millennium approaches, a vacuum in which no intellectual movements have appeared to guide people's thoughts.

In a nutshell, we live in a fascinating but often bewildering era, in the middle (or maybe still just at the beginning?) of a painful, though exhilarating, transition from the complicated concept of Communism to something as yet unknown. The spectacular launch of this journey, in the 1990s, was prefaced by the relatively relaxed, if rather dull, atmosphere of the 1980s, itself inseparable from the agony of fading late-Communism. Preceding that era were the somewhat stricter years of the late 1970s, which in turn succeeded the very promising reform period of the late 1960s and early 1970s. Those reform years had come about as a consequence of the post-Stalinist evolution that began in the early 1960s, after the tragic years following the bloody suppression of the '56 revolution, and so on. Indeed, Hungarians tend to believe their history has been one of constant waves of trauma and disruption.

The Theatre

Compared to the hectic pace of Hungary's history, its theatre seems almost humdrum. For nearly fifty years, since the nationalisation of theatres (and all before 1949 were private, excepting the National Theatre and the Opera), the structure has remained more or less the same.

Ninety per cent of Hungarians now have a state-run theatre less than fifty miles away. These theatres (half of them in Budapest) were mostly built around the turn of the century, and are relatively large, usually accommodating a permanent company of actors, directors, designers, etc. In spite of recent cuts – and in the fear of greater ones to come – they are as yet still relatively well funded by state and local authorities. The companies all perform in a repertory system, rotating productions.

The system had both advantages and disadvantages. In the 'socialist' decades, state subsidy allowed the companies a certain independence from commercial pressures on them to perform easy commercial material. Subsidy enabled theatres to keep ticket prices low, and – with unemployment as unknown in the theatre as in the rest of society, until recently – companies could develop creatively on long-term principles. Within the repertory system, companies could keep productions in their repertoires for many years (as long as there were still audiences for them), and actors could play a very sizeable number of roles in the same season: demanding, but certainly less of a tread-mill than the conventional theatrical 'run'.

Of course, there were drawbacks. Subsidy allowed some companies to become lazy, enabled the state to exercise political censorship to varying degrees, and – together with the generally high estimation in Hungary of notions of 'culture' – encouraged a certain disdain for popular art and entertainment.

These and other elements survived in a system that is now accepted as the norm in Hungary. Though many feel the need for the radical changes that undoubtedly will soon be faced, it would be very sad to 'throw the baby out with the bath water', an all-too-common act in many fields of Hungarian life in these years of transition.

Fringe Theatre

There has traditionally been a gulf between the secure state-subsidized companies and the volatile finances of other troupes, often leading to a definite friction between the two theatre cultures. The non-professionals (often without training) were usually denied access to the stages of major theatres. Some amateur companies turned this to their advantage, found their own voices, and drew loyal audiences who usually avoided the bigger stages. Indeed, there was a time when all that was progressive in theatre happened in these companies. Later, in the mid-1970s, the best fringe artists became part of the theatrical establishment, forming the core of a new wave, though some very important fringe companies disbanded or were banned for 'cultural-political' reasons. Nowadays, the mutual exchange between main-stream and fringe companies is an increasingly healthy one, and despite financial difficulties some new companies have even emerged in the last few years.

Hungarian Drama

In the nineteenth century, national drama and the use of Hungarian on stage were means of defining identity in the struggle for independence, in an age when the nobility spoke German, and German companies dominated the Pest theatres. Much later, the first two decades of the present century saw an exceptional abundance of premieres by contemporary Hungarian playwrights. The plays were often of only ephemeral value, but on such a breeding ground good craftsmen could provide well-made plays, and great talents, such as Molnár (1878-1952), could begin to bloom. Apart from such figures, the repertoire in Hungary has traditionally been international in emphasis. There is obviously a big demand for established international masterpieces; and Hungarian culture is a particularly receptive one to foreign influences, for geographical, linguistic and other reasons.

Such receptivity, however, has not hindered Hungarian fiction writers and poets from gaining recognition – drama seems to be something of a poor relation. In fact, there is a consensus that the Hungarian cultural heritage is written in poetry and prose, rather than in drama. It is also true that there were times when it was hard to name a single play-wright, in the sense of a writer working predominantly in the dramatic form. There have, however, always been brave warriors, led by their instincts or lured into the theatre by directors or dramaturgs, who cut their teeth on drama. Some of these left the stage after a few attempts, while others found joy in the most basic things that theatre can offer: the incarnation of their work on the stage and the fascination of immediate response from an audience.

György Spiró (b. 1946), who, some twenty years ago, at the very beginning of his career, dedicated himself to playwriting, has gained his national and international respect primarily as a novelist, though writing continually for the stage. István Örkény (1912-1979), probably the finest and most celebrated Hungarian dramatist since Molnár, was already a celebrated middle-aged author when, in the mid-1960s, a director *and* a dramaturg persuaded – *forced* – him to adapt his most famous novel for the stage. This play, *The Family Tot*, and his adaptation of another of his novels, *Catsplay*, have been produced worldwide, establishing Örkény as a master of the European 'tender-absurd' or grotesque – while he remained the great novelist and writer of 'one-minute stories' for which he has always been acclaimed.

Other writers, however, have been thwarted in their theatrical careers. Tibor Déry (1894-1977), a great twentieth-century author, wrote a trilogy of expressionist-dadaist plays in the twenties, when he was young. But one part, *The Giant Baby*, received its premiere only after some fifty years had elapsed, while the other two parts remain unstaged. Milán Füst (1888-1967), another classic author of this century, was also a playwright early on. After some works were refused by theatres, and others had bad reviews, his bitterness caused him to abandon the stage. Only posthumously, as late as the early 1970s, were *The Unhappy Ones* (written 1914) and his other plays recognised for the groundbreaking works they are.

It's time, however, to discuss those more fortunate writers, who have had their plays produced during their lives, plays which have contributed so much to Hungarian theatre in recent decades. Let us begin with the current generation, represented in this volume, before looking at their forbears.

The Open Forum Generation: the 1990s

The authors translated here are in their early thirties to early forties, all entered the stage at more or less the same time, the later 1980s, and all write principally for the stage (though Szilágyi and Nagy have turned their hands to prose and essays as well). They've all had a few plays produced in Hungary, received several prizes, and have gained substantial commissions in radio, television, and film. None of them has yet attained the status of a 'great' or 'national' playwright, but their generation is becoming, perhaps, the most influential one in Hungarian theatre today. Yet they cannot be classified strictly as a 'generation', as they have no common agenda, principles, or styles: the spectrum of their themes and approaches is as wide as the rainbow, reflecting the multiplicity in world theatre at large. But in this age of classifications, when we feel safer with applying labels, this latest clutch of writers is often described as the 'Open Forum' generation. The appellation refers to an annual meeting of dramatists, critics, and theatre practitioners, who discuss four or five plays by young authors, and the issues relevant to them. Two of the plays then receive workshop enactments, and possibilities for promoting new drama are then considered. Such efforts are necessary in today's theatre, when new drama is so often exiled to small theatres and studios.

Notable playwrights of this 'generation' *not* included in this volume are Pál Békés, András Forgách and László Márton. Békés has written for children and completed many radio adaptations; his adult plays follow in the light traditions of the Central-European absurd. Forgách has adapted classics and has triumphed with two original plays (while also writing poetic essays on literature, theatre and film). Márton's dramatic output ranges from neo-dadaist experiments to great flows of historical verse drama (his prize-winning trilogy would demand a tremendously large cast and about nine hours for a full production!). In addition, all three are noted translators of classics and modern literature. The 'generation' has also been joined recently by Lajos Parti Nagy, a fine writer of short stories, who has achieved a kind of cult following for his plays produced in the last two years. His unmistakeable style, a peculiar poetry drawn from different levels of colloquial language, is based on the mock-naturalism of his combinations of street idioms.

By the time such writers reached adulthood, political repression had developed a certain more gentle refinement, and life could be said to be generally comfortable, definitely so in comparison with other Communist countries. But there is also a generation of writers only ten years older, for whom the dark years immediately after 1956 were formative. And quite a few of these figures made significant contributions to Hungarian theatre in the 1980s.

The Dramaturgy of Absence: the 1980s

'Absence' is the term by which the tendencies in drama of the late 1970s and early 1980s came to be characterised by one critic in an influential essay: absence of human contact, absence of the past, absence of love, absence of space, absence of self-identity, absence of action. Other critics, too, detected in the drama of the time a lack of linear plotting, a dearth of heroic figures, and considerable scepticism or yearning for action (and there was never any prospect of meaningful action).

In the relatively lax atmosphere of the final period of Communism, the best Hungarian writers were determinedly delving into the secrets and traumas of their country's and their families' pasts, to confront the sin and guilt of their fathers' generation. Their attempts to dramatise the unspoken, and the often unspeakable, led to innovative techniques. Memories, associations, submerged feelings intermingled in these plays; the dramaturgy became less coherent and cleverly crafted, the speeches more abstract or poetic, and the use of time and space more flexible. Plays by Mihály Kornis, Géza Bereményi, György Spiró and Péter Nádas were important mile-stones: their demands for new approaches provoked changes in the aesthetics of theatre. The two plays most illustrative of these times are probably *Encounter* by Nádas, and Spiró's *Chickenhead*.

Encounter (first produced 1985) is an abstract piece, a ritual in an all-white set, with a door into eternity (there are strict stage directions!). In it, a young man provokes a woman into relating an episode from her past – her love affair with his father who, at the time, was the same age as the young man is now. We learn that the father shot himself in the street, while approaching his lover, after having realised how she had been arrested and tortured by the secret police he worked for as a judge. Finishing her story, the woman poisons herself with red wine (a symbolic colour effect when contrasted with the white set), washes the young man from head to foot, lays him on the bed with the now-broken glass in his hand, and leaves through the door. The meaning is clear: with all this knowledge of the past, he now has to decide whether he can live his life cleanly or must commit suicide himself.

Chickenhead (also premiered in 1985) is a savage play, in the mould of Edward Bond's *Saved* and its descendants. The setting is a run-down tenement, the style is naturalistic, the language harsh and coarse, the plot straightforward. Two boys have killed their neighbour's (an old woman's) cat just before the play opens, and will now kill her, although she is their benefactor, before the play's end. The strength of *Chickenhead* lies in its meticulous portrayal of the characters' lives of hard drudgery in the house. Its first production, with its excellent staging and superb acting, provoked very lively reactions from audience and critics alike.

György Spiró is probably the only member of this generation still writing for the stage. For many of his contemporaries there was no point in continuing: the loss of hope in Eastern Europe after the Czechoslovakian events of 1968 coloured the plays they did write, and contributed to their tailing off. The characters of these plays possess, in general, a feeling of having been deceived, unable as they are to take an active part in life.

'Paradise Lost': the 1960s and 1970s

The previous generation, however, had experienced both greater calamities and greater chances for profound change. Thus, in spite of constant frustrations and disillusionment, the characters of plays in the period tend to be full of energy – definitely not heroic, and often grotesque or comic, but nevertheless vital and active.

Indeed, 'Active' is one of Pisti's many incarnations in István Örkény's *Pisti in the Bloodbath* (written in 1969, and produced ten years later). Here the principal character, portrayed as four personas – a metaphor for the absurd schizophrenia of the attempt to adapt to rapid change – makes his journey through all the tragic twists and turns of the past decades. The playwright guides our feelings, and carefully delineates a progress towards catharsis by showing the most tragic events in a very grotesque light. Though not a member of any 'generation', Örkény, the humanist with a distinctively grotesque, tragicomic view, is definitely the outstanding playwright of his era, whose work is frequently revived in Hungary and abroad. *The Family Tot* (1967) is a cruelly comic parable of defencelessnes and servility, in which a neurotic army officer spends his holidays with the family of a soldier under his command, in a small rural house during World War II. *Catsplay* (1969) concerns a funny and touching, but mundane, love-triangle – except this time the characters are elderly. Here the aggrieved party tells, with wit and irony, the whole story in letters and phone calls to her sister, who has left the country and lives a wealthy but unhappy life abroad.

Many Hungarians had similar experiences in those years: endless long-distance calls and letters exchanged with beloved friends and relatives 'lost' when they left the country in successive waves. Some emigrés made a success of it abroad; others never admitted to their nostalgia, sense of loss, and homesickness. And those who stayed behind felt a strange mixture of jealousy and pride – pride for living through a significant era.

This was also a significant period for social, intellectual and artistic movements, when films by Miklós Janesó. István Szabó and others were a revelation to audiences in Hungary and elsewhere in Europe; when artistic expression was in an exceptional accord with its social environment. Writers, film-makers, and theatre-people believed in meaningful action and the power of social critique. Indeed, this was a period when, although the official ideology still held sway over the public expressions of intellectual life, there were no strict rules, and critical behaviour was even encouraged, to a degree. Very common were the peculiar – and in a way very subversive – attempts to cheat the censor and test the limits of official tolerance. Sophisticated ways of writing and reading between the lines were generally employed, thus adding greater subtlety to both the playwrights' craft and the audiences' receptivity. New drama at this time ranged from historical parables on the one hand, to absurd comedies reflecting contemporary problems on the other: indeed, a generally satirical perception of man and society characterised much of the writing. This was also a time when theatres competed with each other in commissioning new plays, and audiences flocked to see performances. The approaches adopted to staging and acting were in tune with both the demands of the plays and the audiences' tastes – in other periods very often the theatrical techniques were not sufficiently adroit to suit the plays, or productions were too doctrinaire to satisfy audiences.

Of the numerous plays by the writers of this period – István Csurka, Tibor Gyurkovics, Gyula Illyés, István Eörsi, Károly Szakonyi and others – the most enduring is probably Csurka's *Deficit, or, In the Red* (written 1969, and, like *Pisti*, premiered in 1979), a distant relative of Edward Albee's *Who's Afraid of Virginia Woolf?*. This sour comedy is a merciless satire on the helplessness of intellectuals, a favourite subject for novels, films, and plays.

This whole wave of post-Stalinist drama could be said to have been inaugurated by Imre Sarkadi (1921-1961). In *Simeon Stylites* (a 1960 adaptation of his own 1949 novel) and his other plays, including the symbolically titled *Paradise Lost*, he put the figure of the impotent and self-destructive anti-hero on stage for the first time. This was a significant change from the 1950s, when the obligatory 'positive heroes' fixed their confident eyes on the Future.

Back to the Future

After having paid tribute to many who deserve it, let me remind the reader that the intention here is not to present plays that have safely established their place in the Hungarian repertoire. We have decided to step on less safe ground, to select challenging and telling new works, fresh from Hungarian stages. And the plays in this volume *are* fresh: the original productions of all but one were still in repertory in Budapest theatres when this selection was made. This emphasis means also that the future will have to be the judge of their importance. But the future of Hungarian drama depends not only on this writer-generation, and the next already knocking on the doors with its promising first attempts, but on the impending changes in the theatre. At a time when new drama moving into smaller spaces is a general tendency, it seems crucial to reinforce a healthy relationship between small and large theatres, and between professional and non-professional companies. And even more important will be the young director-generation's commitment to new writing, in an age when directors often express themselves by re-interpreting classics. And last, but not least, there is the importance – the *need* – to become part of an international exchange, where plays have a chance to travel beyond the boundaries of their own countries of origin. Let's think of the translated plays in this collection, then, as messengers, ambassadors, with responsibilities both to their native Hungarian culture and to the English-language to which they are here addressed. Theirs is a difficult task. But, 'the struggle itself must be the goal', as our classic author Imre Madách put it in his nineteenth-century masterpiece *The Tragedy of Man*. Now, let us leave the four plays to the mercy of directors and audiences. Good luck!

László Upor
Budapest, March 1996

HUNGARIAN PLAYS

THE SEDUCER'S DIARY

by András Nagy

English version by Julian Garner

from a translation by Melis Pálma and András Nagy

'I was born in 1956 in Budapest, just before Soviet tanks started to
blast the city. I grew up here, studied here and live here. Probably the
obligatory "national amnesia" led my attention to historic subjects
when I was young' says Nagy, summarising his background. He
graduated from ELTE University, Budapest, and worked for many
years as a lecturer at the University and as an editor at a publishing
house, before becoming a full-time writer.

By 1996 he had written twelve plays, of which the first opened in
1984. It featured the legendary Elisabeth Bathory, and was followed
by plays about many other figures from cultural history, including:
The 'Anna Karenina' Railway Station, an original adaptation from
Tolstoy's famous novel; *Hungarian Three Sisters*, based on Chekhov's
masterpiece (1991); *The Seducer's Diary*, whose principal character
is Soren Kierkegaard's alter ego (1992); and *Alma*, a one-woman play
featuring Alma Mahler (1995).

Nagy has also published three novels, a collection of short stories, two
studies, and has written several screenplays, including *Café Sarajevo*
(1995), a dystopian vision of Budapest in the grip of civil war; he has
also participated in the work of an international writer's workshop in
Iowa, USA, and shot a documentary in the Himalayas. In his work, he
says, his 'main interest is to find where the sensuality of the spirit ends
and the spiritualisation of the sense starts'.

The Seducer's Diary opened on 5 December 1992, in Budapest Chamber
Theatre, as the closing event of a conference on Kierkegaard. This
philosophical-spiritual love story, loosely based on the Danish philosopher's novel and his diary, centres upon a trivial plot of seduction
and desertion. The principal character, a young intellectual, attempts
to resolve basic questions about God and himself through 'proofs',
that is by carrying out seductions. However, he doesn't dare to eat
the 'fruit' of these seductions, and, by the end of the play, he has dimi-
nished from romantic hero to tragi-comic victim of his own intrigue.

Characters

JOHANNES
CORDELIA
WILHELM
Cordelia's AUNT
EDVARD
JANSEN

The action takes place in Denmark, in the late 1840s.

ACT ONE

Scene 1. Johannes's Apartment.

The stage is in darkness. A shadowy figure, WILHELM, in the room, smoking a cigar. To either side, doors leading respectively to EDVARD's and JOHANNES's bedrooms. Up centre, a door into the bathroom, emitting light, steam and raised voices.

EDVARD (*off*). Denmark is a prison!

JOHANNES (*off*). A prison! Ugh, I'm freezing!

EDVARD. Let me out! Let me out!

JOHANNES. But you're innocent, aren't you?

EDVARD. No one is innocent in Denmark! Not even Juliet Capulet!

JOHANNES. And certainly not as she was played tonight!

EDVARD. Johanne Heiberg was exquisite!

JOHANNES. Exquisite, perhaps. But also thirty-two years old!

EDVARD. And, at last, returned from exile!

JOHANNES. We're all prisoners in Denmark! I've had enough.

EDVARD. Cold water is supposed to be highly effective against sexual arousal, you know!

JOHANNES. Well, it certainly seems to have little effect against political arousal!

EDVARD. Ha! You cannot forgive me, can you, for not noticing your young lady in the foyer, tonight?

JOHANNES. On the contrary, it is you who cannot forgive me, for refusing to accept this evening's vulgar political exercise as theatre.

EDVARD. Wake up, Denmark! Our artists are returning, our actors, our exiles are all returning!

JOHANNES. The System remains impervious; all that has collapsed is our sense of taste! Oh, this country is truly a prison!

EDVARD. Johannes, my towel, if you please. So, suddenly it's the height of good taste, is it, to attribute the presence of a pretty face to the workings of Fate?

JOHANNES (*off*). Why else should Fate contrive my presence at such an indecent spectacle?

EDVARD (*off*). For the sake of Denmark, of course!

JOHANNES (*off*). Nonsense! It was merely Her way of bringing the fair damsel to my attention!

EDVARD (*off, flicking* JOHANNES *with the end of his towel*). You deserve worse than my towel, Johannes! You mean to say that the purpose of this entire occasion – all our initiative and hard work, mobilising the city – was simply to afford you a glimpse of a girl?

JOHANNES (*framed in the doorway*). Absolutely!

EDVARD. All your fine talk of liberty and democracy boils down to nothing but a wench?

JOHANNES. What else!

EDVARD. Take that, sir! (*Flicks* JOHANNES *with his towel.*)

JOHANNES (*backing into the room, wet from his shower, flicking at* EDVARD *with his towel*). A damsel, a maiden, the most beautiful girl ever beheld by man!

EDVARD *pursues* JOHANNES *into the room, flicking at him with his towel. They blunder into furniture in the darkness.*

EDVARD. Behold, the weary philosopher, his theological dilemmas swept aside by the merest sight of a wench!

WILHELM (*stubbing out his cigar, standing*). Down weapons, ye disturbers of peace! He who lives by the towel shall die by the towel! (*We see that he is a priest.*)

JOHANNES. Ah, I am lost – surrounded! Spirituality conquers the spirit!

EDVARD. It's your brother, Wilhelm!

JOHANNES. Wilhelm! This is indeed a surprise! Have you just arrived? (*Embraces him.*)

WILHELM. Surprise? (*Embraces* EDVARD.) Half-brother, actually.

EDVARD. I see. (*Inspecting the hamper.*) I also see half a side of pork!

WILHELM. Your return to Jutland is eagerly awaited, Johannes . . .

JOHANNES. Wilhelm . . . There is something you should know ∴ . .

WILHELM. I envy your high spirits! Two whole days, I've been travelling from Jutland; I'm completely numb from sitting!

JOHANNES. Next time, dear brother, try not to sit on your spirits.

EDVARD (*at the hamper*). There's a whole banquet, here!

WILHELM. Agnete sent it, for the celebration. (*Brings a list from his pocket.*) There are some items I am to obtain for her, also.

JOHANNES. Including me, I suppose? Wilhelm, listen; it's true that something momentous has befallen me, but . . .

WILHELM. Of course; your inauguration as Doctor of Divinity!

EDVARD. I'll fetch the spare mattress . . . (*Leaves.*)

JOHANNES. Wilhelm . . . I should have written to you.

WILHELM. You wrote to me a year ago, with the date of your examination and . . .

JOHANNES. . . . . the truth is, Wilhelm, I . . . I have reached an impasse.

WILHELM. In your studies? Yet, it was you who convinced me, all those years ago, that theology was the subject we had to study . . .

JOHANNES. The study of theology is not the problem, Wilhelm. The problem is theology itself.

WILHELM. Surely, you have teachers to help you over such hurdles?

JOHANNES. Blackfeldt? He's hopeless. He's seems to have taken a vow of silence. He's going to Berlin.

EDVARD *enters with a palliasse.*

EDVARD. Welcome to the guest suite, Wilhelm!

JOHANNES. Fetch the mattress from my bed, instead.

EDVARD *goes out.*

WILHELM. It is theology that's the problem, Johannes? It isn't your faith?

JOHANNES. Yes, Wilhelm, it is my faith. And I'm glad it is that which is the problem! What else could save me – from my doctorate, from roast pork, from the Jutland brethren . . . !

WILHELM. Even if I were inclined to believe you, Johannes, I'm afraid I overheard your conversation in the shower.

JOHANNES. What of it?

WILHELM. I realise it isn't easy to pray when one is in the shower, naked. But, if the idea of a woman's body can banish the Ten Commandments from your mind, perhaps it's fitting also that God keeps his distance.

JOHANNES. That's unworthy of you, brother. You know full well that since that day – an eternity ago, it seems now – no woman has tempted me. (*Pause.*) Well, suddenly, it occurs to me that I might find precisely what I have failed to find in theology, in a woman's love.

EDVARD (*off*). There seems to be a disturbance over by the theatre!

WILHELM. Please, spare me the details.

EDVARD (*entering*). Something's happening at the theatre!

WILHELM. I'm exhausted, suddenly. This revelation . . .

JOHANNES. I'll make your bed.

EDVARD. The revolution has started! I must get dressed. Johannes, are you coming? (*Goes out.*)

WILHELM (*undressing*). My feet are so swollen.

JOHANNES. How is Agnete?

WILHELM. Please, Johannes, it won't help . . . She's well. (*Climbs into bed, pulls the sheet over his head.*) Good night.

JOHANNES. You must try to understand me, Wilhelm!

WILHELM. I understood you before, Johannes; when, together, we chose theology and the service of God in Jutland!

JOHANNES. And what decided our choice, Wilhelm?! We wished to atone for our father. Who once, as a child shivering and starving in Jutland, cursed God. And, though he knew the curse to be justified, still, God would not absolve him!

WILHELM. That's not the whole story, Johannes. Is a woman all it takes for you to forget . . . ?

JOHANNES. I know what you're going to say, and I don't wish to discuss it. (*Goes out.*)

WILHELM. You felt yourself caught in a divine trap, and so you fled to the brothel in search of some counter redemption of your own. But the next day . . . sprawled in the mud . . . your pain and guilt . . . and your vow, Johannes!

JOHANNES (*from the next room*). Will you be comfortable, here?

WILHELM. I pity this poor girl. What is she to you, but a possible solution to your own theological dilemma?

JOHANNES. You shouldn't try to sleep in these spirits, brother.

WILHELM. Then you will have to teach me how to forget, Johannes, as you have taught me so many things!

EDVARD *comes in.*

EDVARD. Are you coming?

JOHANNES (*to* WILHELM). How do you think Isaac felt about being sacrificed on the altar of his father's faith?!

EDVARD. The city's turning upside down, Johannes! You must come!

JOHANNES. He's asleep! My predicament has lulled him to sleep.

EDVARD (*looks in at* WILHELM). Most peacefully, too, it seems. Come on, let's go!

Scene 2. A Street.

WILHELM. Since when did it take four hours to locate an apothecary!

JOHANNES. All I can remember is that she was wearing a green coat.

WILHELM. I still have to find a haberdasher's. Throat lozenges. What are you talking about?

JOHANNES. Your shopping, of course. Lozenges, a quilt, hat-pins, a corset, a scarf, nail-scissors . . . Anything else?

WILHELM. Epsom salts.

JOHANNES. Oh my God, Wilhelm, what has become of you?

WILHELM. Can't you see, my feet are swollen!

JOHANNES. Whatever became of your love?

WILHELM. Of my love? And what about yours? We've been meticulously criss-crossing the city since early this morning. Presumably in the vague hope that we might happen upon your mysterious beauty?

JOHANNES. In the vague hope that we might 'happen upon' the various provisions on your list, Wilhelm. Of course, it would be a happy coincidence if our path did happen to cross that of a certain young lady . . .

WILHELM. I suppose she is beautiful?

JOHANNES. Imagine the sun of all femininity!

WILHELM. Oh, I'm sure I'll recognise her immediately from that description!

JOHANNES. Do you want to sit here and rest your feet a little?

WILHELM. Yes. (*Removes his shoes.*) Now, at least, I understand what fuels your behaviour. Oh, my poor feet! Reflection, you know, is an excellent antidote to reality.

JOHANNES. In theology, yes.

WILHELM. Whereas poetry is an endless detour from reality. Well, let us continue the search, let us follow your dreams.

JOHANNES. Wilhelm.

WILHELM. Let go of my arm, please, you're hurting me!

JOHANNES. Turn around, very slowly . . .

WILHELM. What?

JOHANNES. There she is. She's gone. (*Exits.*)

Scene 3. A Street at Twilight.

EDVARD. Johannes! Thank God, I found you at last.

JOHANNES. I have found her!

EDVARD. You must come! You won't believe what's happening! It's fantastic!

JOHANNES. I might have known it would be music that would lead me to her. No, I won't come with you, what I crave now is female society.

EDVARD. It's not a party I'm inviting you to, Johannes!

JOHANNES. You haven't shaved.

EDVARD. No. And we've occupied the theatre, in protest. Tomorrow, we'll take the prison, and the day after that – parliament itself!

JOHANNES. Now, there's an idea – force power to its knees with the power of your behind!

EDVARD. I've always admired your humour, Johannes; it seemed to me to exemplify your courage. But, now, what am I to think? The only thing that interests you is this blessed girl!

JOHANNES. Your lust, Edvard – for power – utterly dwarfs my little fantasy. Really, your desire for control is pitiable. The Reformation declared itself in the name of Religion, though it was in fact a political movement. Now, we have a spiritual crisis dressing itself up as politics! Edvard, I am closer to God now, with my young lady, than you will ever be in Parliament.

EDVARD. I can't believe I'm hearing this! So, a prisoner needs nothing but a good weekly sermon, is that what you're saying? And the exile, nothing but his rosary beads? Europe lacks nothing today but religious passion? Tell me, is this the effect love can have, even on a mind like yours?

JOHANNES. It's easier, Edvard, if you don't try to understand me.

EDVARD. And what about poor Wilhelm? He's been waiting for you at our chambers for nearly five hours!

JOHANNES. He has? He'd do better to wait at the café by the Stock Exchange, the one with the large windows, where I must make my next move. Tell him to meet me there, will you?

Scene 4. The Café.

WILHELM (*seated*). When are you going to look at me?

JOHANNES (*by the window, standing*). As soon as she goes back in again, I shall have eyes only for you. Until nine thirty-five precisely, when she'll come out again, and I may catch a glimpse of her by the light of the street lamp.

WILHELM. I've been waiting here for you for three and a half hours, Johannes. My boat leaves at ten o'clock.

JOHANNES. She went for a walk, unexpectedly. I had to follow her.

WILHELM. In the meantime, I spoke with your professor.

JOHANNES. What about the things for Agnete? Her lozenges, the corset, the hat-pins, and the eiderdown . . . ?

WILHELM. I have them all, of course. Will you please look at me!

JOHANNES. Wilhelm, except when she is in the vicinity, if you so desire, I will gaze at you constantly! And admire in you a paragon who places his domestic duties above even metaphysical dilemmas. How long were you with Blackfeldt; fifteen minutes? Since when you have been searching, most diligently, for an eiderdown!

WILHELM. Johannes, this is most distressing. You are toying with this girl, as if she were a rat in a laboratory maze!

JOHANNES. What do you suggest I do, instead? Marry her, and become a rat myself, scurrying around a maze of domesticity?

WILHELM. What do you know about marriage, when you can't even tell the difference between a cup of coffee brewed at home by a devoted wife, and this tepid dishwater!

JOHANNES. Yet, I love this café, and I'm glad I discovered it.

WILHELM. Yesterday, I thought I might still persuade you to return with me to Jutland.

JOHANNES. What, smoked and cured, like the pig?

WILHELM. Why can't you grasp the meaning of that gift? That food, Johannes – and the eiderdown, and all the other things – are far, far more eloquent than all your fancy phrases.

JOHANNES. Let us not discuss the eloquence of Epsom salts, please!

WILHELM. In spite of your efforts, Johannes, I do understand you. You don't wish to return home, alone. You've realised that a little matrimonial warmth is necessary if you are to survive the freezing Jutland winters. It was insensitive of me to poke fun at your young lady, this morning. I beg your forgiveness, and hope you will accept this as a token of my apology. (*Gives* JOHANNES *a black ledger.*)

JOHANNES. I'm sorry, I can't look just now. Would you be so kind to place it in my hand?

WILHELM. I understand that these events are significant for you. You could note your thoughts from yesterday – about Grace, and Fate, and Providence . . . Today, you understand them in the light

of a particular young woman: tomorrow, it might be the story of
Abraham and Isaac . . .

JOHANNES. Yes, I'll copy all my theology notes into it! (*Takes out
numerous loose sheets of paper.*) 'At four o'clock, saw her in the
Royal Gardens, by the alleyway . . . Six o'clock, under the
colonnade of the Stock Exchange . . . In a music shop on Vesta
Volgade . . . ' You think Blackfeldt would approve?

WILHELM. Johannes, before I go, one request. Find yourself another
tutor.

JOHANNES. If only it were that simple!

WILHELM. But, surely, you can't accept Blackfeldt's views? That
God is a closed book, a total enigma for all mankind? That it's His
will that we are all kept in a state of perpetual uncertainty? Don't
you revolt at such a concept?

JOHANNES. Against the concept, perhaps – but not the professor.

WILHELM. I think Blackfeldt is ill.

JOHANNES. Here is your book back, Wilhelm; it comes with too
many strings attached.

WILHELM. Johannes, I think you're obstructing . . .

JOHANNES. Yes! I am 'obstructing'!

WILHELM. The door, Johannes, you're obstructing the door.

JOHANNES *spins round. Two* WOMEN *are waiting to come in.*

JOHANNES. Oh my God! (*He drops the ledger.*)

CORDELIA (*treading on it*). I'm sorry . . .

Scene 5. Johannes's Apartment.

Night.

EDVARD. Johannes, Johannes! I think something has happened to
me, too!

JOHANNES (*pointing, on the ledger*). Her footprint!

EDVARD. You must come and join us at the theatre!

JOHANNES (*opens the ledger*). No, she's leading me elsewhere. Just
think; she was on her way to play the piano.

EDVARD. Haven't you noticed the change that has come over the
city? It's wonderful! The forces of tyranny are melting away like a
shower of rain! Liberty is blossoming everywhere, like girls
emerging in their summer frocks!

JOHANNES. She's a musician. You understand? Music is the real language of her heart.

EDVARD. Yes, Johannes, yes, now I do understand you!

JOHANNES. A little Swedish melody, short and sad. And such a feminine sadness! And afterwards, she performed a piano duet. Which, finally, will lead me to her! Or to her partner, at any rate.

EDVARD. But, Johannes, I've also seen a girl!

JOHANNES. And you want to go back to the theatre?

EDVARD. Yes – for her sake! Her father died in exile. Don't you see, this makes the revolution suddenly so much less abstract, so much more real!

JOHANNES. You don't understand me at all, Edvard.

EDVARD. Not only do I understand you, Johannes, but it was your love that inspired me! Her hair is golden; she's not too tall; and her waist is slender as . . .

JOHANNES. You know her well, I see.

EDVARD. I caught sight of her at the theatre. And, Johannes, now I see that Love and Liberty, far from excluding each other, are actually dependent on each other! You're not going to sit and write now, are you?! Yesterday, you told Wilhelm you'd abandoned your studies for Love, and here I am, trying to discuss Love with you and you knuckle down to a spot of theology! What is this – your famous Dialectics?

JOHANNES. I'd rather you didn't try to understand me, Edvard.

EDVARD. You've helped me to understand so much, Johannes. Not least the oppression of the Danish people. Then, yesterday, you introduced me to the idea of Love, and here I am today, burning with desire for a girl! I can't stop thinking about her!

JOHANNES. It will end in marriage – you'll see!

EDVARD. Perhaps you should learn something from me for a change? Oh, what a night we have ahead of us!

JOHANNES. What a night, indeed.

Scene 6. A Sheet-Music Shop.

JOHANNES, *at the counter*. MISS JANSEN, *half way up a ladder*.

JANSEN. Do you know anything else about it?

JOHANNES. That's why I'm here – to discover more.

JANSEN. So – it's Swedish and it's sad. My father might be able to find it.

JOHANNES. I'd rather you found it.

JANSEN. It holds fond memories for you, this tune?

JOHANNES. It's more what it anticipates than what it recalls. (*Hums the melody.*)

JANSEN. Oh my God! It's my friend's tune.

JOHANNES. You're friends with the composer?

JANSEN. No, my piano partner, she plays it.

JOHANNES. Why are you taking down all those?

JANSEN (*descending with a pile of sheet music*). You can help me find it. We also attend cookery classes together.

JOHANNES. There was something about the melody, a forlornness, that quite captivated me.

JANSEN. She's the better pianist, but my cooking is far superior to hers.

JOHANNES. It was like a song of farewell, as if joy had deserted her.

JANSEN. That's rather perceptive of you, actually. Aren't you going to help me?

JOHANNES. Perceptive? You mean, she has been deserted? Such a beautiful woman?

JANSEN. Is she beautiful? Actually, it's usually me that attracts the attention, when we're together.

JOHANNES. Why should she be so unhappy? Has she really been abandoned?

JANSEN. Yes. Did I mention that I'm a better cook than her? Her father. Her mother died when she was small, she was bought up by her aunt. They live alone together, which is why she is able to practise more than I. I have to help my father here in the shop. And then I have my embroidery class, and of course there are my social obligations . . . But I shall be more diligent. We're to perform our piano duet at the Court, on Midsummer's Eve. I've already decided what kind of dress I shall have made for the occasion.

JOHANNES. You play secondo, don't you? In the duet?

JANSEN. That's right. When we were told that we were to play at the Court, we couldn't help smiling. Though we were rebuked for it.

JOHANNES. By whom?

JANSEN. It was at the theatre, the day before yesterday. Her aunt rebuked us.

JOHANNES. The day before yesterday?

JANSEN. Why don't you help me look? Her aunt hasn't been to the theatre for sixteen years. Just think!

JOHANNES. Where shall I look?

JANSEN. Here. On the last occasion she was sixteen years old. It's a brief enough tale; she was engaged to a man who then left her. A puppeteer . . . I'm sorry – a marionettist! But he couldn't get on in Denmark, and so he left the country. Only his puppets remain. Their apartment is full of them! And, still, she – the aunt, I mean – though hardly young any more – she must be your age, at least . . .

JOHANNES. Thank you. I think I'll let you search in peace.

JANSEN. But, there is another story . . .

JOHANNES (*holds up a sheet of music*). I think this is it.

   CORDELIA *enters from the street.*

JANSEN. So it is. Shall I wrap it for you?

JOHANNES. It's not necessary. I'll take it as it is.

CORDELIA. Oh, I thought I might find you alone.

JANSEN. This gentleman was after your melody.

CORDELIA. Do I have a melody? I'm afraid I won't be able to practise with you this afternoon.

JANSEN. Midsummer's Eve is quite soon, you know.

JOHANNES. The secondo doesn't seem to be included here.

JANSEN. Show me. Perhaps it's the wrong piece.

CORDELIA. No. That tune doesn't have a secondo.

JANSEN. Won't your aunt let you practise?

CORDELIA. No. She's been indulging in reminiscences. This afternoon we're going to register my father on the roll of political exiles.

JOHANNES. What might a secondo consist of here?

CORDELIA. Oh, a few major chords would suffice, I think.

JANSEN. But, Cordelia, your father wasn't a political exile.

CORDELIA. Evidently, he was. I only learned of it today.

JANSEN. Would you like to take it, sir? That will be two dalers.

JOHANNES. I would, very much. But I only have a five daler coin.

JANSEN. I must go and fetch some change. Will you wait a little, sir?

JOHANNES. I can wait as long as necessary.

   MISS JANSEN *leaves. Silence.*

Have you ever experienced falling in love with a melody and then having no peace until you could possess it?

CORDELIA. Some tunes affect me that way, yes. Though I don't think of myself as possessing them, rather of them possessing me.

JOHANNES. Oh, happy tunes!

CORDELIA. Though I'm not sure this tune will suit your hands, sir.

JOHANNES. My hands?

CORDELIA. You might find it a little lightweight. Though the major chords would give it a certain depth. Try it.

JOHANNES. Mightn't they prove a little oppressive? The minor would be gentler.

CORDELIA. If it can't take the weight the melody will soon collapse. But sooner that – than soften it artificially – for fear of it breaking.

JOHANNES. Oh my God! It's like Lear's youngest daughter talking!

CORDELIA. I beg your pardon?

JOHANNES. I refer to Shakespeare's drama about a princess without a kingdom, whose greatest sin is to have her heart upon her lips.

CORDELIA. Mr Shakespeare was evidently no anatomist.

JOHANNES. No, he was a very fine dramatist. He shows us how the princess, Cordelia, is surrounded by cripples.

CORDELIA. Well! I'm not exactly spoiled for compliments, but I must say I have had more flattering things said about me!

JOHANNES. I've seen you a number of times during the past few days.

CORDELIA. Does that give you a licence to judge me?

JOHANNES. I've heard you play, too. That little Swedish melody contains everything – your delicacy, reflection, melancholy – *all* your desires . . .

CORDELIA. You might be a little more discreet! First, you spy on a girl whilst she's taking her bath, then you discuss her freckles with her!

JOHANNES. To the trained eye, a secret life, a suppressed desire is far more enchanting than the prettiest freckle on the palest skin.

CORDELIA. Will you please stop! Your compliments are as silly as your offences. These are hardly suitable subjects for small talk. Can't you play any other tune?

She takes up the sheet-music of the Swedish tune from the counter and pushes the rest of the music towards JOHANNES. *It falls to the floor.*

JANSEN (*enters*). Cordelia; are you serving the gentleman?

Scene 7. The Street. Night.

EDVARD. Johannes!

JOHANNES. I've seen her; I've talked to her!

EDVARD. We've taken the theatre!

JOHANNES. My God, I'm floating on air!

EDVARD. She was there, sitting opposite me, whilst I took her particulars!

JOHANNES. Edvard, I am in a state of grace, do you understand?!

EDVARD. Fate has dealt with her very harshly. As she left, she gave my hand a squeeze!

JOHANNES. A young girl doesn't become beautiful, Edvard, she is born so. But her beauty has to be awakened, very tenderly, very gently.

EDVARD. I've been invited to visit them, to collect some documents relevant to their case.

JOHANNES. You're very fortunate. I've not made such progress, yet. My strategy dictates a longer, slower path.

EDVARD. I'm frightfully embarrassed in her presence. I upset the ink pot whilst dipping my pen! Then I smudged her aunt's dress, and gritted my teeth so hard whilst recording her name in the register that my bad tooth came loose. Here.

JOHANNES. Did you say her aunt?

EDVARD. Yes. Her guardian. Though don't imagine some shrivelled old crone; she can't be much older than you!

JOHANNES. Oh my God . . . Edvard.

EDVARD. I so want to visit them, but I daren't! I'm afraid of no one in this city – except, the Wahls.

JOHANNES. Wahl? Oh, you had me worried there for a moment . . .

EDVARD. Worried; you? Why? Her name is Cordelia Wahl. What are you doing?

JOHANNES. I must go somewhere . . .

EDVARD. Oh, I wish I could overcome my fear and visit them.

JOHANNES. Such fears are easily turned to your advantage.

EDVARD. Johannes, if I asked you . . .

JOHANNES. No!

EDVARD. I haven't asked you, yet!

JOHANNES. Yes. You're right. Why not? Perhaps it's some kind of test?

EDVARD. What are you talking about? Johannes, I just wanted to ask you if you would come along and cover for me?

JOHANNES. Cover? Yes. Could I cover, I wonder?

Scene 8. Cordelia's Apartment.

JANSEN. What's come over you, Cordelia? Your playing is almost as wild as your hair!

CORDELIA. I don't know what's come over me. I must let down my hair a little. (*Unties her hair.*)

JANSEN. You're lucky to be able to practise so much. Look at my hair, brittle as twigs! I'm trying this new lotion, though it smells foul.

CORDELIA. Let me smell. Phew! What is it – vinegar, salt . . . ?

JANSEN. Stop it! Didn't you notice, last week at cookery, how the chef kept staring at me?

CORDELIA. Anyway, we're having guests today.

JANSEN. Oh, well that explains everything.

CORDELIA. Not at all! These are official guests; they're coming about my father.

JANSEN. What's got into your aunt, all of a sudden? First, allowing us to practise together and now, guests?

CORDELIA. I don't know, either. She's completely changed.

JANSEN. And your guests; are they revolutionaries? Suddenly, wherever you go in the city, they're everywhere!

CORDELIA. I expect so. And, by the way, I shan't be playing that Swedish song any more.

Cordelia's AUNT *enters.*

AUNT. Cordelia, are you forgetting our guests? They'll be here, any moment.

JANSEN. I must go. (*She remains.*)

AUNT. You look like an unkempt child. Let me do your hair.

CORDELIA. I can do it myself.

JANSEN. What a beautiful dress. It reminds me of my mother's wedding dress; all those little pleats and the narrow waist.

AUNT. Cordelia, what have you done with the pastries?

CORDELIA. Oh! I forgot them at the café!

JANSEN laughs.

CORDELIA. I selected them, watched them being wrapped, paid for them, and then left them on the counter!

AUNT. Yesterday, you bring home some strange piece of music. This morning, you break several pieces of the best coffee service whilst drying it. Then you mope about the house until noon and manage to forget the pastries at the café! What other little surprises may we expect this afternoon, I wonder?

CORDELIA. Those cups were so ugly, anyway. I think I'll do my hair in ringlets.

JANSEN. Perhaps I should go. I can call at the café on the way and tell them to deliver the pastries. (*Goes out.*)

CORDELIA. You look so beautiful in that dress.

AUNT. Fasten me at the back, will you? I haven't worn it for sixteen years; it's like putting on an old skin: extremely uncomfortable but at the same time rather agreeable.

CORDELIA. Oh!

AUNT. Suddenly, in the theatre, I thought: how can I have remained in love, and chaste, for fifteen years?! (*Realises* CORDELIA *has torn the dress.*) Cordelia!

CORDELIA. I'm sorry. I'll repair it.

AUNT. Can you repair the last fifteen years?

A bell rings, off.

They've arrived. I must open the door. I'll have to receive them without a collar! Oh, was ever a person so humiliated by her memories?

CORDELIA *goes out. Returns with* JOHANNES *and* EDVARD, *whose face is very swollen.*

JOHANNES. Good day to you, ladies. My friend's face, as you see, is paralysed by an abscess. He has asked me to be his voice on this occasion. His passions, however, are far from paralysed!

AUNT. His fortitude is much appreciated. I'm afraid we are unaccustomed to receiving guests in our home, but we shall shortly have the pleasure of serving a cup of coffee and some pastries.

EDVARD (*his voice muffled*). This is indeed a home fit for heroes!

JOHANNES. My friend's tooth is sensitive to most forms of heat, though curiously hot air seems not to affect it.

CORDELIA. Oh, the music! I'll fetch some mustard seeds for your tooth. Or some oil of cloves, perhaps? Or hot salt water?

JOHANNES. Marionettes! How wonderful!

AUNT. You're interested in marionettes?

JOHANNES. Madame, you've no idea.

AUNT. Miss: if you please.

CORDELIA *goes out.*

JOHANNES. Not merely as objects; I am fascinated by the whole mechanism, the way the strings facilitate movement.

AUNT. In which case, sir, you are most unusual amongst Danes.

CORDELIA (*enters*). So what's it to be? For your tooth?

EDVARD. Your voice will do, nicely.

CORDELIA. And if I feel disinclined to speak? Salt water, oil of cloves, or mustard seed?

EDVARD. I beg you, just speak!

CORDELIA. I'm sure you didn't come here to listen to me.

AUNT. The coffee, Cordelia!

CORDELIA. I'll go. (*Exits.*)

AUNT. Do you read music? My niece plays the piano rather well. As I trust she will shortly prove. She is to perform in front of the Court.

EDVARD. Ow!

JOHANNES. My Republican friend would sooner hear her play in the courtyards of the poor, I think.

CORDELIA (*returning with coffee cups, etc*). I see you have found your sheet-music, sir.

JOHANNES. Would that I were this melody, that you might play me! Though, I must confess, it surprises me sometimes that young women care for music at all.

CORDELIA. You have no great opinion of our sex? Sir, I brought some mustard seeds for your tooth.

JOHANNES. The magic which music can evoke – with its charm, its poetry, its vibrancy – is present in a young woman as a natural element of her existence. Music is like a marionette: the hand which animates it is the girl herself.

AUNT. Would you like some coffee? Or is the mustard seed sufficient?

EDVARD. Quite sufficient, thank you (*Bites on the seed.*) Ow!

JOHANNES. The subject of music is essentially the genius of the senses; to expound upon it to the world with your hair flying and your shoulders heaving, not to mention the perspiration running down your face, would seem to me rather a perilous exercise.

CORDELIA. Your definition betrays you, sir. What you describe is surely how a deaf man starved of womanly comforts might listen to music?

AUNT. Cordelia! Please, forgive her . . .

EDVARD. I must apologise on behalf of my friend. The fact is, he is in love.

AUNT. I see. A little more coffee?

EDVARD. And as such, he is not free.

JOHANNES. It's the fashion in Denmark to posit false definitions of liberty. What have we known of passion in this country for the past sixteen years? What have we known about the freedom passion brings?

AUNT. Coffee?

CORDELIA. Is she beautiful?

JOHANNES. She is the quintessence of femininity. Imagine all music concentrated into a little Swedish melody. All she needs now, to bring her beauty to full blossom, is the right kind of love. Which would complete her like the series of major chords completes a little Swedish melody.

CORDELIA. Perhaps a few minor chords would be more appropriate?

JOHANNES. If it were just a matter of superficial beauty and charm then, yes, a few minor chords might suffice. But, I am certain, now, that what she needs is something altogether more substantial.

EDVARD. Can we come to the point of our visit?

JOHANNES. Allow me to anticipate my friend's next remark: 'Denmark is a prison!'

EDVARD. It makes my blood boil to watch ladies suffer like this!

JOHANNES. Try not to overheat yourself, Edvard – remember your tooth! Follow my example, instead.

AUNT. It would appear that you are not so much your friend's tongue as his spleen. Here are the documents you asked for. (*Hands them over.*)

EDVARD. Now, I believe, we can win freedom in this country!

JOHANNES. Denmark is certainly a prison, but not necessarily by any design of government.

EDVARD. Well, I think we should be leaving, before my friend here conjures up a theory of the state from the absolute monarchy of his heart! You have my word that we shall return with your documents, once we have triumphed in our cause!

AUNT. In the meantime, I hope you will come to hear Cordelia play.

EDVARD. It would be a great honour! I'll take another mustard seed, if I may. In the Bible, it is used as a measure of faith; I choose to see it as a measure of . . . erm . . . love.

CORDELIA. Take more, if you like. But, sir, I believe I have something of yours.

JOHANNES. Our account is surely settled?

CORDELIA. Your music; I took it home with me . . .

JOHANNES. How can one 'take' music? Or return it, for that matter?

Doorbell sounds, off.

AUNT. Won't you please stay? The pastries have arrived.

Scene 9. The Two Apartments. Darkness.

AUNT'S VOICE. Aren't you asleep?

CORDELIA'S VOICE. I'm too warm.

AUNT'S VOICE. It's past midnight. Try to sleep.

CORDELIA'S VOICE. I have been trying, for hours.

EDVARD'S VOICE. I believe . . . I am very happy. Johannes? Are you working?

JOHANNES'S VOICE. I'm busy creating my lover.

Silence.

EDVARD'S VOICE. Cordelia is so beautiful. So enchanting. So interesting. I think I made quite a good impression, despite my abscess.

JOHANNES'S VOICE. Edvard, a victory gained on a woman's own terms can never amount to much. It's the spirit that she is afraid of, because to embrace that would mean the negation of her very existence as a woman.

EDVARD'S VOICE. What kind of seduction is it that questions her very existence?

JOHANNES'S VOICE. The kind that makes her aware of her own significance. The only genuine kind of seduction there is.

CORDELIA'S VOICE. My bed is so narrow; it might almost be your corset!

AUNT'S VOICE. You must understand, Cordelia, when I put on that corset I re-experience a past embrace, which may not even have happened.

CORDELIA'S VOICE. Why have you never told me what happened to you? Your story?

AUNT'S VOICE. There is no story. There's nothing to tell.

CORDELIA'S VOICE. This man, Johannes – there's something familiar about him.

AUNT'S VOICE. Yes, I thought so, too. What about the other gentleman?

CORDELIA'S VOICE. I know I've seen him before! The other one? Yes, he's quite pleasant . . .

AUNT'S VOICE. You really should try to sleep.

EDVARD'S VOICE. And what about you, Johannes? Did you make any progress at all with your girl, today?

JOHANNES'S VOICE. Oh, I merely adjusted my aim a little. So that when I eventually fire my arrow it will inflict the deepest possible wound.

EDVARD'S VOICE. Well, my plan is to cure, with my love, all the wounds which Fate may have inflicted upon my dear Cordelia.

JOHANNES'S VOICE. Edvard, Edvard – what does Fate know about her? Life is always greater than Fate.

EDVARD'S VOICE. (*yawning*). That sounds like a quote!

JOHANNES'S VOICE. Perhaps it is. Perhaps I just read everything, somewhere. Perhaps this girl of mine is no more than a few pages of notes in my book.

EDVARD'S VOICE. Be careful, or it will be the book you'll fall in love with! Meanwhile, I intend to marry my flesh-and-blood Cordelia!

Scene 10. The Sheet-Music Shop.

EDVARD. I'm sorry; I was hoping to find somebody else here . . .

JANSEN. Well, thank you! You're not the one I was expecting, either.

EDVARD. Perhaps . . . we're looking for the same person?

JANSEN. Usually, in a sheet-music shop, one is looking for music.

EDVARD. A young lady . . .

JANSEN. She's minding the shop whilst her father eats his lunch. But, then, you knew that, didn't you?

EDVARD. What do I need with sheet-music?

JANSEN. What, for that matter, do you need with a young lady?

EDVARD. I have to tell her something.

JANSEN. Well, don't be shy. Tell her!

EDVARD. But . . . she's not here.

JANSEN. The beard is a mark of your politics, I know. But, tell me, what's your blindness a badge of?

EDVARD. I am looking for Miss Cordelia Wahl. I must speak to her.

JANSEN. Oh, I see. Politics?

EDVARD. It's in her interest that she hears what I have to say.

JANSEN. Ah. A pretext!

EDVARD. Will you give her this message?

JANSEN. Is it about sheet-music?

Scene 11. The Beach.

JOHANNES. Be careful. The tide's coming in.

CORDELIA. Oh, it's you. You startled me.

JOHANNES. I was present in the landscape all the while; until a secret force conjured me forth!

CORDELIA. It must be rather unpleasant, to always have an answer to everything.

JOHANNES. Would you rather I said that I, like you, have escaped my duties in order to follow the yearnings of my heart?

CORDELIA. Do you really feel everything so acutely, or . . . ? Are you spying on me?

JOHANNES. We do seem to run into each other rather a lot, don't we? Our duties, and yearnings, seem to dovetail so neatly, we might almost think of them as a kind of embrace. Particularly on Wednesdays.

CORDELIA. Actually, today is Thursday.

JOHANNES. In which case, coincidence has nothing to do with it!

CORDELIA. And what duty, or yearning, brings you to the beach today? To embarrass somebody, perhaps?

JOHANNES. I was following a blind god.

CORDELIA. Oh dear! What a tawdry metaphor! You've been frequenting a certain café, haven't you – with a little marzipan cherub, complete with bow and arrow, in the window?

JOHANNES. Justitia?

CORDELIA. I assumed you were referring to Cupid.

JOHANNES. Of course, the blind god of Love!

CORDELIA. So, you're plotting a rendezvous with Justice, are you, here on the beach?

JOHANNES. During my previous wanderings here, I reached the conclusion that God and Justice could not appear simultaneously. (*Pause.*) I was mistaken.

CORDELIA. I think you'll find most young women prefer their compliments a little less grandiose! (*Pause.*) It seems to have turned out rather pleasant, after all.

JOHANNES. God was simply making a virtue of necessity, when He made Woman capable of that which He is not.

CORDELIA. Why must you invoke God, all the time? Do you so mistrust words?

JOHANNES. Whilst He was creating woman, God cast man into a dream, so that she might appear to him as the substance of his dream. Which explains why you were so familiar to me when I first saw you.

CORDELIA. I think I'll let you carry on dreaming . . .

JOHANNES. But, ever since then, I feel strangely incomplete.

CORDELIA. I must go.

JOHANNES. It's of no consequence.

CORDELIA. Oh?

JOHANNES. My happiness remains. It appears that my desire may be fulfilled.

CORDELIA. If I may say so, that sounds rather alarming, here, on the beach!

JOHANNES. Go then, if you're frightened. If you prefer compliments about your hair, or your eyes, your fragrance – if you think they are more personal. In that case, creation came of nothing; a few fish-bones, some wisps of hair. Mere substitutes.

CORDELIA. Goodbye. And God bless you.

JOHANNES. Yes. He does.

Scene 12. Johannes's Apartment.

EDVARD. How can you eat so calmly?

JOHANNES. Good Jutland crackling; I recommend it.

EDVARD. Didn't you see? Twice whilst she was playing she smiled at me! It was most unsettling!

JOHANNES. Why? Here, have some.

EDVARD. I don't want your crackling! Then she sat beside me as if determined to embarrass me! Whilst you virtually seduced her aunt on the spot!

JOHANNES (*eating*). I went to the library this morning, read a few books about marionettes. I was well prepared.

EDVARD. Must you speak about these things with your mouth full! It's most disconcerting!

JOHANNES. It will be even more disconcerting when the meat is finished! Good Jutland pork, roasted slowly in beer, then garnished with garlic.

EDVARD. Is it true that you met Cordelia on the beach, the other day?

JOHANNES. Yes. Beer?

EDVARD. No! Can't you help me? When I think about the liberation of Denmark, everything is so clear; but when I think about Cordelia, it's just a muddle!

JOHANNES. Put the two together. Conquer Cordelia by liberating Denmark! Political power has its allure, you know.

EDVARD. Of course. An excellent idea! The first boatload of exiles is leaving Stettin, tonight. They'll be home by noon, tomorrow.

JOHANNES. If you tune your voice properly to seduction, you can take any topic you like – parliamentarianism, roast pork, the weather – and you can't fail to hit your target.

EDVARD. Oh, I'm so nervous, just thinking about it! I don't think I can do it on my own, Johannes.

JOHANNES. Don't ask any more erotic favours from me.

EDVARD. Please, just this once . . . Remember, her aunt will be there, too.

JOHANNES. Everything is more dangerous on the beach. Don't forget, I'm in love, too.

EDVARD. Sometimes, I wonder whether you haven't forgotten it.

JOHANNES. Only when my love dictates.

Scene 13. The Beach.

AUNT. Perhaps everything will be the same as it was before?

EDVARD. See the ship, in the distance? My dear Cordelia, can you see the pilot boat! And the naval frigate?

CORDELIA. Dear Cordelia sees well enough.

EDVARD. We are on the threshold of a great moment in Denmark's history!

AUNT. These past sixteen years have been like a single, terrible moment stretched into an eternity!

JOHANNES. How desire intensifies the beauty of the afflicted! It's always the lover, and not the beloved, who is divine. Those passions which you suppress, you never forget.

CORDELIA. I'm cold. Shall we go?

AUNT. Cold? In this warm breeze?

EDVARD. My dear little Cordelia, would you like to borrow my coat?

CORDELIA. A little coat to protect little Cordelia from the little wind? Ugh.

AUNT. What's come over you, Cordelia? You were perfectly happy when we arrived.

CORDELIA. I wasn't happy at all! (*Low, to her* AUNT.) Do you have to give everything away?

JOHANNES. I would happily walk you home, but your temper is so becoming.

CORDELIA. I'm glad to hear there is something about me you like!

EDVARD. A third naval frigate? What's happening?

AUNT. What force lies latent in sixteen years of longing!

JOHANNES. Only time can ripen hope.

AUNT. The desire of Youth knows nothing about hope!

EDVARD. All Denmark's hope is present here! See, Cordelia, how the Danish people darken the shore; they've come to greet their Liberty!

JOHANNES. Nonsense, Edvard; they're incapable of exploiting even the liberty they have, let alone demanding more.

CORDELIA. This is hardly the time or place for such melancholic reflection.

EDVARD. My dear, Johannes just likes to play to an audience. If he and I were here alone, he would no doubt argue for the rights of the people most strenuously, as in the past.

JOHANNES. The mob spat on Christ and mocked His love; Socrates was sentenced to death, democratically.

EDVARD. Cordelia, you love the Danish people, don't you?

CORDELIA. Yes, I do. Most certainly.

JOHANNES. Of course, it's perfectly understandable that a young woman should want to hide her feelings amongst those of the mob.

AUNT. The ship appears to have stopped.

EDVARD. The frigates have surrounded it. Denmark cannot be thwarted now!

JOHANNES. No, not now, it's been thwarted already. Can't you hear it, this multitude, whimpering as one. They are afraid, yes, horribly afraid, of their own feelings. They are not prepared for love at all!

CORDELIA. Please, shut up!

EDVARD. Look . . .

AUNT. We're listening, Johannes.

JOHANNES. Cordelia is right; perhaps I should say it to her, alone. After all, she appeared to me when I was wrestling with my feelings. She appeared like a portent. And since then I know that I am lost, that I love her, desperately, joyfully. And that I no longer have any choice but to reject forever the commandment, 'Thou shalt not love. Ever.' How can it be a sin to feel what I feel now in my heart? Yes, Cordelia – I love you.

EDVARD. Johannes!

CORDELIA. Ah.

JOHANNES. I am yours, with my sins, my desires, my obsessions, my betrayals, my despair, my devotion, my joy. I'm yours, Cordelia. You may journey to the end of the world, you may confer your love on a hundred others, yet still I am yours, even unto death!

AUNT (*embraces her niece*). Cordelia!

EDVARD. Johannes! Oh my God! The ship has been turned back! All is lost!

JOHANNES. Lost?

Scene 14. The Sheet-Music shop.

Enter EDVARD, *more unshaven, wearing an arm-band.*

JANSEN. Can I help you?

EDVARD. I . . . want some sheet-music.

JANSEN. How surprising!

EDVARD. Won't you help me?

JANSEN. With pleasure.

EDVARD. Then give me some!

JANSEN. It might be easier if you told me which piece you desire.

EDVARD. A four-handed piece.

JANSEN. Or, at any rate, two of them?

EDVARD. Is it possible to buy them, separately?

JANSEN. In parts, you mean? Of course. Would you like the primo or the secondo?

EDVARD. Secondo. I'm a democrat.

JANSEN. You'd prefer perhaps the hands themselves to the music they play?

EDVARD. Are you mocking me?!

JANSEN. Not at all. And to prove it, here, I'll give you my own copy. I leave it to you to decide the appropriate payment.

EDVARD. On behalf of the young Denmark, I thank you, but I fear I cannot accept.

JANSEN. Try thanking me on your own behalf – you might find it easier to accept. And also, perhaps, to return the gesture.

EDVARD. Should I accept it as charity, to soothe my grief?

JANSEN. Accept it rather as a sample. Another time, you might come here for some sheet-music, instead of whoever it is you've lost.

EDVARD. There's no justice in Denmark! (*He goes out.*)

Silence. CORDELIA *enters with a sunflower.*

JANSEN. You came too late, Cordelia.

CORDELIA. Yes, I know.

JANSEN. How do you know? Were you spying?

CORDELIA. Look at this flower, isn't it beautiful? I found it this morning, hanging on our front door.

JANSEN. A sunflower. Careful, it's probably infested with blackfly. Is it from him?

CORDELIA. Edvard? No. He'd be frightened of insects!

JANSEN. Yet, show me a more handsome man in all Copenhagen! And passionate! He's alight with conviction!

CORDELIA. The arm-band was very becoming.

JANSEN. Have you come for some piano practice?

CORDELIA. No. Later, perhaps. At our apartment. My aunt is unwell again. Tut, now I've broken the flower. Is that a bad omen, do you think?

JANSEN. It depends where it came from.

CORDELIA. I told you, I found it hanging on the door handle.

JANSEN. It's hardly a generous gift.

CORDELIA. It felt like my own private sunrise!

JANSEN. And if your aunt had left the house before you – then it would have been her sunrise, I suppose?

CORDELIA. It's broken, now. You're right. I'll just throw it away. Can I dispose of it here?

JANSEN. Be my guest.

CORDELIA. It's leaked its sap all over my hand. It stinks! My hand is all wet!

JANSEN. Give it a quick wash.

CORDELIA. No. Actually, it's not such an unpleasant smell. Rather bitter. Natural.

JANSEN. What shall you do now?

CORDELIA. I'll take it. I'm in a hurry. I have to cancel some pastries for this afternoon. I don't think we'll be receiving guests, any more.

JANSEN. You're not going already? Cordelia!

CORDELIA. You know . . . when Johannes looks at me . . .

JANSEN. Don't talk to me about the way men look!

CORDELIA. It's as if he touches me, accidentally . . . holds me . . . presses against me . . . If I close my eyes, I can feel it. Vividly.

JANSEN. Careful, the door is closed!

Scene 15. The Café.

EDVARD *enters with a sword at his side, wearing an arm-band.*

EDVARD. Johannes! At last, I've found you!

JOHANNES. Oh? Did your sword impede your search?

EDVARD. They were issued this afternoon. Our patience is exhausted.

JOHANNES. Do you mind if I finish my coffee? It's the best there is in all Copenhagen.

EDVARD. Don't worry – I shan't burden you with my passions.

JOHANNES. Happy the man who has control of his passions.

EDVARD. There were two betrayals yesterday. The king broke his word about the exiles . . .

JOHANNES. And?

EDVARD. You knew I loved that girl!

JOHANNES. So love her. Take her. There's no betrayal.

EDVARD. I'm going to throw this coffee in your face in a minute!

JOHANNES. Please, try to understand. All I desire is freedom, in the purest sense.

EDVARD. You made me appear ridiculous in front of Cordelia.

JOHANNES. If you can't instil your poetry into a girl such that everything appears to proceed from her desire for you, then you're nothing but a dilettante. Nor will you ever be anything else.

EDVARD. But yesterday you were busy instilling your poetry into her aunt!

JOHANNES. Yes. That was a ploy, to stir Cordelia's emotions.

EDVARD. I didn't come here to listen to you.

JOHANNES. And yet, you know, the other girl has quite taken a fancy to you.

EDVARD. Must you add insult to injury?!

JOHANNES. Some men are only capable of an ordinary, prosaic love. For Cordelia to fall for such a man, would be . . . like peasants feasting on caviar.

EDVARD. Here – have some coffee! (*Dashes the coffee into* JOHANNES'*s face.*)

JOHANNES. I think I prefer it in the usual way, actually. Even this, you manage to spoil, Edvard.

EDVARD. I'm moving out, today!

JOHANNES. As you wish. I had to insult you, so you might leave me alone.

EDVARD. What?

JOHANNES. Do not attempt to judge something which you don't understand, Edvard. Perhaps I shall be the loser here. Perhaps, finally, you will be the one who finds happiness.

EDVARD. I refuse to listen to you any more! (*Leaves.*)

CORDELIA *enters with the sunflower in her hand.*

CORDELIA. Oh. I didn't realise you would be here.

JOHANNES. This is such an excellent café.

CORDELIA. Have you tried drinking your coffee?

JOHANNES (*pointing to the coffee stain on his shirt*). The first stain of passion! Have you noticed that the sunflower is looking straight at you?

CORDELIA. The stalk is broken.

JOHANNES. It seems passion leaves its mark on that, too.

CORDELIA. So, tell me; what is so wonderful about this café?

JOHANNES. You are here.

CORDELIA. You barely know me.

JOHANNES. No. All knowledge worth the name will become available, only from now on.

CORDELIA. You're very sure of yourself.

JOHANNES. Yes, because I observe the slight flush of your cheeks. And your hand, sticky with the sap of a sunflower.

CORDELIA. I've already thrown it away, once!

JOHANNES. Only once? I'm glad to hear it.

CORDELIA. You're much older than me.

JOHANNES. There is precisely an eternity between us.

CORDELIA. Don't you use any other scale?

JOHANNES. Before, I did. But then I hadn't seen you.

CORDELIA. That sounds terrifying!

JOHANNES. Yes, but you have saved me from fear.

CORDELIA. I don't know why I said yes.

JOHANNES. Did you say yes?

CORDELIA. No! I mean, why I didn't say no immediately.

JOHANNES. To what? To my feelings?

CORDELIA. You confused me, though . . . Sometimes I quite like to listen to you.

JOHANNES. A young woman is a miracle of nature; anything you might see in me, is merely a glimpse of yourself in an imperfect mirror.

CORDELIA. Oh my God. How time flies! I must be leaving.

JOHANNES. Please, don't leave like this.

CORDELIA. Don't stop me, please. You'll spoil everything.

JOHANNES. It's wonderful to know that there's something to spoil!

CORDELIA. You really are being most disagreeable!

JOHANNES. I want only the best for you. Even if you leave, you can't deny that you came here precisely to have this conversation?

CORDELIA. I didn't even know you were here!

JOHANNES. Prove it! Have you an alibi?

CORDELIA. Yes. I came to cancel an order of pastries. My aunt has decided that we shall not be receiving guests, ever again.

Scene 16. Cordelia's Room.

CORDELIA. So, you woke up after all?

AUNT. I've found all my old dresses.

CORDELIA. They're lovely. With a little alteration you could easily still wear them.

AUNT. It's me that needs alteration, I think! What's that you have there? Give it to me.

CORDELIA. I found it. So early in the summer, too! I'll put it into water.

AUNT. You must understand that I can't give up so easily.

CORDELIA. Oh, the vase! (*It breaks.*)

AUNT. But how can you understand? You're still so young; perhaps it's right that you shouldn't understand.

CORDELIA. It was such an ugly vase; but these fragments are beautiful . . .

AUNT. Perhaps you think it rather tasteless of me, rather desperate, but I cannot decide otherwise. Cordelia, you'll cut yourself!

CORDELIA. Yes.

AUNT. I was thinking about it all night.

CORDELIA. My fingers are bleeding. The blood tastes good, salty.

AUNT. What has got into you, Cordelia?

CORDELIA. I can feel the shape of the vase in my palm, but inside, where everything is sharp, jagged, painful.

AUNT. This morning I received a message from him.

CORDELIA. From him?! I think I'll just throw out these pieces. And the sunflower . . .

AUNT. Cordelia! Your first love is always the best thing that happens to you, even if it is unrequited.

CORDELIA'S VOICE. I can't hear you!

AUNT. My marionettist; he means to return with the other exiles.

CORDELIA (*appears*). Oh, you're talking about him?

AUNT. I don't mind saying, after sixteen years of fidelity I was sorely tempted. But I was saved by the same grace which now brings me this letter.

CORDELIA. I'll find another vase. (*Exits.*)

AUNT. Did you cancel the pastries?

CORDELIA (*enters*). Yes.

AUNT. Shame.

CORDELIA. I could run back to the café, perhaps?

AUNT. But Miss Jansen is due any minute, for your piano practice.

CORDELIA. Of course. I'd completely forgotten.

AUNT. Last night, I realised it was because of me that the ship was turned back.

CORDELIA. See how beautiful the flower is in this light. Which way it will turn, I wonder?

A doorbell rings, off.

AUNT. Who on earth can that be? I'm still in my corset!

CORDELIA. I'll go and see. (*Exits. Returns.*) That's strange. It was a boy, with the pastries.

AUNT. Cordelia – you've never lied to me before.

CORDELIA. Nor am I now! It's a mistake. I'll send them back. Honestly . . . Someone's making fun of me!

AUNT. Look out, you've got blood on the paper! And the ribbon. Is that a calling card?

CORDELIA. Johannes?

AUNT. He would like to call on us, this afternoon. But you must practise with Miss Jansen. What is it, Cordelia?

CORDELIA. Can't I even sit down?!

AUNT. Must you sit on my dresses? Your hand is bleeding . . .

CORDELIA. Obviously, I can't play the piano – I've cut myself, here . . . and here. Well, can I?

Doorbell, off.

AUNT. Answer that. (*Exits.*)

CORDELIA. Oh my God, he's here, already! (*Exits. Enters with* JANSEN.)

JANSEN. What do you mean, 'only' me? You asked me to come, this morning, in the shop.

CORDELIA. Look what happened to my hand. Have you ever tasted your own blood?

JANSEN. Ugh!

CORDELIA. It's good. Salty.

JANSEN. Salt pastries? Are you expecting someone? Cordelia. Eh?

CORDELIA. He's invited himself. What am I supposed to do about it?

JANSEN. You could do your hair, for a start. Have you got your music?

CORDELIA. We don't even know if there will be a Court by Midsummer's Eve, still less if they'll want us to play for them.

JANSEN. So, what do you want me to do, Cordelia?

CORDELIA. My hair, perhaps? No. Perhaps we shouldn't receive him. Look, the flower looks at me, wherever I go.

Doorbell, off.

JANSEN. I can send him away, if you wish.

CORDELIA. Would you? How . . . How heartless you are! You could show him in, perhaps?

JANSEN *exits, returns with* JOHANNES.

JOHANNES. Good afternoon.

CORDELIA. Your announcement . . . took me by surprise.

JANSEN. We were supposed to practise for our concert.

JOHANNES. May I listen?

CORDELIA. No, no, I think we will spare you from the sight of heaving, perspiring women this afternoon. Or, whatever it was you once said.

JOHANNES. Your memory would be more impressive if you employed it more shrewdly.

CORDELIA. Besides, I've an injury which prevents me practising today.

JOHANNES. They're nice cuts. Good and deep.

CORDELIA. Compassion is clearly not one of your strong points, either.

JOHANNES. Compassion? Are these wounds the result of an accident?

CORDELIA. Our vase shattered!

JOHANNES. I'm glad to see that the flower survived.

JANSEN. The blackfly, also.

CORDELIA. I think you should practise on your own, this afternoon.

JANSEN. I see. Well, don't bother to see me out. (*Exits.*)

CORDELIA. Oh, what have I done? Excuse me, I'll just fetch . . . my aunt.

JOHANNES. Don't hurry, Cordelia. I was mistaken.

CORDELIA. I beg your pardon?

JOHANNES. I was talking to you about love.

CORDELIA. You talked about so many things . . .

JOHANNES. I have a strange secret in the depth of my heart. It's much deeper than love.

CORDELIA. And so? No . . .

JOHANNES. No!

CORDELIA. I must bandage my hands.

JOHANNES. No one can relieve me of this secret, except one particular girl . . .

CORDELIA. And what? You were mistaken about the girl?

JOHANNES. I was mistaken about the feeling. Every word I utter removes me further from that which needs to be said.

CORDELIA. Then, don't talk, Johannes.

JOHANNES. Can silence bear the secret of this love?

CORDELIA. What else can bear it?

AUNT (*appears at the door, exquisitely dressed, beautiful*). Johannes!

Scene 17. The Two Apartments.

Darkness.

CORDELIA'S VOICE. It's nearly dawn.

AUNT'S VOICE. It's time we had separate bedrooms.

JOHANNES'S VOICE. (*reading*). He who loses his love to another, loses also his doubts thereto.

AUNT'S VOICE. What are you eating?

CORDELIA'S VOICE. Nothing. Just the pastries.

AUNT'S VOICE. Was that the rustling of paper I heard?

CORDELIA'S VOICE. There was a letter under the tray.

AUNT'S VOICE. A messenger came with another letter, this evening. How persistent he is!

CORDELIA'S VOICE. That was the third letter, then. He gave me one before he left.

JOHANNES'S VOICE. (*reading*). She was so young, and yet so mature. Like rich and tender nature, her mother would free her with a kiss, a kiss like a seal only one person in the world can break. With their first uttered intimacy, lovers shed their former selves and at once sink into a sea of love, and are as old friends, though they have known each other but an instant.

CORDELIA'S VOICE. Tell me – how can a robe be happy? Or an eiderdown?

AUNT'S VOICE. What do mean, happy?

CORDELIA'S VOICE. By being close to me!

AUNT'S VOICE. What about your aunt – she's close to you, can't she be happy?

CORDELIA'S VOICE. Forgive me.

AUNT'S VOICE. It's too late. It's dawn.

JOHANNES'S VOICE (*reads*). Everything is fragile still, translucent, yet soon it will ripen into light and splendour. The rays will pierce the void, themselves insubstantial, to be gently garnered and multiplied by the sea.

CORDELIA'S VOICE. I'd so like to see the dawn. I've never seen it; that moment when the dawn releases the morning. We could walk along the beach. Shall we? Shall we go?

    CORDELIA *crosses to her* AUNT's *bed*.

CORDELIA'S VOICE. What's the matter? What? Are you crying?

Scene 18. Johannes' Apartment.

JOHANNES (*enters*). An unexpected twist in the plot! Well, what's it to be – Punishment or Pardon?

WILHELM. Neither.

JOHANNES. Wilhelm? Well, well. Are supplies running low in Jutland, already?

WILHELM (*they embrace each other*). It's you that I have come for, Johannes.

JOHANNES. I'm sorry? Did Edvard let you in?

WILHELM. He told me everything.

JOHANNES. Edvard's 'everything' is rather less than comprehensive, I'm afraid.

WILHELM. I would believe you, Johannes, but I have been reading whilst waiting for you to arrive . . .

JOHANNES. You read too much, brother.

WILHELM. If you pack your things, we can leave.

JOHANNES. Leave? Why not? The beach at dawn is beautiful at this time of year. Tell me, what exactly have you been reading?

WILHELM (*goes into the other room, returns with the ledger*). This.

JOHANNES. Where did you find that?

WILHELM. Edvard mentioned that you had recently been working a lot at night. I saw it on your desk. It looked familiar.

JOHANNES. Didn't it occur to you that it might not be my theology notes?

WILHELM. I was surprised that it wasn't. I feel as though I've stumbled on a forger's den: fragments of letters, notes, maps, essays, diary entries. It seems to me, Johannes, that this girl is nothing but a prop in some infernal experiment you're conducting. For God's sake, you're systematically ambushing her soul!

JOHANNES. What is theology, except an attempt to calculate the incomprehensible? Why berate me when I try to do the same thing with love? Or would you prefer that I love Cordelia as Edvard does – by reducing her to banality?

WILHELM. I don't know which I find the more repellent; your salacious accounts of spying on the girl and engineering meetings with her; or the attempts to justify the whole exercise, philosophically. Even theologically! This entire metaphysical arsenal of yours is riddled with Hegel, the Old Testament, Abraham and Isaac . . . And for what? A pair of ovaries?!

JOHANNES. It's easier if you hate me, Wilhelm. And now, if you'll excuse me, I must go.

WILHELM. Edvard is right. You treat this innocent girl as nothing but a drug for your own sick soul.

JOHANNES. Why can't you understand, Wilhelm, that for me Jutland, Berlin and Love are simply different aspects of the same argument?

WILHELM. You are despicable!

JOHANNES. Perhaps your soul is so crippled that you can differentiate between the Old Testament and a lover's look, or Abraham and Isaac, or a stolen kiss. Or, for that matter, Hegel and 'a pair of ovaries'! The only place you can recognise Grace is in a church; if Redemption arrived in the guise of a beautiful girl, you'd simply refuse to recognise it!

WILHELM. Redemption, from a dawn rendezvous on the beach? Please, spare me!

JOHANNES. You think God disapproves of such an explanation? Then, let that be a matter between me and God. These are questions which you can no longer even ask, yet which Fate impels me to answer!

WILHELM. Agnete was right. This isn't love.

JOHANNES. Love? Who knows what that is?

Scene 19. The Beach.

CORDELIA. Ah, so you are here?

JOHANNES. You were expecting me? That sounds promising.

CORDELIA. Well . . . the sunflower . . . the letters . . .

JOHANNES. The light is wonderful, reflecting off the sea onto your face . . .

CORDELIA. You should look at the sea, instead. Watch the dawn reflected in it. Two infinities joined together by light.

JOHANNES. Did you notice how strange the city was? Everything is so quiet. Too quiet. The shutters are closed, the barricades unmanned. It's a tense silence. Dense also.

CORDELIA. I don't know. I don't understand simple things any more.

JOHANNES. In the labyrinth of the heart, every girl is Ariadne, clasping the thread which may guide her out. Yet clasping it in a way that renders it useless to her.

He ties her hand with a golden ribbon.

CORDELIA. You wish to demonstrate the story?

JOHANNES. It's just a piece of thread they use in cafés to tie up cake-boxes.

CORDELIA. I can still talk, even if you chose to take my hand . . .

JOHANNES. But if I were to hold you captive with this golden thread? Then, you could not continue on your way.

CORDELIA. What if I wished to continue standing here, anticipating with my wounds the caress of your thread?

JOHANNES. You do understand, don't you, that all my actions merely reflect your will?

CORDELIA. What was it you said once: a woman is simply a man's dream? We dream most deeply just before the dawn.

JOHANNES. In this dawn there are two dreams interwoven. In the first, love is dreaming of a girl: in the second, the girl is dreaming of love.

CORDELIA. How heavy my hand has become, tied like this. How extremely heavy.

JOHANNES. I'll help you. I'll bear you, Cordelia.

Scene 20. Cordelia's Apartment.

The Swedish melody is played on the piano.

AUNT. Not so loud, Cordelia, you might be misunderstood! You play with such energy, and so loudly! It must sound like an earthquake, outside! How can you play – dinner is ready – with your injured hand? The lights are blinking. The young men have taken to the streets in their hundreds, with their torches! Will everyone return now, in the same way? My dress isn't tight at all any more, Cordelia! The city is flooded with people, like a sea of flame rushing in, lighting up all the grey, sad streets! Dinner is served! So many young men! Why don't you stop, now? There'll be no Court to play for, now! I had another message today – the prison is ablaze! Cordelia! Such light! The dinner has broken out, the revolution will get cold! Can you hear me? Cordelia?

Marionettes dance in the intense light.

Blackout.

ACT TWO

Scene 1. The Café, now in Ruins.

CORDELIA. Johannes? Are you here? Johannes? Where are you? Are you . . . ?

JOHANNES. I just wanted to hear your voice. I wanted to hear . . .

CORDELIA. Why did we have to meet here?

JOHANNES. This is the scene of my love's awakening! Alas, now in ruins.

CORDELIA. Your hands are so hot! The fire spread to this building from the prison. Everything's reduced to ashes. Except this little golden ribbon on my finger; the heat of your love has transformed it into real gold.

JOHANNES. It's over, now. Stray dogs have occupied the ruins.

CORDELIA. I went to the beach hoping I'd find you there. That's where everything fell into place for me. (*She gives him a stone.*) This is for you.

JOHANNES. Were you looking for evidence, too?

CORDELIA. Or my partner in crime, perhaps!

JOHANNES. Is it a stone?

CORDELIA. I don't know. Isn't it metal, like the ring?

JOHANNES. You found it on the beach?

CORDELIA. I think it's truer to say that it found me. The first time I was there, it stopped me blowing away on the storm of your confession! I found it, then, on that momentous morning.

JOHANNES. Cordelia, of the two of us, it is you who is really free. My ring is such a poor symbol of our union. Even if it's understood ironically, its value is questionable.

CORDELIA. You said that what's important between us is the joy of freedom which makes us immune to gravity, both physical and moral.

JOHANNES. How smooth it is. It fits perfectly into my palm. Like an ancient statue, worn down by the sea.

CORDELIA. Or formed by it, perhaps? (*Noticing the ledger.*) Have you been working?

JOHANNES. This way I have you near me whenever I need you. Or my own poetic version of you, at least.

CORDELIA. So, this is the source of all your wonderful letters! (*Reads.*) Berlin? . . . How do I know that these words aren't for somebody else?

JOHANNES. You're surprised that I have loved someone before you? That's understandable. Nor can I deny it. But, Cordelia, just consider; how long did this stone have to wait before you found it? I realise, now, that my love for you is as old as I am.

CORDELIA. Is that all?

JOHANNES. I'm older than you, remember.

CORDELIA. Only by a childhood.

JOHANNES. Look at the stone, Cordelia. I'd say there is an eternity between us.

CORDELIA. Good. That's good.

Scene 2. Cordelia's Apartment.

The marionettes have been rearranged in the room.

AUNT. Please, forgive my tears. I misunderstood your message, completely.

WILHELM. My world has also been turned upside down. I wasn't in Jutland. Though, had I been, I should have come anyway on hearing this news. So, your niece and my half-brother have announced their betrothal?

AUNT. I must take some measure of responsibility in the matter.

WILHELM. Responsibility? Yes, that's a good word.

AUNT. She's here. She wanted to look her best for her future brother-in-law.

WILHELM. Half-brother . . .

CORDELIA (*enters*). May I greet you with a kiss?

WILHELM. It won't make my task any easier if you do.

CORDELIA. Task?

WILHELM. Cordelia: let Johannes go!

CORDELIA. What do you mean?

WILHELM. For your sake – I wouldn't have come, otherwise – but also for his sake. Don't succumb to his charms! See through them instead!

CORDELIA. How charmingly you express yourself, sir. Though, of course, your appeal is too transparent to be at all convincing.

WILHELM. You may believe that capitulation to the power of seduction prior to your engagement in some way makes you more free. But, Cordelia, don't you understand, the act makes a prisoner of your soul! Cordelia, this is your last chance!

CORDELIA. Free, you say? Yes. Johannes is free. In me, he has at last embraced freedom, he said. Those were his very words. If I refuse him now, I'll make him a prisoner, again.

AUNT. Cordelia, don't bite your nails, my dear.

CORDELIA. They're my nails! Nor am I your dear!

WILHELM. Cordelia, the very quality that attracts you to Johannes, which gives his words and eyes their sparkle, may be the very thing which eventually drives him to suicide! Haven't you noticed how overheated his passions are? How emotionally immature he is? Cordelia, Johannes is in the process of losing his faith; by blinding himself with your beauty he thinks he can avoid the issue. But he has to confront it, sooner or later.

CORDELIA. In the beginning, I did think he spoke rather excessively about God, and Creation, Eternity. Until I realised that, actually, he was right. And since then I too see the world in these terms.

WILHELM. Cordelia! Please, understand me. Johannes is incapable of love.

CORDELIA. Nonsense. He has taught me everything I know about love . . .

WILHELM. He doesn't have the strength for love! Why else would he commit himself to theology, which is far less a burden? Yet, even that he couldn't bear. The weight of this will crush him.

CORDELIA. Ah, so that's why you're here! Dear Wilhelm, even if I wanted to help you, if I wanted to relieve Johannes of the lightness of love and force him back into freedom . . . I haven't the strength. I love him, yes. But not because I want to, or choose to, but because my love possesses me. Nothing can rid me of this freedom and no weight can possibly outweigh this lightness.

WILHELM. Oh, Cordelia; I wish I hadn't previously encountered these sentiments in Johannes's diary.

CORDELIA. You hear Johannes's words in my mouth? Quite possibly. But I am perfectly happy to be lost. The more lost I am, the happier I shall become.

WILHELM. I see it's too late for words. I shall try prayer, instead. (*Leaves.*)

AUNT. Cordelia, your nails!

CORDELIA. What about them?!

AUNT. Here you are, on the verge of womanhood, behaving more and more like a child!

CORDELIA. I perspire, continuously. My body is clammy and my lips are sore; I can't help biting them.

AUNT. You neglect your hair, also: not to mention your attire. One day, you study yourself for hours in the mirror; the next, you barely glance at yourself.

CORDELIA. Miss Jansen wears lipstick and paints her eyes. Last time she was here she wore the tightest corset.

AUNT. You've no need of such things. You've only to anticipate Johannes's arrival and your eyes, your skin, and your hair, compete to outshine each other! Yet, you no longer play the piano . . .

CORDELIA. I don't need that, either. The air is filled, constantly, with the most exquisite music.

AUNT. But your nails, Cordelia . . .

CORDELIA. Oh, how can you be so petty!

AUNT. Because, my dear, I too once bit my nails; I've heard the music that you hear; I've felt the love that you feel for Johannes. I, too, have experienced that sudden sense of everything sliding into place . . .

CORDELIA. I don't understand . . .

AUNT. Cordelia, I chewed my nails to the quick, and for what! And all because I dared not believe that the price we must pay for Everything is Everything. Cordelia, to win Everything you must sacrifice Everything! As long as you are disturbed by inaudible music – and perspire, innocently – as long as you chew your nails! – then, you are still a child. But ultimately, Cordelia, you have to become a woman! And I wish you would learn this lesson from my experience, and not from your own.

Scene 3. Johannes's Apartment.

JOHANNES. So. Did you manage to exchange everything for Agnete? It cannot have been easy; cheaper medicines, safer contraceptives . . .

WILHELM. Don't use that tone with me, Johannes; you know nothing of such things!

JOHANNES. You enjoyed the challenge, clearly.

WILHELM. I worry about you. I think you're scared, Johannes.

JOHANNES. Are Jutland clergymen given to such platitudes, or do you refer to something specific, Wilhelm?

WILHELM. Something very specific, Johannes.

JOHANNES. Another time, Wilhelm, I think you'd be advised to leave your shopping duties to me. Come, let's be on our way . . .

WILHELM. I went to see Cordelia. I tried to persuade her to abandon this affair.

JOHANNES. Another item on Agnete's list?

WILHELM. Alas, I appealed in vain.

JOHANNES. Of course. (*To himself.*) Oh, my dear Cordelia . . . My dear Wilhelm, you must understand, the real force that drives this love is poetry! Cordelia feels herself defined by her love for me; the greater her love, the greater her sense of self. You could say, in theological terms, that I am her Continuous Revelation!

WILHELM. You must marry her, Johannes.

JOHANNES. Forgive me, Wilhelm; if I'm to understand that you think seduction, however sinful as a means, is here achieving the perfect ends, then, yes, I would agree with you . . .

WILHELM. What you're to understand, Johannes, is my disgust at a man satisfying himself with a woman's unconditional love – her entire soul! – whilst offering her a love conditional in the extreme!

JOHANNES. And what if I were to tell you that I'm afraid to love her with my entire soul?

WILHELM. Johannes, believe me: the fear that turns you into a seducer is small compared to the terrors that can lurk in the depths of marriage. Yet, matrimony is the only thing that can save you from this fear. To conquer another takes pride, energy, desire: but to retain them requires humility, modesty, patience. I was convinced before that this passion would devour you: now, I realise it offers your only possible escape from despair.

JOHANNES. I hope you neglected to burden Cordelia with this conclusion of yours!

WILHELM. I've only just arrived at it myself. Her love surprised me. It disturbed me.

JOHANNES. And saddened you, it seems. But, Wilhelm, if you're not careful you'll miss your boat. And Jutland will miss you!

WILHELM. Yes, I should leave now, but . . . Johannes, I came back here to convince you that what you are experiencing is not love, that your escape from despair lies in another direction entirely. But, when I read your diary . . . and met Cordelia . . . All Friday afternoon, I was thinking . . . And now, here I am, sitting on my suitcase . . . It's evening . . . and I find that I am lost, not simply for words, but for the conviction which should underpin those words! How can I return to Jutland, in this spirit? I can't.

Scene 4. A Street.

CORDELIA *and* JOHANNES *in the rain.*

CORDELIA. Let's get soaked, Johannes! Please, let's get really drenched!

JOHANNES. Let me just look at you a little longer.

CORDELIA. But you've been looking at me all afternoon! Which might have been acceptable had I been playing the piano, but we were meant to be playing quoits!

JOHANNES. Ah, the golden rings of Aphrodite!

CORDELIA. Huh! The rings were no more golden than I am a Greek goddess.

JOHANNES. But you're so nimble, and strong! I couldn't reach the rings, you threw them too high for me. And, what was it you said, you were looking at me . . . 'Long live love!'

CORDELIA. Johannes, I'm still cold, even with your hand on my shoulder. (*To her amazement, he removes his hand.*) You removed it!

JOHANNES. How close you are to me, and yet so distant! The essence of womanhood may be Devotion, but Resistance is her mode!

CORDELIA. Do you call this Resistance? (*Kisses* JOHANNES.)

JOHANNES. So. Shakespeare really was an anatomist! Cordelia's heart is upon her lips.

CORDELIA. Tell me, is there any way I might get the words off your lips?

JOHANNES. How gently you hold me; how soft your kiss. But this is merely a notion of love, rich and fanciful.

CORDELIA. What else did you expect, in the rain?

JOHANNES. I expected nothing; I just yield to it, swim in it. Like God's grace . . .

CORDELIA. Did you ever see so many stray dogs? Dozens of them.

JOHANNES. Bless them – if it's on their account that you hold me so tightly.

CORDELIA. Mmm, Johannes. This is too close, really.

JOHANNES. You know, Cordelia: Once people lived on earth and they were strong and sufficient unto themselves. They had no knowledge of the unity of love, nor did they crave it. Then, it happened, that they decided to attack heaven, and God, afraid, divided them into two: Man and Woman. And, since then, the Whole may be reconstituted only through love. Albeit, such a union is stronger than the original Whole. Two lovers, united, are stronger than God himself!

CORDELIA. Than God? Look, Johannes, the dogs have gone. Except those two.

JOHANNES. Perhaps once, before they knew desire, they were twice as big as they are now, and twice as strong. Come, Cordelia, let's go.

Scene 5. The Music Shop.

JANSEN. Cordelia, you came at last. I've been waiting for you for nearly four hours. What happened? Your hair, your dress, they're soaked!

CORDELIA. The dress is stuck to me, completely!

JANSEN. What shall we do about Midsummer's Eve?

CORDELIA. Midsummer's Eve? It's the custom for everybody to leap over the fire.

JANSEN. What? I mean the concert, at the Court. Haven't you come to practise?

CORDELIA. I've been practising with Johannes, all afternoon.

JANSEN. You've become so selfish, so distant, since your betrothal. Though, it is the most irregular affair, I must say.

CORDELIA. All my feelings are irregular, now!

JANSEN. Cordelia! Everything's so empty since we stopped playing together.

CORDELIA. I can't even sit at the piano any more. It's seems so . . . pointless.

JANSEN. Is a ring really worth all this, Cordelia? Here you are, soaked to the skin, dressed like a tramp, ready to sacrifice your entire future in society, and art, all for what? Your so-called happiness!

CORDELIA. The ring is worth nothing. I'd exchange it, anytime, for a length of golden ribbon they use to tie cake boxes. That's the only band that can really bind lovers together. But the ribbon, alas, like the café, and the Court, no longer exists . . .

JANSEN. Shall we give our concert for the heroes of the revolution, instead?

CORDELIA. Royal music on the barricades?

JANSEN. Please, for my sake!

CORDELIA. For your sake? Since when did you fight with the Republicans?

JANSEN. I didn't, but Edvard . . . He fought like a lion! And he's one of the pillars of the new administration.

CORDELIA. A pillar? A lion? Poor Edvard . . .

JANSEN. Have you seen yourself in the mirror, lately? If anyone's 'poor', it's you!

CORDELIA. Do I look strange? If only you knew how little my appearance matters, now! But, of course, you cannot. Goodbye.

JANSEN. Cordelia! I beg you! Please, say yes!

CORDELIA. Oh. I see. Yes, yes, of course. But . . . not now, not yet. Hadn't you better ask the new regime first, whether or not they want us to play for them?

JANSEN. I will. I'll put on my new dress, and I'll go and ask them. Now!

Scene 6. The Beach.

JOHANNES. Cordelia. What a surprise. Have you come to see the ships?

CORDELIA. Well . . . I came to look at the sea. What ships?

JOHANNES. The ship they turned away last time is now returning, with many others in its wake. Denmark is falling into the trap of liberty.

CORDELIA. Look at the lights, how they reflect in the wet sand.

JOHANNES. I prefer to see the beach as your backdrop.

CORDELIA. I felt so confined, suddenly, in my room. I wandered the streets, but they were no better. I began to long for the sea. Then, it occurred to me, that I might find you here. But I hadn't considered, Johannes, that you might be ready to betray me with your melancholy.

JOHANNES. Cordelia, my angel, you are mistaken . . .

CORDELIA. Since your brother visited us, I think I understand the link between your possession of me and your sadness.

JOHANNES. You misunderstand my mood, Cordelia, as you misunderstand the possessive pronoun. My God is not 'mine', but He to whom I belong. So it is with anything of importance; one's country, Hope, one's calling.

CORDELIA. In which case, my responsibility is even greater. Or, perhaps you are frightened of my awakening love?

JOHANNES. Cordelia, you are the only hope there is.

CORDELIA. Oh, Sea – did you ever hear a sadder confession?

Cannonfire in the distance.

JOHANNES. The city is saluting the arrival of the exiles' ships.

CORDELIA. If I could turn them back, would you smile then? (*Silence.*) After our betrothal was announced, Edvard suddenly visited my aunt.

JOHANNES. Yes. In Edvard's world, betrothal is the crowning moment of love. Which is how he, and his like, kill love, completely.

CORDELIA. He's accepted an important position in the new government.

JOHANNES. And so repeats his old mistake. Devotion can only be complete if it is offered unconditionally. As in love, a superficial alliance is bound to be an impediment.

CORDELIA. And is that how I should understand your black mood?

JOHANNES. The door of happiness does not open inwards, Cordelia: we cannot open it simply by pushing at it. It opens outwards. We're powerless to affect it.

CORDELIA. Why shouldn't we continue walking together?

JOHANNES. Professor Blackfeldt was my walking companion. He's disappeared.

CORDELIA. Can't you share your melancholy with me?

JOHANNES. I'm afraid to. Of the effect it might have upon you.

CORDELIA. Is that what I have loved in you, Johannes? Is that really what I allowed to seduce me; your passion for despair? Or have I deceived myself? Have you redeemed me from my fate, from my incurable unhappiness, only that I might now force you into a similar state?

JOHANNES. No, Cordelia . . .

CORDELIA. You are not yet free, Johannes. Your sorrow won't release you. Look – I have kept the golden ribbon. When you gave it to me, you were so happy. I'll make you happy again. I can do this, Johannes, I dare to do it, only because I am so certain of our love.

JOHANNES. Cordelia, you are sublime! Though, you don't understand me . . .

CORDELIA (*slips off her ring*). No more words. Unless it's . . . what was it? . . .

JOHANNES. Had I not fallen in love with you before, I would certainly do so, now! Although, I'm afraid you don't understand me . . .

CORDELIA. 'Long live love!' That was it!

She tosses the ring to JOHANNES.

Scene 7. Johannes's Apartment.

JOHANNES. To what do I owe the pleasure of a visit at this hour?

EDVARD. My memory. Or lack thereof. I forgot my best suit.

JOHANNES. So much for the Revolution; now for the party!

EDVARD. The King has sworn an oath of loyalty to the Constitution.

JOHANNES. And to whom, I wonder, has the Constitution sworn an oath of loyalty?

EDVARD. Are you really so cynical? Haven't you seen how the city is transformed?

JOHANNES. Indeed. I noticed it whilst negotiating the barricades, manned by scowling, unshaven youths, all fiddling nervously with their guns.

EDVARD. Typical! The country is free! First, we liberated the press; then, the streets; finally, the Constitution! But your only measure of our achievement is that your daily promenade is slightly inconvenienced!

JOHANNES. I think, Edvard, there is more resignation in your revolution than in all the philosophers put together. Your eventual defeat is inevitable, of course, because politics can never compensate for the deficiencies of religion. Even your barricades are erected in the wrong places; dividing people who in fact weren't so far from each other at the outset! Just wait: tomorrow, you'll be celebrating together with them!

EDVARD. I'm sure it is not too late, Johannes, for you to inform the insurgents how they have lost their way amongst their own barricades!

JOHANNES. You know that in matters of ethics and religion, the mob can never be trusted. Your Democracy will put an end to Justice, forever, because the essence of a human being is liberty, which, in your New Empire, will be constricted on all sides by barricades.

EDVARD. Then the rumours are true. If you have said only half of this to the innocent victims of the old regime . . .

JOHANNES. I haven't met any, yet! And the victims of the new regime have yet to find their voice.

EDVARD. And Cordelia, is she not a victim? She's renounced your betrothal, I hear?

JOHANNES. Ah, now the significance of the suit becomes apparent!

EDVARD. Everything is confused in the upheaval of revolution. Not least, I suspect, Cordelia's emotions.

JOHANNES. Cordelia and I discuss you, sometimes, too.

EDVARD. Perhaps she will be my reward for my part in the liberation? Certainly, if she's broken with you, your plans can be proceeding none too smoothly . . .

JOHANNES. Edvard, I hardly dare to believe that, in Cordelia, I've found such a paragon of love. Who, in the cause of love, is willing to discard all that might bring her temporal happiness, allowing herself instead to be swept towards a deeper, more spiritual love, wherein dull convention has no place. For what is betrothal but dull and conventional? I won't deny that I may have prompted her. My withdrawal encouraged her to make, by her escape, the one gesture that places her forever in my possession. Though, even now, we should bide our time, Edvard. Who knows what outcome the end of the act may bring?

Scene 8. A Beach.

CORDELIA. Did you walk here with Blackfeldt?

JOHANNES. Careful how you step. You can easily lose your balance.

CORDELIA. Have I been too anxious to discover your secret?

JOHANNES. Perhaps your instinct was more to be trusted than my fears . . .

CORDELIA. Feel the sun, how warm it is! I think I'll just remove my coat . . .

JOHANNES. Actually, I subscribe to that early school of religious thought which lists melancholy as one of the Deadly Sins.

CORDELIA. Is it so much worse than loneliness? Or love?

JOHANNES. Love is like a narcotic; it can induce the most intense delight, or the deepest despair.

CORDELIA. My hair has come loose. How hot it is here!

JOHANNES. Do you really misunderstand me to such an extent? Perhaps you don't wish to understand me?

CORDELIA. Or perhaps you are afraid to understand me?

JOHANNES. Possibly. But I must add to your fear, Cordelia. It won't be easy for either of us.

CORDELIA. Look, I've got goose pimples all over!

JOHANNES. Are you cold?

CORDELIA. If I was cold, Johannes, I'd press myself against you. And if you were to hold me firmly in your arms . . . and I were to hold you firmly in mine, then . . . There would be no question in the world that our embrace would not serve to answer.

JOHANNES. And if God were to proscribe the action?

CORDELIA. Why not trust my instincts, now? Can't His will speak as well through me? Feel my heart, it beats so hard, with such longing . . .

JOHANNES. That's precisely . . . what I am afraid of . . .

CORDELIA. If you're afraid, then why not . . . ?

JOHANNES. Why? . . . Not? . . .

Silence.

CORDELIA. Please, Johannes; take me home . . .

Scene 9. Johannes's Apartment.

JOHANNES. What a surprise! Didn't you go home?

WILHELM. Yes, unfortunately.

JOHANNES. Or have you made the road between Copenhagen and Jutland your home?

WILHELM. Is that supposed to be funny?

JOHANNES. Do you have your list with you?

WILHELM. Last time, I left everything on the boat. You were right, Johannes – eiderdowns, hat-pins, medicines; what have these things to do with my life?

JOHANNES. Wilhelm. I don't think you understood me, fully, but . . . I need your help, now.

WILHELM. My help? The other day, I found myself staring at the Communion wafers, unsure what I should do with them. Then, I couldn't answer the simplest questions of one of my confirmands, a thirteen-year-old girl. Finally, preparing my sermon for next Sunday, I felt so empty I simply had to escape.

JOHANNES. Do I detect an accusatory tone?

WILHELM. Agnete has changed! She's completely different! It's terrible.

JOHANNES. Surely, a natural reaction to your doubt.

WILHELM. And what has caused that? Johannes, I'm facing the prospect of being alone forever in Jutland!

JOHANNES. You're not alone, Wilhelm. You have Agnete.

WILHELM. She's alone, too. I understand that now.

JOHANNES. What?

WILHELM. Johannes . . . (*Silence.*) You introduced me to Agnete. I was perfectly at ease with the harmony I could sense between the two of you. I thought only about our future, together. But then, following my unsuccessful attempts to persuade you back to Jutland, with or without Cordelia . . .

JOHANNES. Please, Wilhelm, don't . . .

WILHELM. . . . I realised she was in despair! Were you and Agnete ever intimate, Johannes? Answer me!

JOHANNES. Wilhelm, you are humiliating us both . . .

WILHELM. I'll rephrase the question: Are you and Agnete intimate, now?

JOHANNES. It's over.

WILHELM. What's that, a confession? You know I have no one but Agnete!

JOHANNES. And what, pray, became of the superiority of marriage over the baseness of seduction? The richness of reality compared to the world of dream and illusion? Isn't the Christian gesture of resignation not so much finer than the pagan, erotic gesture?

WILHELM. You're enjoying this, aren't you?

JOHANNES. You have been living with Agnete, Wilhelm; only you can know whether or not she bore a secret which she wouldn't share with you.

WILHELM. The secret, yes, tell me about the secret!

JOHANNES. Do you remember how, at the harbour, you argued so confidently that, of a hundred young men wandering lost in the world, ninety-nine would find redemption in a woman's love, whilst only one would find it through God's grace, directly?

WILHELM. I remember also your objection that I hadn't reserved a single place for the one soul who would remain lost forever . . .

JOHANNES. Well, Wilhelm, what if Agnete did once take it upon herself to save more than just one man?

WILHELM. But I've been a good husband to her! I've given her far more than a seducer ever would! Though perhaps you'd given her that, already? Well, had you?

JOHANNES. Ah. You said it, finally. It's over, Wilhelm.

WILHELM. How could I not suspect it, having read your diary?

JOHANNES. Wilhelm, hear me. Since that fateful morning, following our father's death – because of what occurred, then – I have been incapable of seducing anybody, in the proper sense of the word.

WILHELM. But . . . how . . . ?

JOHANNES. Do you understand me?

WILHELM. . . . . Cordelia?

JOHANNES. Yes, she is losing herself completely in this affair. But I expect to be the one who is finally lost. It is perhaps my fate to be so exaggeratedly metaphysical, that I may be spared the disillusion of fulfilment! Think how dreadful that is! This affair is about grace and redemption. My love is at stake, yes, but also my Faith. The happier I am with Cordelia by day, the more desperate I am at night, alone in my bed.

WILHELM. But nothing can redeem you as long as you are alone in your bed at night!

JOHANNES. I don't want Cordelia to become another Agnete. I don't want to lose my Faith.

WILHELM. There is one link missing from your chain of reasoning, Johannes.

JOHANNES. I know what you're going to say!

WILHELM. Agnete once said that you had never been in love.

JOHANNES. And I know how true that was, only because I am in love, now!

WILHELM. Johannes, with love everything is possible: why can't you believe that?

JOHANNES. Because, Wilhelm, what is Love but God's Grace? And, even if we are worthy of it, how can we bear it?

Scene 10. Cordelia's Apartment.

AUNT. So, the letter came yesterday?

CORDELIA. By messenger.

AUNT. Yet you waited a whole night before giving it to me?

CORDELIA. I clasped it to my breast, all night, trying to feel whether it was a final farewell, or the opposite!

AUNT. And if I've now missed the chance of a meeting I have awaited for sixteen years! Have you read it?

CORDELIA. Yes. During the night. You were already asleep.

AUNT. Tomorrow, he'll no longer be in Denmark. He's waiting for me, forty miles from here. Oh, Cordelia: if only there was one moment which was mine, completely, irreversibly; one moment which I could hold, and never forget . . . But there never was even a single moment . . .

CORDELIA. It's not evening, yet.

AUNT. What do you mean?

CORDELIA. I'm thinking of your story. And its moral. She who wants everything must offer everything. To become worthy of her dearest love, she must first sacrifice him. Is a night on the mail-coach really too much to sacrifice?

AUNT. What? You mean go now? Unprepared?

CORDELIA. You've been preparing for this moment for the past sixteen years, Aunt.

AUNT. No, it's no longer possible.

CORDELIA. There won't be another sixteen years; nor another mail-coach. If you're quick, you can still make the last one.

AUNT. What about you? Should I leave you here, alone?

CORDELIA. Is there any choice?

Scene 11. The Same.

Darkness.

CORDELIA'S VOICE. Don't be afraid of the dark.

JOHANNES'S VOICE. Your message surprised me.

CORDELIA'S VOICE. I felt ashamed, for not having listened to you properly, on the beach.

JOHANNES'S VOICE. If you had listened properly, I'd be feeling ashamed, now. (*A chair crashes over.*)

CORDELIA'S VOICE. What are you doing?

JOHANNES'S VOICE. I must have knocked something over.

CORDELIA'S VOICE. Stay where you are. (*Pause.*) Where are you?

JOHANNES'S VOICE. Your Aunt will come home, soon . . .

CORDELIA'S VOICE. No, she won't. A letter arrived today; one she's been expecting for sixteen years. She's gone out of Copenhagen.

JOHANNES'S VOICE. On Midsummer's Eve? At sunset, all the brush fires will be lit. It's like the end of a story when it turns into a myth.

CORDELIA'S VOICE. I love the sound of your voice.

JOHANNES'S VOICE. Now, I know where you are. I can hear your heart, beating.

CORDELIA'S VOICE. I must light a candle. Otherwise, I'm lost.

JOHANNES'S VOICE. Wait! Let me imagine how you look on this special night, aroused by the beat of your loving heart. I want to be drunk with you; I want to throw myself into the depths of your love, I wish I could . . .

CORDELIA'S VOICE. Oh God, where's the candle?! (*Lights it.*) Light! At last!

JOHANNES. My dear Cordelia . . .

CORDELIA. My dear Johannes . . .

JOHANNES. Mine . . . Yours . . . These concepts frame all our letters, like parentheses. And all the time, the intervals between them shrink, but their significance . . .

CORDELIA. Please, Johannes . . . sit down. Why do you look at me like that?

JOHANNES. I've always been frightened of Midsummer's Night.

CORDELIA. I've received no message from you, not a single line, since that day on the beach.

JOHANNES. Let me look at you.

CORDELIA. I nearly fell there, do you remember? I think we may only regain our balance together, Johannes. (*Gets out of bed.*)

JOHANNES. Cordelia, you'll catch cold . . .

CORDELIA. Do you remember what you said about sacrifice? And I, childishly, refused to grasp your meaning . . .

JOHANNES. It's quite cool, tonight . . .

CORDELIA. Yet I am on fire, Johannes! As if I had all your unwritten letters pressed against my body. Please, Johannes, cool me with your hands . . .

JOHANNES. Love fills me, it burns, pulsates in every nerve. Yet my soul feels frozen. As if I had taken a glass of poison . . .

CORDELIA. Poison?

JOHANNES. Oh, Cordelia! I've never experienced such depth of feeling before! My whole life is compressed into this one instant! Before you, everything I knew and felt was shared only with my own faithful melancholia. Which I must now bid farewell!

CORDELIA. Let me take its place, Johannes! And when you were united with your melancholy, did you feel stronger than God, as it says in the myth?

JOHANNES. I think God has ordained this fear, so that He may not be overwhelmed.

CORDELIA. Johannes, why are you so afraid of my warmth?

JOHANNES. What if the myth is true? If the unity of Man and Woman in Love really is stronger than God himself?

CORDELIA. Why can't I reach you, Johannes?

JOHANNES. Because you are stronger than me, Cordelia!

CORDELIA. Then, take some of my strength!

JOHANNES. Mind the light!

CORDELIA *knocks over the candle, extinguishing it.*

JOHANNES'S VOICE. What's that light?

CORDELIA'S VOICE. It's me. My body.

JOHANNES'S VOICE. My God . . . (*Pause.*) There is no grace!

CORDELIA'S VOICE. Yes! Yes!

JOHANNES'S VOICE. No! He is so petty, so mean!

CORDELIA'S VOICE. Who is?

JOHANNES'S VOICE. He is! Him! Him! Cordelia! Your body shines, like reason!

CORDELIA'S VOICE. Him? Me? Who? Johannes . . . ?

JOHANNES'S VOICE. Him! Him, of course . . .

JOHANNES *leaves.* CORDELIA *weeps in the darkness.*

Scene 12. The Same. Later.

AUNT'S VOICE. (*entering*). Cordelia? (*Pause.*) Are you here? (*Pause.*) What is it?

CORDELIA'S VOICE. Nothing. It's nothing.

AUNT. It's light outside. (*Opens the window.*) What happened?

CORDELIA. Nothing. Nothing happened.

AUNT. Why is the candle on the floor? Writing paper, everywhere . . . What is this, ink?

CORDELIA. Oh, well something happened to them. Lucky them.

AUNT. Why are you in bed? Naked?! Did he . . . ?

CORDELIA. No. Did he what?

AUNT. Steal your honour and abandon you?

CORDELIA. If he had, at least I would have a memory to hold onto, however painful. But, by rejecting me, he's taken everything.

AUNT (*pause*). I wish I could feel some pain, at least.

CORDELIA. Please, don't . . .

AUNT. He stood there, in the night, on the icy sand. His face, once so animated and alive, was hard and fixed. Like a mask of his former self he'd put on, so that I might recognise him.

CORDELIA. There's no light any more. Look, the sheets are shining, like reason . . .

AUNT. To avoid looking at his face, I stared at his feet. A pair of old, tired boots sinking into the sand. It was him. Why did you give me his letter?

Doorbell rings, off.

CORDELIA. Perhaps . . .

AUNT. Who can that be, so early?

CORDELIA. I was wrong! Perhaps I misunderstood him, it was all just a lesson. It's my fault, I had no faith in him, I deserve my punishment! But, see, he forgives me, he loves me! I've so much to learn! Wait, I'm almost ready. I understand, now, how deep our love is. That was the purpose of this night!

AUNT. Stay here. I will open the door. (*Goes out.*)

CORDELIA. Yes. This joy, undeserved as it is, like grace, would probably overwhelm me . . .

AUNT (*returns with an envelope*). Your messenger. He has returned it without opening it . . .

Scene 13. Johannes's Apartment.

Darkness. Someone knocking at the door.

AUNT'S VOICE. Hello? Is anybody there? Please. Answer me.

JOHANNES'S VOICE. What can I say?

AUNT'S VOICE. I know it's improper to arrive like this, unannounced, but . . . May I pull back the curtain? (*She does so.*) What's happening?

Light from the window reveals luggage and packing cases.

JOHANNES. I received a letter.

AUNT. Yes, and you returned it. (*Puts down a large bag she has brought with her.*)

JOHANNES. This one I couldn't return. It was from Blackfeldt.

AUNT. I'll make some tea. Clean your face with this.

JOHANNES. What are these?

AUNT (*taking marionettes from the bag*). I can no longer live with them in my house.

JOHANNES. Did he return?

AUNT. Just a pair of old boots, sinking into the sand.

JOHANNES. You see what you've done to him.

AUNT. No! . . . I've come now, to avert another tragedy.

JOHANNES. You're too late.

AUNT. I don't know what was in your letter, Johannes. I don't know what happened or why it must end like this.

JOHANNES. The envelope contained a ticket of passage, but no explanation. There are no explanations in love, either. Why do you ask?

AUNT. If only you had seen how beautiful Cordelia was this morning . . .

JOHANNES. I know.

AUNT. To break from fulfilment is terrible, but at least then the pain is finite. If you interrupt something which might have been, the pain is eternal. Johannes, you will cripple her for life! Please, abduct her, live with her in sin, make her pregnant, anything but this . . . false poetry!

JOHANNES. Yes, marriage can disguise a multitude of horrors. But I'd rather kill Cordelia than . . .

AUNT. Kill her! I know she too is responsible for this. She wanted an impossible love; she broke off her engagement, she wanted . . .

JOHANNES. There is no one to blame and nothing to explain. I pulled her into the midst of a fearful river; she could swim, I could not.

AUNT. But, Johannes, you still love her!

JOHANNES. Why should I leave her, but because I still love her? (*Pause.*) She'll find happiness soon enough, in another's arms.

AUNT. This is absurd! You torture yourself because you love her?

JOHANNES. Look. (*Continues packing.*) We know from Aristotle that women are not susceptible to tragedy; not least in matters of the heart. Their 'tragedy' abates with the arrival of a new lover.

AUNT. Nonsense!

JOHANNES. Then just think of this as the oldest and simplest story in the world: A girl offers everything she has, and loses it. Innocence, in a man, is a negative attribute, but take it from a woman and what is left?

AUNT. Stop it, Johannes! This isn't helping anyone!

JOHANNES. Remember, it was I who poeticized Cordelia. I invented her, adored her, worshipped her. She merely received my admiration.

AUNT. Do you really believe you can find consolation in this disdain? Even self-pity would be preferable!

JOHANNES. Perhaps you would make some tea?

AUNT. What?

JOHANNES. May I borrow your handkerchief. Such fragrance.

AUNT. Wipe yourself there, as well.

JOHANNES. You've such a delicate touch.

AUNT. Did you hit yourself? Where's the tap?

JOHANNES. Don't worry about that, now. It's strange to see the marionettes, here.

AUNT. I couldn't forget what you said about them, once.

JOHANNES. Since then, I have said the same thing over and over again, to myself.

AUNT. Do not say it, now. Love is strong, it is stronger than the whole world. But the moment doubt creeps in, it perishes. It is like a lunatic who may tread in complete safety the most precipitous paths. Until someone calls his name, and then he falls.

JOHANNES. Your own story could be precised just so.

AUNT. It could?

JOHANNES. I realise, now, that everything has led to this moment. Your sixteen years of waiting – my entire life! – our common despair . . . have led us to this handkerchief in your hand. That we might find each other, thus.

AUNT. Johannes . . . (*Pause.*) Damn you!

JOHANNES. Do you understand me, now?

AUNT. Is there nothing you wouldn't exploit for the sake of your diabolical project? You're doing this simply to make Cordelia hate you!

JOHANNES. You don't understand . . .

AUNT. My hands are trembling!

JOHANNES. I'm exploiting nothing, I'm sacrificing it . . .

AUNT. Yes: honour, morality, other people's feelings . . .

JOHANNES. Sacrifice is by nature amoral, and inexplicable.

AUNT. Shut up! At least until I can get out of here!

JOHANNES. Nor do I sacrifice everything, only that which is most dear to me. Like Abraham, on God's orders, preparing to execute his own son . . .

AUNT. God, how I hate those gruesome Old Testament stories!

JOHANNES. Or Christ himself. The sacrifice of one's dearest love, in an act beyond reason, beyond morality, as proof of one's boundless, eternal devotion!

AUNT. I'm not staying here!

A knock at the door.

JOHANNES. At last. Come in!

EDVARD (*enters*). Your message came most inconveniently.

JOHANNES. Edvard, I believe you remember this lady.

AUNT. May I pass?

JOHANNES. Edvard has risen in the world since last you met. He is one our national heroes. Yet, your memory of him remains rather uncomfortable, I suspect? Due not least to his failure to keep his promise to you.

EDVARD. What?

JOHANNES. I . . . don't recall . . .

EDVARD. One moment, Johannes; if this is a matter of my honour . . . Dear Lady, please stay until I have had a chance to repair any misunderstanding . . .

JOHANNES. Yes, or she might remind Cordelia of your betrayal . . .

AUNT. Must I listen to this?

JOHANNES. Edvard, the apartment is yours. I hope you'll be happy here. Why not get married?

EDVARD. Your cynicism is pitiful!

JOHANNES. But, surely, you promised this lady and her niece that you would return their documents as soon as you had assumed power? Edvard, listen to me carefully: Now Is The Time.

AUNT. I can't endure any more of this.

JOHANNES. Why don't you trim your beard for the occasion?

AUNT. I'm leaving.

Scene 14. Cordelia's Room.

JANSEN. Cordelia! I'm glad I've found you alone! Are you still in bed?

CORDELIA. In bed. Alone.

JANSEN. I'll sit here, if I may? I couldn't stay at home, I had to get out, and when I heard the nightingales in the gardens I felt it was my heart, singing! What's the matter with you?

CORDELIA. You're squashing me.

JANSEN. I just knew it would be a wonderful Midsummer's Night! Can you smell it, the woodsmoke still in my hair? And guess who jumped over the fire, Cordelia? There is something wrong, don't try and deny it.

CORDELIA. Is it visible, then?

JANSEN. But, let me just tell you, first: I borrowed my sister's corset, and I let my hair down, and put flowers in it, it was the first time in my life that I had ever worn . . . You're not even listening to me!

CORDELIA. Can you see it on me? Or out there, amongst the trees? Or in the distance, on the water?

JANSEN. Shall we play some music?

CORDELIA. Music is no more real than love.

JANSEN. Come on, come and sit at the piano.

CORDELIA. Piano? What piano? All I see is a mass of wood and iron, felt, wire, ivory . . .

JANSEN. It looks pretty much like a piano to me . . .

CORDELIA. Some people are changed by their first night of love, it sets them alight! Well, tonight, I have been changed as well. Except it is not love that has burned me, but rejection! All that remains is this little heap of ashes. And who can love that, a heap of ashes?

JANSEN. But . . . what happened, Cordelia?

CORDELIA. What's happening is disintegration! If only I had a single moment . . . But I was robbed, totally, denied even a moment to enjoy my treasures!

JANSEN. Cordelia, you may have been drowning in this ridiculous affair, but, believe me, love is something else, entirely! Last night, Edvard squeezed my hand; as I jumped over the fire the hem of my dress was scorched a little; and Edvard caught a glimpse of my ankle! He said that, tomorrow, he will pay his respects to me!

CORDELIA. You mean there'll be a tomorrow?

JANSEN. Cordelia! It's summer! If this is the affect unrequited love has on you, how on earth could you have endured the real thing?! The soul isn't made for this. If we're vain, and try to catch a poet, we risk ending up with even less than the commonest girl deserves! Now, get up. Wash your face. Look – the sun is shining!

AUNT (*enters*). Cordelia!

CORDELIA. Say nothing! Your expression tells me everything.

AUNT. And does it tell you this, perhaps? Get up.

CORDELIA. The marionettes? Doesn't he want those, either? Nothing to remind him of me?

AUNT. Don't deceive yourself, Cordelia.

JANSEN. No, at least don't do that!

CORDELIA. He hasn't deceived me. He no longer loves me, that's why he left me. If he'd stayed, not loving me, that would have been deceit.

AUNT. There is no easy consolation, Cordelia.

CORDELIA. He loved me, didn't he? He loved me more than I was able to love myself. I shall get dressed.

JANSEN. My God, Cordelia, you're never going to forget him this way!

CORDELIA. Forget him? What do you mean? Can Pygmalion abandon her memory and become just a block of stone again?

JANSEN. You were hardly a block of stone before he came along. A statue, perhaps; more refined than you are now, in some ways, but . . .

AUNT (*sorting through the marionettes*). The material can be used for patches. The stuffing will make good kindling. I'll keep the string. The faces are broken. They were only masks, anyway.

CORDELIA. What happened? You mean, it really is all over, he doesn't love me any more?

AUNT. Cordelia, he's a man; sufficient unto himself. A man can never know the same happiness as a woman; but neither can he match her unhappiness . . .

CORDELIA. No! It can't just end like this . . . !

AUNT. Pull yourself together, Cordelia. You may have a visitor.

JANSEN. Oh?

AUNT. It's not who you think it is, but even so. You must pull yourself together.

CORDELIA. Why all this mystery? Tell me, is there still hope? Does he still love me?

AUNT. I think there is no hope, Cordelia. He still loves you.

Doorbell rings, off.

JANSEN. Obviously, I'm the only one who can open a door around here . . . (*She goes out.*)

AUNT. For the time being.

CORDELIA. He loves me! Of course, how could it be otherwise?

WILHELM (*enters with* JANSEN). Ladies, how can I possibly excuse my previous imposition, except with a greater one . . . ?

CORDELIA. You? What have you come for, to gawp at me? Please, feast your eyes!

AUNT. We were not expecting you, sir . . .

CORDELIA. Why have you come? Haven't I made Johannes free enough? Shouldn't I feel any pain at losing him? Should I simply forget him? Have you come to reclaim his words, his smiles, his caresses?

WILHELM. I admit that last time I asked you to set him free; but my entreaty was for your sake, also.

CORDELIA. Well, you were wrong about freedom. Johannes isn't free, now. He's trying to escape the freedom of our love into what he thinks is his fate . . .

WILHELM. Yes, I know. Therefore, following my last visit here, I went to Johannes and begged him to marry you.

CORDELIA. You . . . What? You did? Oh, you dear, dear man!

WILHELM. Which act, I think, has played a part in all that has followed . . .

CORDELIA. Sir, I beg, for the sake of my niece, that you come to the point of your visit.

WILHELM. . . . I mean, of course, concerning my own fate . . . But that is not why I am here . . . Johannes intends to try again to find in religion what he has failed to find in love. Alas, his experience with love has so shaken his faith, that I fear he'll gain nothing from that quarter.

CORDELIA. You want me to save Johannes? Do you hear that?

JANSEN. But, that's not love!

WILHELM. Johannes is trying to order his own destiny, such that all possible routes of escape are closed to him.

CORDELIA. Oh, God. I don't know what made him leave me, but I saw that it was painful to him. He didn't want me to enter his pain, and so he left me as he did. How could I be so blind? Nor was it the blindness of love but of selfishness, and inexperience. Whilst his love made him creative and selfless. Oh, I see now just how small and petty I was!

WILHELM. You must summon up all your strength, forget your own pain, think whatever you will, what matters now is that he is saved! If once he captured your soul – as, years ago, he captured mine – our task now is to capture his, and return it to him. Life is bigger than Fate; most women realise that.

The doorbell rings, off.

CORDELIA. Perhaps . . . ?

AUNT. Don't raise your hopes, my dear . . .

CORDELIA. I'll open the door.

She goes out. Returns with EDVARD.

Firstly, I am not 'Little Cordelia'. Secondly, how on earth can you think me 'beautiful' – I'm a perfect fright!

JANSEN. Edvard! Did you know I was here, or did you just feel it?

WILHELM. Edvard; you've changed! What on earth is that smell . . . ?

AUNT. You were quick. You've trimmed your beard, I see.

CORDELIA. Have you two met earlier?

EDVARD. Why should I deny it? It was at Johannes's apartment.

WILHELM. What was his mood when you left him?

EDVARD. I beg your pardon, but it is my own mood which concerns me, now. As far as one could tell, he was in the process of moving. For good, I believe.

CORDELIA. For good? No!

JANSEN. Please, Edvard, talk about your mood; what brings you here?

EDVARD. As you will no doubt be aware, I have long owed this house a visit.

CORDELIA. Rest assured, we had forgotten.

AUNT. Cordelia, manners, please!

EDVARD. I had not forgotten my obligation, even without Johannes's prompting.

CORDELIA. Johannes? I'm listening . . .

EDVARD. As long as one is fighting for freedom, it is impossible to heed one's heart. But, when all other rights are guaranteed, forever, the demands of the heart must be met.

JANSEN. Oh, well said!

CORDELIA. What are you talking about?

EDVARD. I gave my word, here in this room, that once we had stamped out injustice in Denmark, I would return. What begins as a political and social process – religious, too – can only be brought to completion in love.

CORDELIA. Johannes would never say such a thing.

EDVARD. No. The guilty party always thinks differently to one who would repudiate him.

WILHELM. I think you've misunderstood Johannes . . .

AUNT. Sadder still, I think he has understood him!

EDVARD. Who cares about Johannes! I understand full well what is in my heart!

JANSEN. No, you don't!

CORDELIA. So tell me, do you visit all victims of injustice like this, with your beard freshly trimmed and perfumed?

EDVARD. You are upset, I understand. You must excuse my weakness . . .

JANSEN. Edvard, what is this? Can you feel love only for victims of injustice? Well, what's this, if not gross injustice? Then you can love me, too! Oh, what am I saying . . . ?

EDVARD. From now on, the rights of the heart are also sacrosanct, even against those of other hearts! Down with the tyranny of deceitful passion! I love you, Cordelia! I love you with all the constitutional guarantees of my heart!

CORDELIA. Oh, shut up!

JANSEN. There will never be justice in this world, not ever!

AUNT. No, fortunately not.

Scene 15. Johannes's Apartment.

WILHELM. I was knocking on the door for five minutes; why didn't you open it?

JOHANNES. I was preparing what I should say to you.

WILHELM. What's this? Are you packing?

JOHANNES. Moving.

WILHELM. Johannes, at least take off your coat. (*Pause.*) Please, hear me: The last time I was here, I was upset. Forget everything I said. In Jutland, we await you with open arms. Truly. All I care about now is saving you from your own rash conclusions.

JOHANNES. They're not rash at all.

WILHELM. I can't bear to see you like this, Johannes! I'll take off your coat . . .

JOHANNES. Look, it's raining.

WILHELM. Take your hands out of your pockets, at least. What's that?

JOHANNES. An envelope. Containing a ticket.

WILHELM. To Berlin?

JOHANNES. From Blackfeldt. He once said that most people reach the final conclusion like schoolchildren, copying it from a textbook. He refused to be a copyist.

WILHELM. They say Berlin is a nice city.

JOHANNES. Do you think it even exists?

WILHELM. What's that smell?

JOHANNES. Or does the word simply define a place you may reach only through dialectics, and not at all by way of faith or grace? It's horrible, isn't it?

WILHELM. You stink, Johannes! Have you been wearing this since last time I was here?

JOHANNES. My sorrow, you mean? Perhaps.

WILHELM. Have you eaten anything? But . . . What does Blackfeldt write?

JOHANNES. 'By the time you receive this I shall no longer exist. I do not consider suicide an act of triumph, nor do I commit it out of vanity. It is my conviction, however, that nobody can glimpse infinity and bear it. I have always understood this, intellectually; that is, I have been ignorant of it, yet what is ignorance but the negative expression of knowledge? Similarly, suicide is but the negative expression, a negative form, of freedom. Good luck to him who is able to find a positive form. Yours sincerely: Ludwig Blackfeldt.'

WILHELM. No, Johannes . . . No . . . (*Pause.*) It's raining so hard!

JOHANNES. How do you mean, 'no'?

WILHELM. I'm . . . going to get some food . . . And you must take a shower. It will help you feel better. Let me take your coat . . . and . . . You can't do this, Johannes . . . I'll buy some cheese, shall I? The shower will give you a new lease of life! It is not over, Johannes, not yet . . .

JOHANNES. No. That is what I'm afraid of. That it's not over.

WILHELM *pushes JOHANNES into the shower and switches on the water. Steam billows out of the bathroom. WILHELM goes out. Silence. CORDELIA appears, dishevelled, her hair wet. JOHANNES sneezes, off.*

CORDELIA. Johannes. I'm here.

JOHANNES (*off*). Is anybody there?

CORDELIA. I'm wet. And cold.

JOHANNES (*off*). I cannot hear you!

CORDELIA. I know a girl shouldn't do this. Be alone with a gentleman, in his apartment. But . . . I can no longer go anywhere where you are not.

JOHANNES (*off*). Cordelia?

CORDELIA. You told my Aunt that you would rather kill me than make me unhappy. Well, here I am.

JOHANNES (*off*). I can't hear you!

CORDELIA. Why postpone it any longer? Johannes . . . I can't call you 'my Johannes' because you were never mine. And I've been punished most severely for daring to hope that it could be otherwise. Yet I'm still yours, Johannes. You may journey to the end of the world, you may confer your love on a hundred others, yet still I am yours, even unto death . . .

JOHANNES (*off*). I'm just drying myself, Cordelia.

CORDELIA. I'm cold. Drenched. Do you remember our rain, Johannes? I'm not asking you to be mine; I just want you to sit beside me and dry me, talk to me so that I might cry. I can only cry through you, Johannes.

JOHANNES (*enters wearing a bathrobe, carrying a towel*). No, Cordelia.

CORDELIA. Then, may I dry myself upon you? (*Places her forehead into his chest.*)

JOHANNES. Here, this is better. (*Dries her with the towel.*)

CORDELIA. No . . .

JOHANNES. You're wet, you'll catch cold.

CORDELIA. Yes, and I'm also distraught, and ugly and unhappy and nervous! I know! (JOHANNES *dries her with the towel.*) Mmm, Johannes. Good. That's good.

JOHANNES. No, Cordelia.

CORDELIA. It isn't good?

JOHANNES. No, I shan't kill you.

CORDELIA. I will go with you, Johannes, to Jutland, to Berlin. Forever. I'll make my home in your suitcase; if that is to be your world, it shall be mine, too.

JOHANNES. No, Cordelia. You shan't live in my luggage, but in our past. That I will take with me wherever I go, and in it you shall be immortal.

CORDELIA. I don't want to be immortal, I want to be yours!

JOHANNES. No, our love cannot be left to Life – it is infinitely more precious than that.

CORDELIA. See, Johannes – you are killing me!

JOHANNES. Our love will turn into a myth, Cordelia!

CORDELIA. And all myths require a human sacrifice.

JOHANNES. You're here, in this book. And perhaps love will come to mean this for you, also. Justified forever, before God, instead of a mere passion left to perish in Time.

CORDELIA. Johannes, I'll do anything . . .

JOHANNES. You're making this so hard, Cordelia. If two people fall in love and feel that they are destined for each other, they must have the courage to part. If not, they will lose everything and gain nothing.

CORDELIA. I don't accept your words, Johannes!

JOHANNES. Then, I beg you, please, forgive one who is willing and able to do anything in the world . . . except bring you happiness. (*He continues packing.*)

CORDELIA. I believe in our past. My memories of it are clear, and beautiful. But how am I to accept that in seduction only the seduced remains without sin?

JOHANNES. Try and see it as the moral of the story, if it makes it any easier.

CORDELIA. In which case I must compensate you for all the suffering I've caused . . .

JOHANNES. Just understand me; that will be compensation enough. Will you help me close this trunk?

CORDELIA (*sits on it*). I was so selfish, so immature . . .

JOHANNES. Cordelia. Listen . . . (*Opens his ledger.*)

CORDELIA. Your book?

JOHANNES. Yes. Everything is preserved here, between these pages.

CORDELIA. Your face has changed, Johannes. Is it a diary?

JOHANNES. More than that. It's a protocol, a strategy, a record of a scientific experiment, a psychological dissection. When I get to Berlin, I shall elaborate on my findings, and publish it.

CORDELIA. At least you've stopped packing.

JOHANNES. What would you like to know of your story? The first time we held hands? (*Reads.*) Oh, young lady, a handshake may betray many intentions. You will assume that my intentions are honourable, but I will indicate by my handshake that they are anything but!

CORDELIA. You made notes about that? I rather like that . . .

JOHANNES. Or our first meeting? Here. (*Reads.*) Oh, she has entered into this so carelessly. Be careful, young lady, to camouflage your desires; they are so obvious, in the sunshine, on the beach.

CORDELIA. I don't remember how it was, but . . . I don't care, I love you, anyway! I've no regrets. Listening to you now reminds me of your letters . . .

JOHANNES. The letters? (*Reads.*) My letters continue to hit their targets. The subtle poison is slowly infecting her blood. The more erotic they are, the shorter I can make them. With a little manipulation, she'll end up believing that these feelings originate in her own heart . . .

CORDELIA. Why do you torture yourself like this, Johannes?! Only champions of reality, like Edvard, could be disturbed by your remarks, whereas I . . .

JOHANNES. Edvard! Will you hear my version of him? (*Reads.*) Somewhere, I must find a love-poacher, seeking his opportunity. But where shall I look, in this great monastery? There! There he is, moping around like a rat in love . . .

CORDELIA. Stop it, Johannes! How do I know there's anything written there, at all? That you aren't simply poeticizing your own pain?

JOHANNES (*reading*). When I begin my withdrawal, she will offer anything in her attempt to keep me. But the only tool left to her will be desire. What I have taught her with my fire, will be confirmed now by my coldness.

CORDELIA (*weeping*). Johannes!

JOHANNES (*pretending to read*). Might it be possible to manipulate events in such a way that, finally, her pride would oblige her to abandon the affair? That might be an interesting epilogue. Though not one for me, I think.

CORDELIA. Why is it so important to you that the myth of our love should end in your complete callousness? What else is there left for you to sacrifice?

JOHANNES (*continues packing*). Not 'what else', but 'who else' . . .

CORDELIA. Our memories, our feelings, our secrets? I'm prepared to sacrifice anything for you . . .

JOHANNES. You don't understand me at all, Cordelia! The whole point of Abraham's sacrifice of Isaac, is that the act utterly confutes his desires yet leaves him in a world which will condemn him, forever, as a murderer.

CORDELIA. Then be a murderer!

JOHANNES. God denies me that solution.

CORDELIA. Solution? But . . . Wait! The act confutes his desires? . . . Confutes . . . ? Johannes, I understand! I understand. You do love me!

JOHANNES. Isaac also asked, 'Where is the lamb?'

CORDELIA. Where is the lamb?

JOHANNES. His father couldn't tell him. Fathers never can; it is part of their sacrifice. You are the lamb, Cordelia.

WILHELM (*enters with a basket of food*). You should see the loaf I bought, Johannes! Oh, Miss Cordelia . . .

JOHANNES. Not a moment too soon! I'm as hungry as a wolf!

CORDELIA. You may journey to the end of the world, you might confer your love on a hundred others, you may forget about me, completely . . . yet still I am yours, even unto death.

WILHELM. Look, smoked goat cheese, fresh white bread. Won't you join us, my dear?

CORDELIA. And I might journey to the end of the world, confer my love on a hundred lovers, forget about you, completely . . . yet still you are mine, even unto death.

JOHANNES. Mm, this cheese smells wonderful! And the bread, I can't wait to taste it! (*Takes a huge bite of bread.*)

CORDELIA. Remember me, Johannes. (*Leaves.*)

WILHELM. What has happened here? Johannes?

JOHANNES. Go to hell with your damned cheese! (*Throws down the food and rushes into the bathroom, retching.*)

WILHELM. I have never seen her look more beautiful. But what price such beauty? (*Lays the table.*) I don't think that you ever had the courage to love life, Johannes. (*Eats.*) Has it never occurred to you, that obduracy and sentimentality are one and the same thing?

JOHANNES. Perhaps I should pack, instead . . .

WILHELM. Surely, a girl's unhappiness is too high a price to pay for the verification of your own despair? This cheese is wonderful. (*Eats.*)

JOHANNES (*goes into his room*). Her future happiness depends on her present unhappiness. Everything unjust in her must be rooted out, in order to vindicate the divine rejection.

WILHELM. Johannes, please, please, please can we distinguish between Providence and your failure to love?

JOHANNES. I wish I could. But how may I run away from God? He would trap me forever, in love.

WILHELM. Johannes, you are suffering from impotence of the soul; which condition can be cured . . .

JOHANNES. Why is it so important for you not to understand me, Wilhelm?

WILHELM. And why don't you understand, Johannes, that you cannot subject a sensitive spirit like Cordelia to your foul human experiments?

JOHANNES. I prefer to think of it as a divine experiment. (*Goes into his room, continues packing.*) We can never justify ourselves in the face of God: what thought is graver than that? Yet, our father's curse against Him was justified: and that is our appalling heritage!

WILHELM. I am able to accept it, quite well, in fact.

JOHANNES (*enters*). Yes, because you believed in our self-redemption in Jutland, and managed so to redeem yourself. But I wished to continue our father's revolt, against God Himself. For which reason, I was obliged, that fateful morning, to tumble from the heights of blasphemy into the hand of the living God.

WILHELM. Majestic words indeed, for a failure in love, Johannes! I understand, perfectly; you still love her.

JOHANNES. How else could I leave her?

WILHELM. I think, brother, that you need your head examined!

JOHANNES. Ah, the logic of the theologian! Examine your head, examine God, calculate God, calculate impotence, calculate love. Reduce everything to mathematical formulae! Everything is curable!

WILHELM. Now you're being tasteless. Come, taste this cheese, instead.

JOHANNES. Religion expresses the conviction that, with God's help, man is lighter than the whole world. The same belief makes it possible for us to swim.

WILHELM. I'd contest your analogy, I think, but . . .

JOHANNES. But, I was not lighter, don't you understand? At the crucial moment in my love for Cordelia, my weight dragged me down and I found myself drowning! Do you have a cure, perhaps, for such death-by-water of the soul?

WILHELM. You're distressed, Johannes.

JOHANNES. By posing questions superficially, in the manner of a non-believer, I appeared to have answers for everything. Yet I bore the cross of Christ only as Simon of Cyrene bore it; superficially.

WILHELM. And now you wish to collapse beneath the weight of the real cross?

JOHANNES. Yes. But first I must understand the nature of the sacrifice. Not from a book, nor according to the tenants of theology. How else am I to understand He who was sacrificed, on the cross, by his father? And yet . . . I don't really know whether I'm collapsing or not . . .

WILHELM. For which knowledge you must travel to Berlin?

JOHANNES. No. If I go to Berlin, then I am already lost, and there is no such thing as grace.

WILHELM. But your ship leaves in a few hours . . .

JOHANNES. Brother, I think you still have much to learn about theology. God has yet to decide whether or not He will accept my sacrifice. As He put me to the test, on that night, then so will I put Him to the test, in this rain.

WILHELM. How?

JOHANNES. By his sacrifice, Abraham regained not just his son, but also his faith. Similarly, our father was survived by nothing but his two sons: yet we have survived him.

WILHELM. What sacrifice are you talking about?

JOHANNES. Cordelia, of course.

WILHELM. She was prepared to sacrifice herself for you. Would you do the same for her? And if so, how?

JOHANNES. She deserves to be touched by grace. Because she offered herself without condition, like Isaac, she'll be able to withstand the sight of infinity. And I sacrificed her, who was dearest to me, without condition or explanation, so that I should appear willing to abandon her as absurdly as God once abandoned me.

WILHELM. You humiliated her. You sent her away. Unless, of course, you wish me to run after her with this explanation of your cruelty . . . ?

JOHANNES. No! Wilhelm, you still do not understand me! If I am to be touched by grace, I must regain Cordelia and my faith, and in her my love must be fulfilled. Then I will be capable of anything, even bearing the sight of infinity.

WILHELM. But, how can you get her back, Johannes? Or are you talking about your diary, in which you may make her yours through poetry?

JOHANNES. Of course not. The diary is to be the work of my despair, my last sacrifice for her sake. It will make her despise me. She no longer has anywhere else to go. Not physically, of course, but metaphysically. She abides in this love; it is her home, her body, her life, without it, she's no longer whole. If the statue of Pygmalion can't come to life, nor can it simply become a block of stone again. If she can realise this, if love assumes for her the same meaning it has for me . . . then she will return, transformed, and redeem me.

WILHELM. This sacrifice is infinitely selfish. How can you use a young woman, not only for seduction, or as the object of scientific experiment, but, worse, for your own spiritual self-defence?

JOHANNES. If no miracle occurs, then nor is there anything to fear. And now, please, allow me to finish packing. (*He goes into his room.*)

The door opens, slowly, and CORDELIA *comes in.*

WILHELM. Johannes!

EDVARD (*enters*). Wilhelm?

WILHELM (*closing and barring the door to* JOHANNES's *room*). Oh, Edvard, it's you . . .

EDVARD. Yes, I'm coming back here to live. Or, perhaps I should say, we are coming here to live.

WILHELM. What?

EDVARD. May I borrow a towel? Here you are, my dear Cordelia. She doesn't move. In which case I'll . . . (*Dries her with the towel.*)

WILHELM. Edvard, I think perhaps . . .

EDVARD. She's completely drenched. Why don't you let me . . . ? She was standing on the street, stock still. I offered her my umbrella, which she accepted, then my arm, which, likewise, she accepted. And although she said nothing, I knew immediately that her silence signified her acceptance of me, indeed her anticipation of this very moment, when she would enter my home . . . our home . . .

WILHELM. Cordelia!

CORDELIA *sneezes.*

EDVARD. Oh, my dear, don't catch a cold, now, at the end of the act! Who knows what the end of the act will bring?, Johannes once said! Well, it has brought me this apartment, and Cordelia! And, now, I can see that this entire drama has described the exquisite unfolding of our love. The Revolution, my anguish, everything which Cordelia has suffered, all has led up to this moment beneath my umbrella, and the beginning of our common story!

WILHELM. She's so wet.

EDVARD. And so beautiful! Only love can make a girl as beautiful as this! Propitious, passionate love . . .

WILHELM. I think she's just flushed from all the wind and rain . . .

EDVARD. I love you, Cordelia. Much deeper, and more sincerely than I was able to before. I'm indebted to those events which stole you away, only to return you to me, more beautiful than ever, now, when the long penitence of my unhappiness makes me worthy of your love. Will you give me your hand? (*Takes it.*) How hot it is.

WILHELM. Perhaps she has a fever.

EDVARD. Yes. I know this fever, and it makes me happy. It shall provide warmth and light for our home. Won't it, Cordelia?

WILHELM. Edvard . . .

EDVARD. And now it's time for us to leave. Wish us luck, Wilhelm. I shall inform her Aunt. We shall be the happiest prisoners in the whole of this new, free Denmark! Cordelia, aren't you going to bring the towel with you, my dear?

They leave.

WILHELM (*opens door to* JOHANNES's *room*). Johannes . . .

JOHANNES (*fists clenched*). Did you see her? She's going to live. Did she smile?

WILHELM. I didn't notice . . .

JOHANNES. She believed what I said . . .

WILHELM. Finish packing, Johannes.

JOHANNES. What will happen when she learns that nobody could love as much as me? As, sooner or later, she will discover.

WILHELM. I'll accompany you to the harbour.

JOHANNES. Henceforth, everything will be for her. Even the diary. To help her find freedom. Did she offer him her hand? Did you notice? Did she?

WILHELM. I can help you with your luggage.

JOHANNES. There was no miracle.

WILHELM. Johannes! If you knocked but received no answer, if you searched but could not find, if you laboured but were not rewarded, if you sowed and watered but did not reap, if the heavens remained closed against all assurances to the contrary . . . how then can you remain so sure in your convictions? We can never justify ourselves in the face of God!

JOHANNES. Can't we, Wilhelm? You were never mine, so you I shall have, you forever.

WILHELM. Only God can fulfil the greatest desire of lovers; you cannot go against His will. Is it not your curse that you can never love as much as you are loved?

JOHANNES (*opens his fist to reveal* CORDELIA's *stone*). Look. Do you see it, Wilhelm?

WILHELM. Yes. I see a stone . . .

JOHANNES. Yes. A stone. She has turned back into stone.

UNSENT LETTERS

a play with life by

Andor Szilágyi

English version from a translation by Ildikó Patthy

Andor Szilágyi was born in 1955, in Szolnok, a town about 80 km east of Budapest. He graduated as a history teacher in Eger, and subsequently worked there as a journalist. Later he moved to Budapest, and took a variety of jobs: for years he made his living by delivering newspapers, cleaning windows, and so on, before he began working for Hungarian radio. He now lives in a small town near Budapest with his family. These details apart, nothing much is known about the playwright, as he insists on his privacy.

In 1989 he published a novel, *The Blind Eyewitness*, and in 1993 a collection of short stories, *Esoterema*. His first play, *The Dreadful Mother* (written 1988, and produced 1990), foretold the chaos which has accompanied the recent transformations in Eastern Europe. Eleven stage and radio plays have followed, and a few screenplays for television and the cinema. His writing is surreal in tone: in his sour, grotesque comedies and strange tragedies he creates a unique language based on constant inventiveness with words. His dialogues are filled with mock-archaic phrases and distorted idioms or newly created expressions. It is no wonder, then, that Szilágyi also feels at home writing beautiful and humorous plays for children and the puppet theatre.

Unsent Letters, perhaps his most accessible play to date, opened on 8 May 1993, in Radnóti Miklós Theatre, Budapest. 'A Play with Life' is its subtitle; but it also plays with time, with mistaken once-in-a-lifetime decisions and consequent yearnings to turn the clock back. There is no great plot development, but the basic situation of the play is clear, and has the innocence of a fairy tale. Two people (two 'angels', as the author has described them) meet at a railway station, fall in love, and part. They think they'll never meet again, but in consequence they are seeking each other in everyone they meet subsequently (and they actually meet each other many times, but always in a different time). This is a typical Szilágyi play – funny, enigmatic, and poignant.

Characters
ANGELUS
ANGELINA

PART I

In the entrance hall the anguished song of a woman mourning her love is heard.

1st Scene

On the stage, centre right, there is a rustic seat with a small withered tree behind it, illuminated with bluish light.

Leaning on his scythe the hooded Death is listening to the woman's song on the seat.

At a distance a train is arriving from the left, its smoke engulfs everything.

2nd Scene

When the smoke has cleared, there is no trace of Death.

The elderly ANGELINA is sitting in a wheelchair wearing a bonnet, with battered suitcases around her.

She is knitting.

She puts eye-glasses on her nose and produces a Keepsake Album with a hasp.

She is turning the pages and reading.

ANGELINA. One early evening when twilight sheds its blood and the sun, may it be blessed a thousand times, is about to sink into the purple billow of the sea encircled by its distant horizon – oh, delirious moment – the poisoned sting of a bewildered lead wasp bursts the window of my heart into a blood rose, My All, My Dearly Beloved, my Eternal Angelina, you should know that I will be thinking of you, even in the hour of death, Captain Angelus . . .

Outside ANGELUS snaps angrily.

ANGELUS. Oh, may Archabel put you into the fire with his hideous shaggy-haired cock.

ANGELINA listens in a fluster.

ANGELUS. . . . Or at least may the fizzling thunderbolt strike between
your jug ears, you damned blockhead! You abominable mother's
nightmare grabbing your smutty, filthy stove pipe!

*A stooping tramp with a great beard limps in. In his right hand
there is a stick and a battered tin water-can, in his left hand there
are two cases. He puts his things down. He beats some dust out of
his shabby overcoat, then pulls a bottle of red wine, half empty, out
of his pocket, wipes its mouth and drinks out of it. ANGELINA
looks utterly dejected. She hides behind her knitting again.*

ANGELUS (*wipes the mouth of the bottle, slips it back into his pocket
and dusts his coat, grumbling*). A blow. A heavy blow. A heavy
blow of fortune! (*He looks down at his clothes.*) Urgh! I'm an
eyesore. Just like a wart-hog! (*He looks round and catches sight
of* ANGELINA.)

ANGELUS. Isn't that true? . . . (ANGELINA *makes no response.*)
Don't you think I'm an eyesore? Once a year you decide to – and
then – there you are! Along comes a clodhopping (*He is at a loss
for words.*) millet like him! There he comes with his smutty stove
pipe and the game is up! It's all up! A furnace with his blastpipe
squeezes his way up to you . . . (*Words fail him.*) – stupid bumpkin.
He sprawls all over you. He rolls his sickening body onto you!
Such a boorish oaf. And he has the cheek to put me in the wrong
if I venture to say: 'Now now, Mr Kettle, what d'you think you're
doing?'

*He has a drink and plonks himself down exhausted. Still gasping,
he looks down at himself. He waves his hand with resignation and
drinks again.*

ANGELUS. Pure brute beasts! . . . But even they have better manners!
They at least (*Groping for words.*) don't have (*Still at a loss for
words.*) sooty stove pipes! . . . And then they have the cheek to put
you in the wrong, should you dare to open your mouth! (*He gives a
sigh and muses.*) What a great change has come over the world . . .
(*He looks at* ANGELINA *for support. She squirms with indigna-
tion. She puts away the album and takes up knitting. ANGELUS
shrugs his shoulders offended.*) A bitching change . . . (*He pulls
out the bottle, wipes its mouth all round and drinks. Having wiped
the bottle again he slips it back into his pocket.*) But at least it
could have changed for the better! I shouldn't give a damn . . . (*He
scrutinises his overcoat again.*) Archabel, with his long and shaggy
haired . . . He blinks at you as if he were the Virgin Mary of
Ravenna himself! He looks at you like a stuck pig and asks: 'Are
you in pain . . . (*Speaking through his nose.*) chum?' (*He looks at*
ANGELINA.) He called me . . . chum . . . You know what I told
him? (*He wants to give a clever answer, but then he falls back
upon making a discouraged gesture.*) Well, I'd better not tell
you . . . (ANGELINA *does not seem to have heard the question.*)

Of course, you're consumed with curiosity. (ANGELINA *takes no notice at all*. ANGELUS *looks her in the face*.) Your insides are being eaten up with curiosity. Well, let them be eaten. (ANGELINA *can't even hear the question*. ANGELUS *suddenly blurts it out jabbering*.) 'Stick it up your arse!' that's what I said to him. (ANGELINA *takes no notice at all*. ANGELUS *waits and then repeats it almost melodiously*.) St . . . i . . . ck, it . . . up . . . your . . . r aaarse! (*He bends forward to* ANGELINA *and shouts to her*.) Stick, it up your arse.

ANGELINA (*does not look up but continues to knit*). Very impressive!

ANGELUS (*turned sulky*). Alright. Everybody gets worked up sometimes, don't they? I wonder, what you would do, if you were covered in soot by a bullnecking ass like him. I really would like to know . . .

ANGELINA. I wouldn't squeal like a stuck pig to be sure . . .

ANGELUS. You wouldn't squeal, you wouldn't squeal . . . But what would you have done in my place, may I ask? Would you have thanked him for it? (*He bows repeatedly, mockingly*.) Let me offer you my humblest thanks, Mr Brainless, for being kind enough to smut me and nobody else, with your filthy stove pipe. For being kind enough to smudge me . . .

ANGELINA. I would have budged up a bit, if you want to know.

ANGELUS. Why should I move? Why shouldn't he move with his (*He can't think of the word again*.) stinking what-the-blazes is it?

ANGELINA *peeps out from behind her knitting, scanning the old man demonstratively*. ANGELUS *stops talking offended*.

ANGELINA. Because you were the eldest.

ANGELUS. God has created a mouth for man to make him able to spit out whatever weighs upon his heart.

ANGELINA. Has he told you this personally? The Creator, personally?

ANGELUS (*pointing at his mouth*). Why would he have created it otherwise?

ANGELINA. To have something to keep closed occasionally.

ANGELUS (*considering the matter*). I see . . . I have never really thought of that. (*He weighs the idea carefully feeling his mouth*.) There's something in it though . . .

ANGELINA (*continues to knit with satisfaction*). You see . . .

ANGELUS (*looks round, regaining his composure*). Are ye travelling far?

ANGELINA. Who? Me?

ANGELUS. You, of course you! Who else, may I ask?

ANGELINA. What's nearby and what's far away? Where do you draw the line between the two? What used to be distant seems to have drawn nearer now and the things nearby seem to have become inaccessibly displaced . . .

ANGELUS. May I ask you where you have heard this brilliant idea?

ANGELINA. Wouldn't you have thought me   capable of it?

ANGELUS (*bends forward suddenly and as if he wanted to stand on his head and looks back between his legs*). Well, I would, in this position. Would you like to try it? In this way you can catch a glimpse of things standing on their feet again. The roots of the trees disappear in the earth and their branches grow up to the skies! Just like in our day! There are no rocks drifting in the sky but clouds like years ago, in our day. And people aren't walking on their heads, but on their feet again! I can hardly believe my eyes! Well, how about you? Don't you have a mind to try it? In this way everything is as beautiful as it used to be . . .

ANGELINA. In our day.

ANGELUS. How do you know?

ANGELINA. You have just told me, just now . . .

ANGELUS. Yes, of course . . .

He draws himself up, has a look round and makes a wry face.

It's not the real thing (*He takes a swig.*) It looks real, but it just isn't. Somehow you just lose interest in life . . . (*Takes another gulp, sits back and starts twisting his foot. Making a terrible face he appraises his shoes.*) These shoes . . . What are they for? They are anything but footwear.

ANGELINA. What have you got against them?

ANGELUS (*imitating* ANGELINA *angrily*). 'What have you got against them?' What have you got against them? Shoddy workmanship! Each and every one of them! That's what I've got against them! Trouble is you can't walk in them! My problem is, you hardly take one or two steps wearing them, but you have the feeling that the job has been made a mess of. That you have been made a mess of, not your shoes. Formerly the poor mucked up fellow took his mucked up legs and put his feet in his shoes. He never became an Adonis but he could at least believe that he looked like something. (*He feels his feet.*) In those days cobblers were real poets. Of course, in those days everybody was a bit of a poet . . . However, I'll never have the kind of shoes that I had in those days. Look at my feet. Are they worthy of the name? They have been worn to fit my shoes. Just because the world has fallen into the hands of bungling cobblers. (*He keeps squeezing his ankles.*)

ANGELINA (*peers into the sky*). How beautiful the full moon is!

ANGELUS (*looks at the sky*). Oh, yes, isn't it? Have you noticed even that has become smaller?

ANGELINA (*looks at* ANGELUS *with disbelief; begins to shake her head slowly*). Oh . . . ! No, no!

ANGELUS (*nodding his head with conviction*). It really has. So help me . . . The Russians . . .

ANGELINA (*she simply can't believe her ears*). Oh no, it's . . .

ANGELUS. The Russians have established that it's getting smaller.

ANGELINA (*shaking her head*). And you believe it . . .

ANGELUS. What I'm surprised at is that other people don't seem to have noticed it. The Russians are peaceful, meticulous people. The Poles are also like that, but they're Russians too. If they say it shrinks like a pair of long johns, then it does shrink just like a pair of long johns. And that's all there is to it. You may take poison on it.

ANGELINA *makes no reply. She gapes at the moon.*

ANGELINA. The moon? Long johns?

ANGELUS. You women have no sense of the abstract. That's what is wrong with the world. You have no sense of the abstract . . . It's awful. This is the seedbed of all troubles.

ANGELINA. Tell me, where did you get that curse from?

ANGELUS (*grinning*). Which one? My vocabulary contains quite a few . . .

ANGELINA. The one you have used just now . . .

ANGELUS. Archabel, with his shaggy dick . . .

ANGELINA *nods her head.*

Do you like it?

ANGELINA. I seem to have heard it before . . .

ANGELUS. That's it! The complete absence of abstraction skills. This is an example!

ANGELINA. I heard it from someone very long ago . . .

ANGELUS (*putting out his hand*). Perhaps I could strain my mind a little bit for a nominal fee . . .

ANGELINA (*angrily*). It's not important at all!

ANGELUS (*shrugging his shoulder again*). I'm not in a position to start thinking just for anyone.

ANGELINA (*angrily*). I see that . . .

ANGELUS (*offering the bottle to* ANGELINA). There's no ill feeling . . .

In response to ANGELINA'S *gesture of rejection* ANGELUS *shrugs his shoulders and drinks.*

ANGELINA. Well then, enjoy yourself. (*She starts rolling out.*)

ANGELUS. Don't take the wrong train, missus! I often do.

ANGELINA. At my age there are no wrong trains.

ANGELUS. I'd rather say there are no right trains. There are only wrong trains or worse. But the right trains – they're things of the past! (*Massages his feet.*)

ANGELINA *starts rolling out, but stops on her way once again. She digs out some small change from one of the bags. She offers it to* ANGELUS.

ANGELINA. Buy some drink with it, and drink to my health . . .

ANGELUS *takes the money, clicks his heels and gives a salute.*

ANGELUS. Thank you.

ANGELINA. Just take it . . .

ANGELUS. It's only proper to introduce myself. I'm Captain Angelus.

ANGELINA *looks at the tramp, shocked.*

ANGELUS. Do you feel unwell?

ANGELINA (*tries to regain her composure*). No, I don't really. Just my heart misses a beat occasionally . . . And sometimes there are more beats than necessary . . . It's nothing . . . Doctors say it happens to everybody once in a while . . . Immaterial. Of course, if you have no heart, you don't know this feeling . . . (*She looks at* ANGELUS *lost in her fantasies.*) Well then, enjoy yourself, Captain Angelus! (*She rolls out.*)

ANGELUS. Have a good journey and thank you very much. Thank you ever so much. (*He puts away the money and feels his chest at his heart.*) What a weird thing she said . . . as if she had wanted to say that I have no . . . (*He sits back. He throws his shoes off, and then, wearing the expression of a sinner whose punishment has been remitted, he starts moving the toes of his bare feet. He bends down and gets some folded paper out of his shoe. Starts reading it out.*)

My dearest Angelina,

It's just a few hours since I had the good fortune to meet you for the first time in my life, and I seem to have lost my individuality, my present, my past and my future! The only thing left for me is you, my dear Angelina. I no longer exist, I have become YOU!

Only YOU, no one else! I haven't got a family, a brother or sister any more, I have nobody left in this world. Only YOU! You are the air that braces me, my hope, my All. I hope you will never leave me. You won't, will you? My dear, sweet Angelina, I think of you such a lot! And when I do, my heart is so stricken with despair that in my grief I often don't know what I'm doing. Hopefully you are not angry with me. You aren't, are you? And if our single communion bore its fruit, would you give him my name, my lovely little Angelina? If the baby was a boy, of course. If we had a baby girl, I would like her to bear your name. The most beautiful, the dearest and the holiest name that my ears have heard and my mouth has pronounced . . . I love you. I love you, I love you a thousand times and forever,

Your faithful and doomed

Angelus.

3rd Scene

In her snow-white wedding dress the twenty-odd-year-old ANGELINA *flies onto the stage. On her head there is a veiled hat, as large as a mill-wheel, decorated with a garland. In one hand she has a bunch of myrtle, in the other there is a white wicker case. She is beaming and dancing with happiness.* ANGELUS *hurriedly puts his feet into his shoes and stands up.* ANGELINA *catches sight of the old man and suddenly stops short.*

ANGELINA. Oh, excuse me! I didn't notice . . .

ANGELUS (*he can hardly believe his eyes*). Angelina . . .

ANGELINA (*startled*). Pardon? Do you know me?

ANGELUS (*confused*). oh, nothing. There's a full moon, you see . . .

ANGELINA. Full moon! (*Dancing.*) Full up, full up, completely full up!

ANGELUS. Just go on, keep dancing! A girl is beautiful, when she is in high spirits.

ANGELINA. Then I must be beautiful! (*Spinning.*) Then I must be the most beautiful girl in the world! Because there's no one happier than me on the globe! I've been proposed to!

ANGELUS. I hope you're not rejecting him, are you?

ANGELINA. Rejecting him? I'm his! Only his! (*Spluttering.*) My heart, my soul, my mind, my hands and my breasts are all his. And so is . . .

ANGELUS. Whoa, whoa! Don't go on with the list, you might regret it later! And who is the lucky blighter, may I ask?

ANGELINA. Of course, you may. It's not a secret. Captain Angelus!

ANGELUS (*his jaw nearly falling*). Angelus? . . . Captain Angelus?

ANGELINA. Why yes! Captain Angelus!

ANGELUS. Captain Angelus . . .

ANGELINA. Do you happen to know him?

ANGELUS. Oh no! Quite the contrary! Although anything is possible . . . Why don't you describe him? What kind of a man is your Captain Angelus?

ANGELINA *draws herself up. She twirls her non-existent moustache, and struts past the old man.*

ANGELINA. That's what he is like . . .

ANGELUS (*amazed*). Like that?

ANGELINA. Precisely.

ANGELUS. I see . . . Wouldn't you like to sit near me and tell me about him? . . .

ANGELINA (*suspicious again*). Why are you so interested in him?

ANGELUS. I am consumed with curiosity about him . . .

ANGELINA (*giving in*). OK, what are the questions?

ANGELINA *sits down.* ANGELUS *thinks hard and ultimately blurts it out.*

ANGELUS. Is he dashing?

ANGELINA. He's beautiful.

ANGELUS. It's enough for a man to be only a bit more handsome than the devil.

ANGELINA. But he is very handsome!

ANGELUS. I understand.

ANGELINA. Oh, no, you don't understand! Even I can't understand how anyone can be so . . .

ANGELUS. Beautiful, I know. Could you give a bit more detail? Has he got brains?

ANGELINA *frowns.*

ANGELINA (*when she hits upon the most striking metaphor, she becomes as happy a a lark*). He's got a sea of brains!

ANGELUS. I see. And . . . ?

ANGELINA. I have already told you that he is as beautiful as a sculpture.

ANGELUS. Yes, you have told me so.

ANGELINA. And he is brave, too.

ANGELUS. And what else?

ANGELINA. He is honest. (*Spluttering*.) straightforwardchastesincerefascinating, a real charmer . . .

ANGELUS. Of course, of course . . .

ANGELINA. Why do you say that?

ANGELUS. Why do I say what?

ANGELINA (*imitating the old man*). 'Of course, of course' . . .

ANGELUS. Just because . . . Well, I don't know . . .

ANGELINA. Are you making fun of me perhaps?

ANGELUS By no means, young lady.

ANGELINA. He is like a God . . .

ANGELUS (*he runs his eye over himself*). Well . . .

ANGELINA. You are sceptical only because you don't know him . . .

ANGELUS. And what if I said that I knew him?

ANGELINA (*kisses the old man on the face*). Do you know him?

ANGELUS. No, I don't. But let's suppose I say that I did.

ANGELINA. But why would you say that if you don't know him?

ANGELUS. Because I know these mustachioed fops who pluck fragrant flowers.

ANGELINA. I don't really understand why I am talking to you about this . . .

ANGELUS. Because it's nice to talk about 'him', even to me. In fact, anyone would do . . .

ANGELINA (*blushing*). It's true . . .

ANGELUS. But if you don't feel like it we don't need to talk about him. We can talk about something else . . .

ANGELINA (*sincerely baffled*). About something else?

ANGELUS. Let's talk about . . . how nice the full moon is.

ANGELINA. Well . . . it appears to be shrinking . . .

ANGELUS. Oh, don't say so!

ANGELINA. Haven't you read that? . . .

ANGELUS. No, I haven't.

ANGELINA. The Russians have worked it out.

They look at the full moon.

ANGELUS. Do you think so? (*No reply.*)

ANGELINA. The Captain has told me . . .

ANGELUS. Captain Angelus?

ANGELINA. Yes, on a mysterious summer night . . .

ANGELUS. Your captain must be a strange man, Miss . . .

ANGELINA (*crossing her heart she gives a heart-rending sigh*). Absolutely! He is a strange and every inch an exciting man! I can hardly wait for him to clasp me in his arms again!

ANGELUS (*impishly*). Again?

The woman breaks into tears. ANGELUS puts his hand on ANGELINA's shoulder.

ANGELUS. Excuse me, Miss, but I thought . . .

ANGELINA (*still weeping*). Do you think I don't know what you were thinking?

ANGELUS. Hasn't Captain Angelus told you that nobody is supposed to weep under the full moon?

ANGELINA. Yes, he has told me . . . (*She calms down gradually.*) So many times.

They are looking at the moon.

ANGELINA. How beautiful . . .

ANGELUS. Yes, Miss, beautiful . . . Really beautiful . . . And yet very lonely . . .

ANGELINA. How strange. My Angelus also put it this way: lonely.

ANGELUS. This is strange indeed.

ANGELINA. And he also said that the full moon was a beacon of fulfilled love.

ANGELUS. Your captain is a man of delicate feelings. Such a man is a rarity these days.

ANGELINA. Oh yes, he is, isn't he?

ANGELUS. I too think that the full moon is a beacon of fulfilled love. That is, if fulfilled love continues to exist in the world.

ANGELINA. It shall exist! For example, the captain's and mine!

ANGELUS. Oh yes, I had almost forgotten. The love of you, young lady, and Captain Angelus . . .

ANGELINA (*noting the sad voice*). Why did you say that so sadly? Are you suffering from unhappy memories, perhaps?

ANGELUS. Who hasn't got unhappy memories?

ANGELINA. I haven't! (*She flutters round the seat.*) And even if I did have some my captain has made me forget them all! My dear, sweet Angelus . . .

The old man looks sadly at the happily dancing ANGELINA.

ANGELINA. My all! My only one! The Lord and King of my heart! (*She suddenly stops short looking at* ANGELUS *beseechingly.*) Ask me some more questions! I love talking about him! Talking and talking and talking and talking! (*She starts dancing again.*) About him, about him, abouthimabouthim . . .

ANGELUS. God has created a mouth for man to talk with . . .

ANGELINA (*thinking*). How strange . . . It seems as if I have heard that somewhere . . .

ANGELUS. The world is a mystery, Miss . . .

ANGELINA. The world in itself is simple. Only the people living in it are mysterious. And these mysterious people with their mysterious eyes . . .

ANGELUS. I used to think the same. But now I have lived enough to know how untrue it is . . .

ANGELUS *is about to set off.* ANGELINA *stands up to say goodbye.*

Oh, yes! I nearly forgot. If you happen to meet Angelus, the Captain of your Heart, tell him he is very lucky in case he doesn't know it . . . (*He looks at the girl lost in his thoughts.*) And, in addition, tell him also . . . (*Trying to get the right word.*) the message I'd like to leave him is . . . that he should take care of you, young lady . . . he should take good care of you . . .

ANGELINA (*deeply moved*). That's very kind of you. I will tell him . . .

ANGELUS *quits and* ANGELINA *is dancing round the tree daydreaming. She strikes her head and runs after the old man.*

ANGELINA. Your name sir please, at least your name . . . ! (*She stops short.*) He's got on the train . . . He hasn't even told me his name . . .

She sits down, takes the Keepsake Album out of her handbag, turns the pages and reads.

ANGELINA. When the ears of grass are shooting in the marshy meadows, and the branches of the trees are putting forth green leaves, you, Golden Swallow of Hope, my dear Angelina, can always take shelter under the eaves of my heart! Captain Angelus. (*As if she couldn't have enough of the spoken words, she reads the lines again melting with emotion.*)

When the ears of grass are shooting in the marshy meadows, and the branches of the trees are putting forth green leaves, you, Golden Swallow of Hope, my dear Angelina, can always take shelter under the eaves of my heart! Captain Angelus.

Under the eaves of my heart! (*She hugs the Album to herself.*) Oh, God, what beautiful words! (*She turns some new pages eagerly, looking for something.*)

If you see a monkey in a tree / Close the blue lake of your eyes / Pull its tail and think of me.

(ANGELINA *hugs the Album to her.*) My sweet Captain Angelus.

4th Scene

As if he was fleeing from pursuers, ANGELUS, *in his forties, rushes in wearing a silk raincoat with a turned-up collar and a wide-brimmed felt hat pulled over his eyes. In one hand he has a briefcase, in the other, a revolver. He keeps looking back in terror and hides behind the thin tree. Scared to death he entreats the girl.*

ANGELUS. Please hide me. For Christ's sake, please, hide me!

ANGELINA (*looking round unable to grasp the situation and pointing at herself*). Me?

ANGELUS. You, you! I'll explain everything! (*He emerges from behind the tree, rolls his eyes terrified and squats down behind the seat.*) Don't worry, I'll explain everything . . . For God's sake, hide me, I beg of you!

ANGELINA. Where, I'd like to know?

ANGELUS. I'll explain everything young lady. But now I have no time! They are chasing me! (*He throws himself at* ANGELINA*'s feet entreating her.*) I have no time. Can you hear that? I can already hear their steps. They will be here in no time, and then I am lost. What a wretch! Please, conceal me!

ANGELINA. I'd be willing to help but . . .

ANGELUS (*threatening* ANGELINA *pointing his revolver at her face*). I am not a man to waste time! It's cocked. This is a demand!

In an unguarded moment, ANGELUS *creeps under the flared wedding dress.* ANGELINA *gapes with surprise.*

ANGELINA. But Sir, I am . . .

ANGELUS (*pokes out his nose from under her skirt*). Let me warn you. I am not a man to waste time, Miss! One false move . . .

ANGELUS *retreats to the safe haven of the frills of her dress. For a time* ANGELINA *tries to behave as ordered, but then she lowers her eyelashes.*

ANGELINA. But Sir, I . . . (*She sighs.*) I am betrothed . . .

ANGELUS (*heard from under the skirt*). I promise you, Miss, I'll respect your status quo . . .

ANGELINA *is like a statue made of stone. After a time, however, peaceful snoring can be heard from under the skirt.* ANGELINA *gives an unobtrusive little cough, fidgeting a bit and then makes some vague attempts to call the man.*

ANGELINA. Sir . . . Please, Sir . . . Hallo . . . Sir . . .

ANGELUS (*startled*). What's that? . . . who's that?

ANGELINA. Only me . . .

ANGELUS (*irritated*). Who's me?

ANGELINA. Well, I don't really know . . . me.

ANGELUS (*emerges from his shelter angrily*). I hate this blessed egotistical chatter.

ANGELINA *drops onto the seat as pale as a ghost with exhaustion.*

ANGELUS. May I ask you to stand up for a moment. (*He kneels down and searches for something, his lower forearm disappearing among the frills of the wedding dress.*) It must be somewhere here.

ANGELINA (*roused*). But Sir!

ANGELUS. My mistake . . . I'll be finished in a moment! (*With a happy smile lingering at the corner of his mouth he produces his bag, which he had left under the skirt. He rubs it carefully and puts it on the seat.*) Because good order is the soul of all good things . . . isn't it? (*He looks up at the sky. Changes subject.*) A nice evening we're having, isn't it? (*He looks at* ANGELINA.) I feel I owe you an explanation, Miss . . . for my somewhat eccentric behaviour!

ANGELINA *wants to speak but* ANGELUS *cuts her short with a gesture.*

ANGELUS. Well, I'm being pursued. You naturally ask the question, young lady (ANGELINA *listens to him with naive interest.*) by whom or what, what forces are motivated to pursue somebody, specifically me in this case. And whether you have done the right thing to offer me, an unknown person, shelter, guided merely by general philanthropic feelings, a secure hiding-place to protect me from an enraged pack of wolves. By your gesture – and these are not idle words, dear lady – you have saved my life. Please tell me if you felt even for a moment that I have taken even the slightest advantage of the charming and disarming fact that you have admitted me to the heavens of your confidence. Please, dear young lady, tell me plainly.

ANGELINA (*shy and blushing*). No, I didn't.

ANGELUS (*as if a great load had been taken off his mind*). I'm very glad that we have got over this . . . Aren't you tired, my dear. I don't really know what to call you. Or is it perhaps a secret?

ANGELINA (*protests, ready to drop*). Oh, no, it isn't – Angelina.

ANGELUS. 'ANGELINA'? . . . Have I got it right? Have I heard it correctly? 'ANGELINA'?

ANGELINA (*losing confidence*). Yes . . .

ANGELUS (*giving her an order*). Halt! Stand up. Like that. Don't move.

ANGELINA *is paralysed with fright.*

ANGELINA. What's this about now?

ANGELUS *gives* ANGELINA*'s features a searching look. Then starts speaking in an extremely detached voice, while arranging his clothes.*

ANGELUS. Oh, nothing really . . . You may sit down now. I ought to tell you that I have mixed you up with somebody else . . . There used to be a lady, very close to my heart and whom I seem to have recognised in you a few minutes ago. But then I realised I was mistaken . . . but never mind.

ANGELINA. I'm very sorry, really . . .

ANGELUS. Believe me, it's better this way . . . It's a bit difficult, but my conviction is getting firmer and firmer that it is better this way.

ANGELINA. It may be . . .

ANGELUS (*stealing a glance at the girl, with hazy eyes*). After so many years . . . Oh, God . . .

He feels like touching ANGELINA*'S face, and under the influence of the moment the girl is too weak to protest but his hand stops short a few centimetres before* ANGELINA*'s face in mid air and is numbed.*

ANGELUS. Angelina . . . your name has a mysterious, heavenly ring – has anyone ever told you this?

ANGELINA *passes her hand over her own face, distracted.*

As if I heard bells tolling . . . AN-GE-LI-NA . . . AN-GE-LI-NA . . . As if the bells were chiming for you . . . (*Cupping his hands in front of his mouth preparing to call out, but he fails to do so.*) AAANGELINAAA! AAANGELINAAA! And soon the answer peals forth, AN-GE-LI-NA . . . AN-GE-LI-NA . . . Has anyone told you this, young lady?

ANGELINA (*weak with emotion*). Somebody . . . has . . .

ANGELUS. Isn't it strange that after so many years precisely you and precisely me . . .

ANGELINA (*waltzes round enchanted*). It's very strange . . .

ANGELUS. It's strange and beautiful.

ANGELINA (*carried away by the moment continues to waltz*). Oh, yes . . .

ANGELUS. And the coincidence is especially strange . . . Isn't it especially strange? Don't you think so?

ANGELINA (*having lost control*). Oh, yes I do . . .

ANGELUS. After so many years . . .

ANGELINA (*waltzing with her eyes shut*). After so many years . . .

ANGELUS. After so many years frittered away . . .

ANGELINA (*waltzing, beside herself with enchantment*). After so many years frittered away . . .

ANGELUS. And here, at the same place.

ANGELINA (*waltzing passionately*). Here, at the same place.

> *As if coming out of his dream,* ANGELUS *gives a barely noticeable start, his hands dropping.* ANGELINA *stops and is coming round.* ANGELUS *continues to speak whilst walking. He only stops to relax for a few stolen moments, occasionally resting his eyes on the girl's face, when there is a slight break in the rhythm of his speech – and then he continues to speak. With an experienced man's bitterness in his voice he asks:*

ANGELUS. Are you travelling far?

ANGELINA (*with a girlish reaction*). I don't really know . . .

ANGELUS. You don't know? How is that possible?

> ANGELINA *still feels embarrassed, almost letting her legs swing.*

ANGELINA. Everything is so relative . . . Distant? . . . Near? . . . where do you draw the line?

ANGELUS. Who have you heard such things from?

ANGELINA. I don't really know . . . Perhaps from my fiancé . . .

ANGELUS. What's your fiancé called, may I ask.

ANGELINA. Captain Angelus.

ANGELUS. Captain Angelus? How strange . . .

ANGELINA. Strange?

ANGELUS (*ill at ease*). Angelina and Angelus. Isn't it strange? I mean, the two names together. Don't you find them strange? Angelina and Angelus . . . like two stars ordained to be side by side in the sky . . .

ANGELINA. Angelus and Angelina . . . I find this order nicer.

ANGELUS. You're right. They're nicer that way.

ANGELUS's *face becomes suddenly convulsed.*

ANGELINA. Oh, Sir. Do you feel unwell?

ANGELUS. Only my shoes. (*His breathing is heavy.*)

ANGELINA (*frightened*). Your shoes?

ANGELUS (*choking*). They pinch . . . (*His voice fading away.*) Sometimes I feel they are pinching my heart . . .

ANGELINA (*crying out in alarm*). Oh, dear me, how can I help?

ANGELUS. Pah, it's nothing. It'll soon be over . . .

ANGELINA (*on the verge of utmost despair*). Dear Lord, what shall I do?

ANGELUS. You seem to know very well who you should turn to!

ANGELUS *is gasping for breath.* ANGELINA *tries to pull the man's shoes off his feet.*

ANGELUS. Oh, no! I cannot allow you to do that!

ANGELINA. Please, let me help you!

ANGELUS. No, don't touch my shoes!

ANGELINA. But I have to, Sir!

ANGELUS. You mustn't touch the shoe-laces!

ANGELINA. But that's the only way!

ANGELUS. I forbid you to undo my shoes!

ANGELINA. But I only want to loosen them!

ANGELUS (*he releases his leg*). No, I won't have that! (*He jumps up, looks round and starts lacing his shoes hurriedly.*) And what if they take me by surprise? (*He has recovered.*) You insidious snake bird. How shall I make my getaway? With undone shoe-laces? What do you think you are doing. Do you want me to be killed?

ANGELINA. I only want to help you . . .

ANGELUS. You wanted to trap me, young lady. That's what you wanted!

ANGELINA. Me?

ANGELUS. You, of course you, Miss Angelina! You, yourself!

ANGELINA. But, but . . .

ANGELUS. Did you or did you not want to pull my shoes off?

ANGELINA. But . . .

ANGELUS. Did you or didn't you?

ANGELINA. I did.

ANGELUS. You are not even trying to deny it!

ANGELINA. I did, because you said that they were pinching your heart.

ANGELUS (*suspiciously, as if he was facing a raving maniac*). My shoes . . . ?

ANGELINA. You said that your shoes were pinching your heart!

ANGELUS. My shoes? My heart? Did I say that?

ANGELINA. You did, you did!

ANGELUS. You wanted to give me up to my pursuers, Angelina!

ANGELINA (*on the verge of bursting into tears*). I only wanted to help!

ANGELUS. But the question is, who? Who did you want to help, young lady? Who?

ANGELINA. You! A man who was choking . . .

ANGELUS. A choking man, by dragging his shoes off his feet? (*Ironically.*) But my dear young lady . . .

ANGELINA *picks up her handbag. She keeps looking about nervously.*

ANGELINA. I must be going . . .

ANGELUS (*sarcastically*). Where to?

ANGELINA. My train is leaving . . .

ANGELUS *approaches* ANGELINA *with a menacing attitude.*

ANGELUS (*as before*). Nobody can ever miss their own train! 'My train is leaving.' And can you tell me, my sweet, where your train is going?

ANGELINA *retreats.*

ANGELINA (*pointing to the right hesitating*). In that direction . . .

ANGELUS. In that direction. Are you sure, Miss?

ANGELINA (*pointing to the left*). Or perhaps in that direction . . .

ANGELUS. In that direction . . .

ANGELINA. Well, yes . . .

ANGELUS. 'Well, yes.' But you do know where you are going, don't you?

ANGELINA (*confidently*). To my fiancé . . .

ANGELUS. So you are going to your fiancé . . . Do you think you can be sure of that, young lady? Don't you think the opposite is true?

ANGELINA. No, that is impossible! (*She rushes off the stage.*)

ANGELUS *shrugs his shoulders resignedly. He goes to the seat and sits down. He rubs his sore right foot. He manages to tug the shoe off it. Turning it to the light he looks into it. He dips his hand into it and pulls out a folded sheet of paper. He starts reading it out.*

My Love, my All, my sweet Angelina,

To me my life is like a pot with a hole in it, with the minutes of my days passing uselessly through it. You don't write to me, there's no news about you. My dearest, I don't know if you are dead or alive. Perhaps you love another? Believe me, even that wouldn't hurt me as much as the total silence. This murky black silence! I have to know, you must understand this. I need certainty to go on living, not to die of your absence, my only one! These days I think a lot of you between battles, as the meaning of my life, my All. Life does not matter a chipped pebble here. The fields are strewn with unburied dead bodies, as if they were melons left in the melon fields at the end of August. They don't play for love here, that I know. But I still don't know what would happen to me if I did not have you, and your sweet memory did not feed the red rosebuds of hope bursting in my heart . . .

ANGELUS *keeps looking at the paper for a long time. He folds it up and slips it into his shoe. He puts on his shoes and looks round nervously.*

5th Scene

ANGELINA *comes in. She is a middle-aged lady with a dignified gait, wearing a black dress. She has a medium-sized black suitcase and a black umbrella in her hands. On her head there is a beautiful black veiled hat.*

ANGELUS (*stands up politely giving up his seat*). Madam, please.

ANGELINA. Thank you, Sir. (*She sits down with a straight back.*)

ANGELUS. How sad the evening of a full moon can be . . .

ANGELINA (*coolly*). Yes, it can, can't it?

ANGELUS (*looks round nervously. He runs his hand down his coat, resting it for a moment on the pocket where he has put his revolver*). Sad and infinitely bleak . . .

ANGELINA. Sad and infinitely bleak . . .

ANGELUS (*casting helpless side-glances at the gloomy elegance of the lady in mourning*). Still, we have to live . . .

ANGELINA. Certainly, we have to live . . .

ANGELUS *starts to feel his sore foot.*

ANGELUS. And however hard we may find living sometimes and however painful it might be – we have to do our duty and our duty is nothing else but to carry on . . . (*He takes a careful look round.*) – our lives.

ANGELINA (*heaving a sigh*). . . . . our own lives.

ANGELUS. Yes, our own lives . . . Yes, Madam, that is the truth and it continues to be the truth, even if both of us see clearly that it's not such a marvellous idea. (*He feels his feet.*)

ANGELINA. As long as there is a single, living being breathing on the earth, the dead souls breathe with them.

ANGELUS (*jerks up his head, surprised*). How strange . . .

ANGELINA. The world itself is strange.

ANGELUS. 'As long as there is a single living soul breathing on the earth, the dead souls breathe with them.'

ANGELINA. It's a sublime and engaging thought. It gives comfort to those who need it, and support to those in need of support. Whoever conceived this idea has every reason to be proud of it.

ANGELUS (*passes his hand over his head*). May I ask you who you have heard it from?

ANGELINA. A man told it to me. A real man, Sir. I loved that man. I loved him more than myself . . .

ANGELUS *stands up, embarrassed. He tries to look behind the veil.* ANGELINA *does not stir but continues to sit there with a straight back.*

ANGELUS. I see, Madam. Please excuse me, I did not mean to offend you by stirring up memories.

ANGELINA. You did not offend me, Sir.

ANGELUS. You're encouraging me to ask you: what has happened to the man?

Slowly retreating, ANGELUS *gets behind* ANGELINA.

ANGELINA. He's dead.

ANGELUS. Is he?

ANGELINA. Yes, he's dead.

ANGELUS (*craning his neck to look behind the veil*). Are you sure?

ANGELINA. For me he is definitely dead.

ANGELUS. I did not mean to upset you, Madam.

ANGELUS *looks round carefully and then bends quite near her.*

ANGELINA. There's no storm that could ruffle a frozen lake . . . Sir.

ANGELINA *suddenly looks at the man, who shrinks back in alarm. He draws his hands nervously over his pockets and then rests them on the revolver.*

ANGELUS. I guess that you are mourning that man, Madam.

ANGELINA. You guess wrongly. I'm mourning my baby. I had a miscarriage here . . . a few years ago . . . I also conceived here . . .

ANGELUS *bends down as if some air had got stuck behind his ribs. He spreads his hand on his chest. He gasps for breath like a fish washed ashore.*

ANGELUS. Oh my God, I am choking . . .

ANGELINA (*without turning back or stirring*). Is something wrong, Sir?

ANGELUS *straightens up, his forehead sweating.*

ANGELUS. My shoes . . . My shoes are pinching, Madam . . . Sometimes they . . . sort of . . . stifle me.

ANGELINA. God may appear even in the form of an uncomfortable shoe, Sir.

ANGELUS. But I am hurt by two shoes, Madam, although God is one and indivisible . . .

ANGELINA. But we do not understand the ways and intentions of God at all, Sir. You don't think, I suppose, that it's a problem for God to be two shoes at once, if he wishes to, do you!

ANGELUS *does not seem to know what to think. He keeps shifting from foot to foot, scrutinising his shoes.*

ANGELUS. I don't know, Madam . . . (*He repeatedly looks away from the stage, then suddenly goes to the seat and picks up his case.*) I'm sorry, I must be leaving . . . I wouldn't like to miss my train . . .

ANGELINA. No one could ever miss their train, even if they wanted to. Wouldn't you of all people know that, Captain Angelus.

ANGELUS *halts benumbed. Through his coat he grabs the stock of his revolver with a sense of fear.*

ANGELUS. Do you know me?

ANGELINA (*motionless*). You are asking me if I know you?

ANGELUS. Who sent you?

ANGELINA. Me . . . ? Captain . . .

ANGELUS (*pulling out his revolver*). Who are you?

ANGELINA. Act your age, Captain Angelus . . .

ANGELUS. Who are you?

ANGELINA (*still motionless*). You ought to know that better than me, Captain . . .

> ANGELUS *levels his revolver and pulls the trigger once, twice, three times, four times* . . .

> ANGELINA *stays motionless, as if the bullets couldn't harm her. She recites a quotation;.*

ANGELINA. My sweetest Angelina, you're an angel with your inviting lips, a fragrant flower blooming on my heart. You're my life, I love you!

> ANGELUS *strains his hands to his ears.*

ANGELINA. I love you, as I have always loved you and will continue to love you until my heart beats . . . its last . . . Captain Angelus.

> ANGELUS *rushes off the stage.* ANGELINA *pulls a letter out of the pages of the book. She starts reading it aloud.*

> Because I have to live, dear Captain! Because I can't just die . . . I can't just take my own life, because I don't dispose of it in my own right any longer . . . because I'm expecting a baby. Because I'm expecting your baby, Captain Angelus. Please, write to me or send me a message, I beg you! I don't expect anything else, just a signal! A tiny light in this frosty night! You shouldn't deny me this, as I'm bearing your child under my hoar-frosty heart . . .

> I remain yours forever and only yours – Angelina.

She gets out an apple. She bites into it behind the crêpe. She chews it. The song of the woman mourning her love is heard again. Darkness.

PART II

6th Scene

In deep mourning, ANGELINA *sitting on the seat, reading a letter.*

ANGELINA. . . . I don't know what to think of you, of myself, of us
both and of life any more, if I can say at all that life still exists for
me without your beloved person . . . dear Angelus. Because I can
only think of the passionate moment for body and soul, when you
kissed me. Since then I only live in that moment. Because that
moment is everything to me . . . But you should know, my own
love, that I would like to rip out the memory of that moment from
my heart as many times . . . a million times! As I wish I could see
your face, which is so dear to me, touch your beloved hands or hear
your deep-toned silky russet voice . . .

Swearing is heard from outside.

ANGELUS' VOICE. Oh may Archabel cast you into the fire, you
hideous shaggy-haired, prick . . . Or at least may the fizzling
thunderbolt strike you between your jug ears, you wooden
jackanapes.

ANGELINA *rises and listens to* ANGELUS, *who is just coming in,
turning towards him.*

ANGELINA. You abominable mother's nightmare grabbing your
smutty, filthy stove pipe! Oh may the crucifix and all the
sacraments pierce this perverted world!

ANGELUS *enters brushing the soil off the sleeves of his coat. He
is middle-aged, tired and worn out, with matted hair. He puts down
the heavy trunk that his shoulders have been bending under and
settles on it, fagged out. Looking round, he casts a searching
glance at* ANGELINA.

ANGELUS (*politely*). How much did your ladyship hear of all that?

With a dignified air ANGELINA *settles back on the seat. She gives
no answer.*

ANGELUS. Because I'd like to apologise according to how much
your ladyship has deigned to hear of it . . .

ANGELINA *avoids looking at* ANGELUS. *She is sitting straight-
backed with downcast eyes.* ANGELUS *shrugs his shoulders, dusts
off the sleeves of his coat again and starts massaging his feet
repeatedly. He continues to grumble.*

ANGELUS. May he be struck dumb with his sooty nozzle . . . wherever he is . . . Don't you agree?

ANGELINA. Isn't it like as if it were breathing? . . .

ANGELUS *looks at the woman unable to get her meaning and continues to stroke his feet.*

ANGELINA. . . . the full moon. I mean, isn't it as if it were breathing?

ANGELUS *looks a ANGELINA, puzzled.*

. . . As if it was watching the earth and breathing quietly . . .

ANGELUS *keeps stroking his sore feet.*

ANGELUS. Are you talking to . . . ?

ANGELINA (*not looking at* ANGELUS). Isn't it as if . . . ? Don't you think it is like that?

ANGELUS *rolls a cigarette.*

ANGELUS. I'm not a poet. I'm just a homeless pedlar, Madam . . .

ANGELINA. A pedlar may be a poet in his soul, my friend . . .

ANGELUS. It is more feasible the other way round . . .

ANGELINA (*she turns her veiled face to the man and starts quoting*). My sweet Angelina, the fat, toothless full moon, he pries into all the secrets of faithless lovers!

ANGELUS *jerks his head up in surprise. He looks at* ANGELINA, *deep in thought, and lights a cigarette.*

ANGELINA (*sharply*). Don't those lines seem familiar to you?

ANGELUS. If your brain recorded everything that your ears hear . . .

ANGELINA. I think it's rather a question of the heart, my friend. And its memory.

ANGELUS (*ironically*). The heart's memory. I'm flabbergasted. I don't know what the attraction is. The heart is a worthless, worn out piece of meat. (*He pulls at his cigarette and strokes his chest over his heart.*) And on top of all that, it is not very hard-wearing . . .

ANGELINA (*sighs with resignation*). You really aren't much of a poet, are you?

ANGELUS (*throwing away his butt*). I have told you, Madam. I am a pedlar.

ANGELINA. And what do you peddle?

ANGELUS (*as if he were hesitating to answer*). . . . Prostheses, Madam . . . Prosthetic eyes, prosthetic hearts, prosthetic heads . . . and things like that . . .

ANGELINA. It must be very exciting . . .

ANGELUS. Some people don't think so, Madam . . . Lots of people shy away from me when they find out what this trunk holds . . . Although there's nothing peculiar in it, nothing very striking . . .

ANGELINA. Personally I can find nothing objectionable in that.

ANGELUS. That is because you probably know life.

ANGELINA (*gloomily*). Well, yes, life is something I know . . .

ANGELUS. You can't imagine how much, how very much I suffer from this. People can be very wicked if they don't make an effort . . .

ANGELINA. . . . And if they do, they can be even more wicked.

ANGELUS. Exactly, Madam. (*He casts a long glance at the woman.*) Somebody from your family?

ANGELINA (*slowly turning her face towards* ANGELUS). Who do you mean?

ANGELUS. The person you are wearing black for.

ANGELINA (*with wounded dignity*). I'm wearing these clothes because of my profession, my friend.

ANGELUS (*opens his eyes wide*). What d'you mean?

ANGELINA (*slowly turning her face towards* ANGELUS). You know very well what I mean . . . (*She fixes her eyes on* ANGELUS *from under the veil.*) Don't you? (*Only after taking a deep breath can* ANGELUS *bring himself to say the following.*)

ANGELUS. To help people to suffer . . . guaranteed work, as sure as fate . . .

ANGELINA. I deliver people from suffering, my friend.

Long silence.

ANGELINA. Could you show me a heart, old man?

ANGELUS (*sincerely surprised*). . . . You, Madam?

ANGELINA. I'm interested.

ANGELUS. Oh, there's nothing interesting about it in itself . . .

ANGELINA. You know, sometimes things can be interesting in themselves.

ANGELUS (*looking into the distance*). Well, I think we still have enough time . . .

ANGELINA. No one can ever miss their own train . . . dear Captain . . . Angelus! . . .

ANGELUS (*shocked*). You know me, Madam?

ANGELINA *does not answer for a long time. Then she points at the trunk.*

ANGELINA. It's there, on the side of the trunk . . . (*She reads, pronouncing the syllables distinctly.*) 'Captain Angelus'.

ANGELUS (*relieved*). Of course, it is!

ANGELUS *opens the trunk. After a prolonged search he produces a heart, with the pride of a salesman. He breathes on it, polishes it with his sleeve and hands it over to* ANGELINA.

ANGELUS. Even a real one is not as glossy as this, Madam . . .

ANGELINA. I don't know . . . (*She receives the prosthetic heart handed to her as carefully as if it was a painted Easter egg.*) So this is it, is it?

ANGELUS. Yes, it is, Madam . . .

ANGELINA. The HEART . . .

ANGELUS. The PROSTHETIC heart, Madam . . . The PROSTHETIC heart.

ANGELINA. Of course, of course . . . (*She turns it round and looks at it.*) Dazzling . . .

ANGELUS. Sometimes I myself am really tempted . . . to have certain organs of mine replaced . . .

ANGELINA. Your heart, for instance . . . is that right?

ANGELUS (*his brow darkens*). Why my heart in particular?

ANGELINA (*pertly*). Just because . . .

ANGELUS. One doesn't say things for no reason.

ANGELINA. Do you think so, Captain? Do you really think so, or are you just saying so?

ANGELUS. I never talk purposelessly for no reason.

ANGELINA (*with an edge*). That is no small virtue these days.

ANGELUS (*glancing at the woman suspiciously*). What exactly did you mean by that?

ANGELINA. I meant what I said, my friend.

ANGELUS *gives the woman a nervous and searching look. she lowers her veil again.*

ANGELUS. Haven't we met somewhere? . . . I've such a strange feeling, Madam . . .

ANGELINA. Skip it, my friend, forget it . . . The world itself is rather strange. Why should our feelings be an exception . . . ? (*She lifts up the heart.*) I'll buy this . . .

ANGELUS. Don't we know each other?

ANGELINA (*she snaps drily*). It's impossible!

ANGELUS (*slightly hurt*). You don't need to bite my head off!

ANGELINA (*holding out the heart for* ANGELUS *to see*). I said I'll buy it . . .

ANGELUS. But what do you need it for?

ANGELINA. A souvenir of you . . . remembrance of a beautiful night with a full moon . . .

ANGELUS *nods his head, completely sure of himself.*

ANGELUS. I do know you . . .

ANGELINA. Now now, my friend . . . (*She stands up.*) I must be leaving . . . I don't want to miss my train.

ANGELUS. No-one can ever miss their train.

ANGELINA. How much do I owe you?

ANGELUS *keeps shaking his head, hardly able to speak.*

ANGELUS. Nothing . . . you haven't answered my question . . .

ANGELINA. What question?

ANGELUS. Whether we know each other . . .

ANGELINA. I'm sorry, Sir, but there really isn't any answer to that question.

ANGELUS. But why?

ANGELINA. Perhaps you too will come to understand everything one day . . .

ANGELUS. Have you got anything against me?

ANGELINA (*scanning* ANGELUS *from top to toe*). Nothing, my friend. Nothing.

ANGELINA *produces some money. She throws it on the trunk, in front of the man.*

ANGELINA. Count it, please . . . It may be enough for a heart . . .

ANGELUS *is sitting with his face buried in his hands, ignoring the money. He keeps nodding his head.*

ANGELINA. I wish you all the best my friend . . . I must be leaving . . . Have a nice journey . . .

ANGELINA *leaves with the prosthetic heart under her arm.* ANGELUS *slowly pulls himself together. Cramming the notes into his pocket he pulls out a letter with the same movement and starts reading it.*

ANGELUS. My Golden Oriole, my Ruby-Red Dove . . . Why is it that the sun and the moon cannot be united? Why is it that the boundless ocean and the illimitable sky can never be wedded? Why is it that fire and water cannot combine without extinguishing each other? Why is that so? Maybe some will unknown to both of us does not allow such closeness . . . My Fragrant Rose, my Own Love, my All! Nowadays I think of you even more often than before. You're with me when I get up and when night falls. But I also think of you whilst marching, when on guard and in battle. I think of you and only you when the Russian cannonballs as big as my fist whiz past me, like the May hailstones around the innocent downy yellow ducklings, which have been turned out to grass and left there. My sweet Angelina, can you forgive me? Can you forget my sin? Can you forget that I have been so uncouth and immensely foolish? I have not a moment's rest because of this! Please tell me that you can! Tell me that you can forget my heinous act! I can't die without the assurance that you have forgiven me. That you have absolved me from the weight of my terrible sin. Please be kind enough to tell me you have. And I will shut my eyes but through my heart I will see and hear it as your cherry lips pronounce the words, which will be blessed a thousand times: 'I do. I do forgive you.' Your golden balm-cricket, Captain Angelus . . .

PS. If I were to die, I would like you to know, to be aware that . . .

7th Scene

ANGELINA *enters. One of her hands is on her strongly bulging tummy, in her other hand she is holding a light case. She is standing about, wavering and listening to* ANGELUS.

ANGELUS. . . . I have always loved only you. I did not even know that You, your Body and Soul had taken shape somewhere on earth, but I loved you already at that time. Only you, always and forever.

ANGELINA. It's beautiful . . . The woman these lines are addressed to must be the happiest in the world . . .

ANGELUS *quickly folds the letter. He rises. He stares at the girl, her hand stretched to her mouth, as if she was an apparition.*

ANGELINA. Please, excuse my overhearing you. I didn't mean to . . .

ANGELUS (*amazed, spontaneously*). Angelina . . . my dear . . .

ANGELINA. Do we know each other?

ANGELUS (*clearing his throat*). Well . . .

ANGELINA. I'm talking rubbish . . . How would you know my name otherwise? You might just as well have mixed me up with somebody else you know, whom I resemble or who may resemble me . . .

ANGELUS (*settling on the seat, still paralysed*). But it might also easily . . . (*He looks at* ANGELINA's *tummy. For a moment he hesitates whether to continue.*) . . . happen that I have a pact with the devil . . .

ANGELINA. That I find hard to believe . . .

ANGELUS (*as if he had taken it badly*). You wouldn't have thought me capable of it?

ANGELINA. No, I wouldn't! . . . (*Dismayed.*) That is to say . . .

ANGELUS (*feeling his face, offended*). Is my face so horrible?

ANGELINA (*even more alarmed*). You misunderstand me!

ANGELUS (*breathes into his palm and smells it*). My breath smells like brimstone.

ANGELINA (*in despair*). Oh, God!

> ANGELUS *has mercy on her. He lifts his first finger, smiling.*

ANGELUS. You should be careful, though . . . (*He squints at* ANGELINA's *tummy, hesitating.*) . . . Madam.

> ANGELINA's *mind is relieved of an immense weight. She does not even notice* ANGELUS' *hesitation.*

ANGELINA. I trust people . . .

ANGELUS. Man is just a peculiar animal, nothing else . . .

ANGELINA. The world in itself is very peculiar, Sir. People are just visitors here, kinds of wingless angels . . .

ANGELUS (*springs up from the seat and wipes it with his sleeve. He offers* ANGELINA *a seat*). Why don't you take a seat? . . . er . . . Madam.

> ANGELINA *sits down modestly, pulling her legs under the seat. Locking her fingers together under her tummy she smiles gently.*

ANGELINA (*correcting him*). Miss . . . If you have been wondering . . .

ANGELUS. Yes, I have . . .

ANGELINA. . . . whether I am married.

ANGELUS. I must confess, I have . . .

ANGELINA. Well, I'm not, Sir.

> *They are sitting on the seat. He casts sidelong glances at* ANGELINA.

ANGELUS. Well, these days such things happen easily. Along comes some fellow in the moonlight and you're in trouble.

ANGELINA (*proudly*). The baby's father is a captain!

ANGELUS. A captain . . .

ANGELINA. Yes, he is, a captain!

ANGELUS. That can't be true . . .

ANGELINA. Oh yes, it is, he is a captain! A real, angelic captain!

ANGELUS. A wingless, angelic captain! I have always known that captains are great womanisers!

ANGELINA. But he is different!

ANGELUS. A braggart, a petticoat-chaser.

ANGELINA. But you don't even know him!

ANGELUS. You may be right. (*He looks at* ANGELINA *immersed in thought*.) I wonder where your captain can be . . .

ANGELINA. He is doing his duty, Sir.

ANGELUS (*with genuine bitterness*). I see.

ANGELINA. He is fighting . . . (*She takes her handkerchief and blows her nose hard.*)

ANGELUS. I understand.

ANGELINA (*she blows her nose again*). How could you understand when I myself can't understand?

> ANGELINA *bursts out sobbing.* ANGELUS *feels like stroking the woman's shoulders, but whenever he lifts his hands, they fall back, inert.*

ANGELUS. And tell me, does he write letters to you at least?

ANGELINA (*speaking while blowing her nose*). If somebody fights day and night, how could be possibly write letters?!

ANGELUS (*grinding his teeth*). Oh, what a wretched fellow I am . . . (*He changes his tone.*) A strange life if, young lady . . .

ANGELINA (*with tears in her eyes*). Very strange . . .

ANGELUS (*gently*). You know, I also met a girl once. A glamorous girl like you.

ANGELINA (*sobbing*). It's very strange, I can tell you . . .

ANGELUS (*trying to smile*). It certainly is.

ANGELINA (*setting her hat straight with a gentle gesture*). Do you mean to say she was as beautiful as I am?

ANGELUS. Exactly, just like you . . .

ANGELINA. And what's happened to that girl, tell me!

ANGELUS (*bending his head and failing to answer for a long time*). I don't know.

ANGELINA. Did you leave her or did she leave you?

ANGELUS *nods his head.*

ANGELINA. Now I see . . .

ANGELUS. I was young . . . (*He lights a cigarette.*) young and foolish. Very foolish . . .

ANGELINA. You never met again?

ANGELUS *takes a long draw on his cigarette.*

ANGELINA. Never?

ANGELUS. I dream about her . . .

ANGELINA (*stretching herself*). It's nice to dream. I like it too.

ANGELUS. I was as young as you are. I thought life was ahead of me.

ANGELINA. Did you love her?

ANGELUS (*nods his head*). She was my whole life . . . she was EVERYTHING. But I realised it too late.

ANGELINA. You haven't heard anything from her?

ANGELUS. Only several years later.

ANGELINA (*sadly*). That is very sad.

ANGELUS (*gloomily*). It is very sad indeed.

ANGELINA. You didn't even look for her? Didn't you want to meet her?

ANGELUS. Things lost are never the same once found again. (*He turns to* ANGELINA.) Have you noticed that yet?

ANGELINA. It sounds terribly unfair, but I can only hope that you are wrong.

ANGELUS. Unfortunately this is the kind of injustice that you yourself will have to face.

They are sitting on the seat.

ANGELUS. How nice the full moon is . . . Extra-terrestrial and mysterious!

ANGELINA. There was a time when I was very afraid of the full moon . . .

ANGELUS. But they say the full moon is the lovers' friend, Mademoiselle.

ANGELINA. 'It pries into all the secrets of loving hearts!'

ANGELUS (*springs to his feet, dumbfounded*). Do you know the first line, too?

ANGELINA (*impishly*). That's my secret.

ANGELUS (*roused*). Do you know it?

ANGELINA. I think so . . .

ANGELUS (*controlling himself*). Please, Mademoiselle.

ANGELINA (*wrinkling her forehead*). . . . the fat . . .

ANGELUS (*aroused but fully controlling himself*). Carry on! (*almost hissing*.) For heaven's sake, Mademoiselle, get a grip!

ANGELINA. But you're continually interrupting me! (*Fixing her eyes on the sky she concentrates. A train whistle can he heard from afar*.) 'Fat . . . '

ANGELUS (*keeps looking away from the stage. He can't help prompting*). 'Toothless full moon!' . . . 'Fat, toothless full moon . . . ' Come on, get a move on, what are you waiting for?

ANGELINA (*in agony, looking exasperated*). 'Fat, toothless full moon . . . ' I don't know . . .

ANGELUS. Have you read it somewhere? (*Shouting at her*.) Spit it out for God's sake!

ANGELINA (*frightened*). Well, I'm doing my best . . .

ANGELUS (*infuriated*). That's not true! You're not trying to do anything! If you were, you'd manage it!

ANGELINA (*shaking her head in anguish*). . . . 'fat, toothless full moon . . . '

ANGELUS *grabs the girl's arm, enraged. He shakes her.*

ANGELUS. I have no time! My train is coming! ' . . . Fat, toothless full moon, unwanted, unwanted . . . !' How does it go?

ANGELINA (*sobbing*). Why are you tormenting me?

ANGELUS (*pulling the girl towards him savagely*). Because you are accusing me! The way you look at me and talk to me!

ANGELINA (*whining with fright*). Who are you?

ANGELUS. The poem! Once you have started it, you should recite it to the end! Come on!

ANGELINA. The lovers . . . the full moon, the buffoon . . . (*She weeps*.) . . . the old . . .

ANGELUS (*rages*). Where have you heard these lines? Try to remember! You must remember! And you must forgive!

He rushes away from the stage and then rushes off it, picking up the case. ANGELINA *remains there alone.*

ANGELINA. 'The old, fat . . . full moon . . . old buffoon' . . . (*She snivels and blows her nose*.) 'The full moon . . . fat buffoon . . . unwanted . . . pries into . . . ' (*She blows her nose and snivels*.) 'The unwanted full moon . . . loving . . . old . . . fat . . . '

She produces the Keepsake Album, turns some pages and reads from it.

ANGELINA. My sweet Angelina, the fat, toothless full moon, this unwanted old buffoon! He pries into the secrets of loving hearts! (*She blows her nose and wipes her face. She takes a letter out of the Keepsake Album.*)

'My sweet Angelus, the consecrated bell-ringer of my heart's church, my All . . . My sweet Shepherd! Tell me why you treat my chaste feelings so unkindly, tell me why! Have I wronged you, even in thought? Was it perhaps harmful to you when our forsaken hearts united like two red-hot volcanic eruptions in the middle of the icy Arctic Ocean? I don't know what to think of you treating me the way any right-thinking gentleman wouldn't treat a stray dog! Are you casting me off? . . . I can understand you, as I fell into your strong arms at that trysting-place at the railway station., my head reeling with the unknown secret spell you cast upon me which I had never experienced before, like the nocturnal moth falling into the deadly flames of a nightlight . . . '

8th Scene

ANGELUS *enters. He is wearing black glasses and his face is covered with bandages. His gloves are white and there is a white scarf round his neck. In his hands he is holding a silver-topped cane and a small case. He stops, turns his head round and listens attentively. He is listening for the crying.*

ANGELUS. Can I be of any help? Do I hear . . . ? Is there somebody here?

ANGELINA *overcomes her fear and hesitation, stands up and touches* ANGELUS' *arm. She leads him to the seat.*

ANGELINA. Thank you, it was nothing to speak of, just a passing nothing . . .

ANGELUS. All my life my miseries have been associated with passing nothings.

They sit down.

ANGELUS. Thank you very much . . . Where am I?

ANGELINA. In some god-forsaken hole . . .

ANGELUS. I have been at a god-forsaken railway station once before . . . It was so small, it didn't even have a name . . .

ANGELINA. This place hasn't got a name either, it's so small . . .

ANGELUS. It's strange . . . a small withered tree and a seat . . . That's what the whole station was, nothing more . . .

ANGELINA. A small withered tree and a seat, there is nothing more here either.

ANGELUS. It may be as many as 50 years ago that I was at that station last. But I remember it as if it had happened yesterday . . . There was a full moon. (ANGELINA *looks up at the moon.*)

ANGELINA. There is a full moon now . . .

ANGELUS. It's very strange . . . Don't you think so? Fifty years, that's not a short time, but I feel as if just a second separated me from then. There was somebody there, a girl . . . Angelina . . . who was also waiting for a connection . . .

ANGELINA. I'm also called Angelina . . .

ANGELUS (*after a short pause*). This is perhaps more than strange . . . Don't you think so, dear . . . Angelina?

ANGELINA*'s hands are on her belly. She cranes her neck curiously.*

ANGELINA. Oh yes, I do . . .

ANGELUS. Not that the world is not strange enough in itself, but its strangeness will become even stranger in the light of such strange occurrences. Don't you think so?

ANGELINA. Well . . . yes.

ANGELUS (*courteously*). May I hope that you will place your confidence in me if you should feel that I can help you in some way?

ANGELINA. You could help a lot by not standing there . . .

ANGELUS. You're most kind, Mademoiselle. (*He sits back.*) Could you tell me what the weather is like . . . outside?

ANGELINA. It's a beautiful night with a full moon . . . (*She keeps glancing at the man, with curiosity filled with sympathy.*) Was it an accident?

ANGELUS. You could say that . . .

ANGELINA. That's too bad . . .

ANGELUS. Yes, you could put it that way . . .

ANGELINA. Do say if I'm being indelicate.

ANGELUS. On the contrary! I am pleased by your enquiries, Mademoiselle. They are rather endearing . . .

They both remain silent.

ANGELINA. Yet it seems you find it hard to talk about.

ANGELUS. It's difficult to get enough air in here . . .

ANGELINA (*with sympathy*). Oh, God, poor man!

ANGELUS (*feeling for his case*). There's something here that could help . . . (*He gropes about.*) something . . . that . . .

ANGELINA. May I help?

ANGELUS (*fumbling about, he manages to open the case*). No, no, thank you . . . Everybody has to learn sooner or later . . . (*He is feeling for something in the case.*) . . . how to get about by themselves . . . The world is like that . . .

ANGELINA (*stroking her tummy*). Yes, it is . . .

ANGELUS. Got it! Here it is! (*He pulls out a funnel. He puts it to the opening in front of his mouth.*) What were we saying?

ANGELINA. That my enquiries are . . . endearing . . .

ANGELUS. Yes . . . yes . . . very much so.

They both remain silent. ANGELUS *breathes through the funnel.*

ANGELINA (*cautiously hesitating*). But if you didn't feel like talking about it, I would, of course, understand . . .

ANGELUS (*removes the funnel from his mouth and locks it in the case*). I can assure you, Madam, that it is quite the contrary . . . But my experience is that if I suddenly get air, I always feel a bit dizzy . . .

ANGELINA. That must be rather nasty!

They remain silent.

ANGELUS. Are you saying that there is a full moon?

ANGELINA. Yes, I am. The full moon is shining beautifully.

ANGELUS. Does it have a halo?

ANGELINA. I beg your pardon?

ANGELUS. Could you look if there is a halo round it?

ANGELINA (*still uncomprehending*). A halo round what?

ANGELUS. The full moon, Mademoiselle. You know, my neck . . . and my eyes.

ANGELINA. Oh, I see! (*She is looking up.*) I think, there is . . .

ANGELUS. A transparent circle . . .

ANGELINA (*looking at it*). Yes, there is . . .

ANGELUS. That does it!

They are sitting.

ANGELINA. Is there a problem if it has a halo?

ANGELUS. It means it will be freezing, Mademoiselle.

ANGELINA. In the middle of August? . . .

ANGELUS. In the middle of August, Mademoiselle.

ANGELINA *strokes her tummy protectively. They are sitting.*

ANGELUS. Is there a draught?

ANGELINA. A draught? Here?

ANGELUS. I can feel it inside here, but you never know. My doctor told me that I might be killed even by a draught.

ANGELINA (*moistens her forefinger and turns it round above her head*). No, there is . . . no draught . . .

ANGELUS. It is very kind of you . . .

ANGELINA. Not at all. It's really nothing . . .

ANGELUS. I wouldn't want to bother you for all the world but haven't we met somewhere? Your voice seems so familiar . . .

ANGELINA (*looking at the man*). It's interesting, yours also seems familiar to me . . . Perhaps if I could see your face . . .

ANGELUS. Oh, well, yes . . .

ANGELINA (*looking at* ANGELUS *with interest*). Faces are very important . . .

ANGELUS. Well, yes . . .

ANGELINA. One remembers some faces to the end of one's life . . .

ANGELUS *does not answer. They are sitting and staring at the moon.*

ANGELINA. If I could see your face . . . perhaps . . .

ANGELUS. I'm well aware of the fact that my appearance doesn't make the situation easier . . .

ANGELINA. Yet I have a feeling that we have met somewhere . . .

ANGELUS. I don't think so . . . But you look very much like somebody . . . I used to . . . here.

ANGELINA. Really?

ANGELUS. Yes, You know when you are young there is nothing you like sharing with somebody so much as your loneliness. And we were young and attractive.

ANGELINA. You chanced upon each other by accident . . .

ANGELUS. Do you think there is any such thing as an accident?

ANGELINA. . . . and you fell in love with each other . . .

ANGELUS Well, yes.

ANGELINA. . . . and then you suffered like abandoned dogs . . .

ANGELUS. Yes.

ANGELINA. . . . and you were separated from each other forever.

ANGELUS. Yes, we were.

ANGELINA. It's a very beautiful story, Sir.

ANGELUS. Nevertheless, the story has a flaw, Mademoiselle.

ANGELINA. Every story has a flaw . . .

ANGELUS. But this is not that kind of flaw . . . it is much more than that . . . I seduced that girl.

ANGELINA. But a girl's heart is not a plaything, Sir.

ANGELUS. I seduced her and abandoned her . . . (*He rises, goes round the seat and stops behind* ANGELINA.) Would you forgive me? Could you forgive me?

ANGELINA *gives no answer but waits numbed.*

ANGELUS. Since that night I haven't had a peaceful moment, Mademoiselle . . . I am always on the run, but wherever I flee, I sense people peering into my face! . . . Can you understand that? I feel that everybody can see on my face that it was me . . . (*He raises his gloved hand.*) That they can see it on my hands that they were the ones . . . (*His hand droops.*) I can't bear those glances . . . (*He sinks beneath the burden.*)

ANGELINA *shudders to look at him.*

Could you forgive me?

ANGELINA. I cannot give you absolution on another's behalf. (*She stands up.*) I think my train is here . . .

She lifts up the case and loses her balance for a moment.

ANGELUS (*looking up*). Can I help you . . . dear Angelina?

ANGELINA. Thank you . . . I'd better do it myself . . .

She overcomes her weakness and leaves. ANGELUS *follows her with his eyes for a long time. He takes off his shoes and rubs his feet. He pulls some folded paper out of his shoe. He opens it and starts reading it out.*

ANGELUS. My sweet Angelina, scarcely a minute passes that I don't think of you and the wonderful night that I spent with you, far away from here, at that god-forsaken place. My dearest Love! I know my sin is grave and I cannot be forgiven for what I have done to you. I beg you not to think that I did it because I did not love you enough. I did love you . . . But you must understand that I couldn't have done anything else! I was young and foolish! Almost a child! My sweet Angelina! I thought that if you wanted to be happy in this world, you had to make your fortune and be a success.

*He suddenly creases up and throws down the letter. He puts his
shoes on. He leans on his walking stick with a straight back. He is
sitting turning his bandaged face towards the moon. Outside dogs
are howling.*

9th Scene

A radiant young ANGELINA *comes in. On her head there is a straw
hat, in her hands there are two heavy cane cases and a folded silk
frilled parasol. She catches sight of the man with the bandaged head.
She lingers, rather frightened, as if she wanted to turn back but then
she squats on one of the cases.*

ANGELUS (*without looking at the girl*). They are howling. Can you
hear them howling, Angelina?

ANGELINA (*giving a little embarrassed cough she looks round*). You
know me? Do you know me?

ANGELUS (*does not stir*). They are barking at the full moon . . . But
maybe somebody has died . . .

ANGELINA. Do you know me?

ANGELUS. A good question . . . Do I know you? (*He sighs.*) But let
me ask you, can you get to know someone? Or yourself, for that
matter? Can anyone believe that they know themselves? And can
the full moon be known at all? The earth? The dogs? Life? And
you, dear Angelina? Or me? Just think of it. Even if I knew you,
could I say yes to this question with a clear conscience?

ANGELINA. Have we met somewhere?

ANGELUS. Here is another difficult question, Angelina. This is a new
problem but appears to be simpler than the previous one at least. Is
it possible for two or more different people to exist at the same
time and in the same space?

ANGELINA. I wouldn't think it was so complicated . . .

ANGELUS. Things, Angelina, will not become complicated or simple
because you or I think about them this or that way.

ANGELINA. An encounter . . .

ANGELUS. Two people at the same time and in the same space!

ANGELINA. Have we met or haven't we?

Outside the dogs stop howling.

ANGELUS. They have stopped howling. Don't you think there is
something archaic, something extra-terrestrial in this howl? (*He
turns towards* ANGELINA, *who looks at him expectantly*.) And if
I tell you that we have met? . . .

ANGELUS *rises and stands behind* ANGELINA.

ANGELINA. The bandage . . . I ought to see your face . . .

ANGELUS. We have met, more than once . . . but you will meet me for the first time only later.

ANGELINA. I think – I don't understand . . .

ANGELUS. An encounter. Two different people at the same time, in the same space, there, at the same place.

ANGELINA (*shaking her head uncomprehendingly*). . . . What?

ANGELUS. We have already met. In the same space, here, at the same place, several times, but always at a different time.

ANGELINA (*still failing to understand*). Who are you?

ANGELUS. Another good question . . . Just like the others.

ANGELINA. Then why can't I see you?

ANGELUS. Because I'm invisible . . .

ANGELINA *looks at* ANGELUS, *flabbergasted.*

ANGELINA. Invisible?

ANGELUS. That is to say, I've lost myself . . . though I used to be a man like anybody else . . . You'll see it for yourself . . .

ANGELINA. Shall I see it for myself? When?

ANGELUS. I think, my little Angelina, quite soon . . .

ANGELINA. Why has your voice become so husky?

ANGELUS. I don't know . . . Please, go away . . .

ANGELINA. Pardon?

ANGELUS. I mean well, believe me!

ANGELINA. But where shall I go?

ANGELUS. Take a train and leave this place!

ANGELINA. But what do you mean?

ANGELUS (*beginning to lose his patience*). Take the next train and don't look back! That's what I mean!

ANGELINA. But who are you to tell me this?!

ANGELUS. If you promise to leave, I will tell you . . .

ANGELINA. You want me to promise to leave?

ANGELUS. In your own interest . . .

ANGELINA (*thinking*). I can't do that . . .

ANGELUS. Please try to understand this. This is our only way of escape . . .

ANGELINA. Way of escape? Whose?

ANGELUS. Ours, my dear Angelina!

ANGELINA. I don't understand . . .

ANGELUS (*picking up* ANGELINA'*s cases*). You don't need to understand! That's how we can stay free! You can be happy and I don't lose my self! I beg you to leave! The train is coming!

ANGELINA. Who are you?

ANGELUS. Don't be stupid, I can't tell you if you are not leaving!

ANGELINA. But why not?!

ANGELUS. If you get on the train and things don't turn out in the way they have turned out, I will be able to tell you! But if you stay here, and everything stays as it was, I won't be able to speak . . . Please, hurry up, the train is here!

ANGELINA *does not move.* ANGELUS *can't believe his eyes.*

ANGELINA. You haven't told me yet . . .

ANGELUS. Because you haven't got on the train . . . (*He embraces the girl gently.*) Oh, poor . . . poor little Angelina . . . I think I can no longer tell you . . . Won't you change your mind?

ANGELINA. It may have to happen this way . . .

ANGELUS. For a moment it felt pleasant to believe that it didn't . . . (*He looks out.*) The train is still here . . .

ANGELINA *shakes her head.* ANGELUS *picks up the walking stick and his case.*

ANGELUS. I think – my heart has never felt so heavy.

He leaves.

ANGELINA *sits on the seat. She catches sight of* ANGELUS'*s creased up letter on the ground. She flattens it out and starts reading it.*

ANGELINA. I used to believe that if you want to be happy in this world, you had to make your fortune and be a success, climb the social scale, get a title and make a career. Perhaps other people need these things . . . but I don't. For my happiness I would have needed a single person during my life, you, my dear Angelina, only you. Now I know. I also know that it is too late. I have left you, so I have to be brought to punishment, I have to suffer, stand the pain, fall into the dust again and again until my heart takes pity on me and beats its last . . . (ANGELINA'*s voice is joined by* ANGELUS' *from outside.*) My dear, dear Angelina, now I don't want God to do anything else, just give you as much happiness, as he gives me suffering . . .

ANGELINA *stops speaking. Her eyes are searching for the source of the man's voice.*

10th Scene

ANGELUS' *curses are heard from outside.*

ANGELUS' VOICE. Oh, may Archabel throw you into the fire, that
hideous shaggy-haired cock or may at least the fizzling thunderbolt
strike between your jug ears, you damned blockhead!

*ANGELINA quickly folds up the letter and puts it away. She
listens nervously to the voice.*

You, abominable mother's nightmare grabbing your smutty sooty
stove pipe! Oh, get the crucifix and all the sacraments, dig a hole
and throw it all in.

*ANGELUS comes in. He is handsome, good-looking and young.
There is a sword at his side and a feathered soldier's shako on his
head. With his snow-white glove he is rubbing the sleeve of his
jacket. But as soon as he sees ANGELINA, the anger disappears
from his face and is replaced by an engaging smile.*

ANGELUS. Look how that old pot has smudged me . . . Excuse me,
Miss. (*He nods his head and clicks his heels.*) Captain Angelus
reporting for duty . . .

ANGELINA (*holding out her hand, embarrassed*). Well, I don't
know . . . Pleased to meet you, Captain . . .

ANGELUS (*kissing her hand*). Pleased to meet you too. May I take
the liberty of asking your name, Miss?

ANGELINA (*hardly able to speak*). Angelina . . .

ANGELUS (*still holding the girl's hand*). ANGELINA . . . Angelina
and Angelus! What a nice ring the two names have together . . .
(*With elegant sensuality he imprints another kiss on ANGELINA's
hand.*) What lovely little hands . . .

ANGELINA (*on the verge of fainting away*). Oh, they're nothing to
speak of . . .

ANGELUS (*still not letting go of ANGELINA's hand*). Shall we rest
here awhile?

ANGELINA. With pleasure, Captain . . .

They are sitting hand in hand.

ANGELUS. How lovely the full moon is . . .

ANGELINA. I have noticed it, too . . .

ANGELUS. Have you also noticed it? Isn't it fantastic?

ANGELINA. And it was just as shiny when I arrived here . . .

ANGELUS. May I ask how long you have been here, dear Angelina?

ANGELINA. I've just . . .

ANGELUS. And did it immediately strike you how beautiful the full moon was?

ANGELINA. I was just going to read . . .

ANGELUS (*lifting the Keepsake Album*). Saint Habakkuk! A keepsake album.

ANGELINA. Oh, this is just girlish nonsense . . .

ANGELUS *elegantly pulls the glove off his right hand.*

ANGELINA (*bashfully*). I have never seen a captain before.

ANGELUS. And is he to your liking?

ANGELINA (*blushing*). I haven't discussed this with myself yet . . .

ANGELUS (*kissing* ANGELINA's *hand and looking long into her eyes*). You'd better discuss it, because I'm very interested . . .

ANGELINA (*amazed*). Why are you interested?

ANGELUS. Just because I have already talked to myself . . .

ANGELINA. And what did you tell yourself?

ANGELUS. Would you really like to know? (*He kisses* ANGELINA's *hand.*)

ANGELINA (*with her eyelashes lowered*). Yes, very . . . very much . . .

ANGELUS. I told myself that I had never seen such a wonderful girl. Such a beautiful, clever and nice girl as you are . . . (*He steals a kiss from the girl's lips.*) And such sweet lips . . .

ANGELINA (*faltering in a swoon*). How strange . . . I said to myself literally the same thing. (*She returns the kiss.*)

ANGELUS (*while kissing*). Mercibeaucoupmademoiselle . . .

ANGELINA. How did you come to know such things, my dear sweet Captain?

A long kiss.

ANGELUS (*between two kisses*). You haven't kissed before?

ANGELINA. No, never . . . Is it a problem?

ANGELUS. No, no! It isn't a problem at all, my dear sweet girl . . . (*He kisses* ANGELINA *passionately.*)

ANGELUS. I wish the trains would never come . . . (ANGELINA *suddenly extricates herself from the Captain's embrace.*) Have I said the wrong thing?

ANGELINA *whips out the Keepsake Album.*

ANGELINA. Sign it here please. (ANGELUS *laughs.*) You're laughing at me! Laughing at me! Laughing at me!

ANGELUS. Oh, no! (*He kisses the girl.*) Of course I am not laughing at you!

ANGELINA. But you are laughing now!

ANGELUS. I'm not laughing at what you have done, you silly little thing!

ANGELINA (*turned sulky, disbelieving him*). What are you laughing at then?

ANGELUS (*lying*). Well, the moon! Can't you see what a foolish face it has?

ANGELINA. I don't believe you!

ANGELUS. I don't think I could ever lie to you.

ANGELINA. They all say that. But then they tell you a pack of lies!

ANGELUS (*trying to affect seriousness, but still laughing*). And how do you know this?

ANGELINA. Why are you laughing now?

ANGELUS. You haven't answered me.

ANGELINA. Everybody says so.

ANGELUS. And you believe everything you hear? Are you such a seagull?

ANGELINA (*correcting him*). Just gull . . .

ANGELUS. A seagull is a seagull. Just gull, OK, just gull!

ANGELINA (*suspiciously*). Who is the gull?

ANGELUS You are! Where is the Keepsake Album? Shall I fill it with rhymes? May I? (*He takes a pen, laughing.*) What would you like? Happy ones or sad ones?

ANGELINA. One to make you laugh, three to make you cry.

ANGELUS. Anything you care to name, Madam . . . (*He is thinking.*) Just sit here . . . (*He indicates his lap.*)

ANGELINA *hesitates, unsure of herself.*

Oh, are you afraid? Or have you heard something about this too?

ANGELINA *shrugs her shoulders defiantly and sits on* ANGELUS' *knee.*

ANGELUS. Well done, that's it, there's a big girl. (*He puts his hand on the girl's knee and starts writing.*) Let's get the happy one over and done with. Well, what do you say to this?

ANGELINA (*reading*). If you see a monkey in a tree / Close the blue lake of your eyes / Pull its tail / And think of me.

ANGELUS. How's that?

ANGELINA (*enthusiastically*). Wonderful!

ANGELUS. Do you think it's worth a kiss, my sweet Angelina?

    ANGELINA *gives the captain a joyful kiss and looks at his hand
which keeps crawling up her thigh. She puts her hand on the
captain's.*

ANGELINA (*reading out what he is writing*). My sweet Angelina, the
fat, toothless full moon, this old buffoon! He pries into all the
secrets of loving hearts! (*She looks at the moon.*) It really is
toothless and fat . . .

    A train arrives. Its smoke engulfs the scene.

ANGELINA (*looks away from the stage*). I ought to be going (*But she
does not stir.*)

ANGELUS And shall we have a sad one?

    ANGELINA *kisses the captain obediently.* ANGELUS *reads out
what he is writing.*

    And one early evening, when twilight sheds its blood and the sun,
may it be blessed a thousand times, is about to sink into the purple
billows of the sea encircled by its distant horizon – oh, delirious
moment – the poisoned sting of a bewildered lead wasp bursts the
window of my heart into a blood rose, My All, my dearly beloved
one, my Eternal Angelina, you should know that I will be thinking
of you, even in the hour of death. – Captain Angelus . . . Where is
my reward, sweetheart?

    ANGELINA *kisses him.*

ANGELUS. Why are you watering the mice?

ANGELINA. This is very sad.

ANGELUS. We'll write another happy one! (*Writing.*) When the ears
of grass are shooting in the marshy meadows, and the branches of
the trees are putting forth green leaves, you, my Golden Swallow
of Hope, dear Angelina, can always take shelter . . . (CAPTAIN
ANGELUS *kisses the girl passionately.*) . . . under the eaves of my
heart!

    *They both droop on the seat and when the slowly wreathing smoke
has engulfed them,* ANGELINA'*s Album thumps onto the ground,
suggesting finality.*

MÜLLER'S DANCERS

by Ákos Németh

English version by Daniel Mornin
from a translation by Pálma Melis and Lásló Upor

Ákos Németh was born in Székesfehérvár, 50 km south-west of Budapest, in 1964, and graduated from the History and Literature Faculty of
Budapest's ELTE University. In characterising his background, he has
commented: 'I come from the narcissistic/self-worshipping generation
born in the '60s "welfare society". Ours is a spoiled generation'. He
lives currently in Budapest.

Németh wrote his first play, *Lili Hofberg*, when he was 22. Set in
Austria in 1933, the play concerns an imaginary theatre and its leading
star, exploring all the petty intrigues in the company and the necessary
political compromises of the time of its setting. It was first produced in
1990, and was followed by six other plays. The earliest of these were
historical works, such as *The Last Days of the Heidler Theatre* (written 1987), a sequel to *Lili Hofberg*, and *Red Ball* (written 1989), an
original view of the short-lived 1919 Communist revolution in Hungary.
Later he turned his attention to the most private aspects of everyday
life. *Julia and His Lieutenant* (first produced 1993, then adapted for
radio, television and film) is a cruel love-story centred on a stripper
and a discharged army officer, in the context of all the ambiguities of
the early post-Communist era. *Anita* (1994), his latest to date, is again
about the endlessly absorbing difficulties of male-female relationships.

Müller's Dancers opened on 20 November 1992, in Katona József
Theatre, Budapest. Müller, an exceptional talent, has deserted the
company he's founded, and his dancers find themselves with no
leader. Their careers and private lives fall apart without him; but they
must find ways to survive and stand on their own feet. Their chaotic
love affairs and failed attempts to make a living by their art (or by
corrupting their ideals) articulate their sense of loss, and the debt owed
to their leader. As the play's director commented, making explicit the
social and political theme, 'For forty years we had been held tightly by
the hand – and it was comfortable. Now "they" let our hands go and
we all feel confused and are spiteful towards each other'.

124

Characters

Members of Muller's Dance Group
It should be noted that the dancers are very young.

FERI HORVATH, *male*
BARON, *male*
RABBIT, *male*
ERIKA, *female*
RITA, *female*
JUTKA, *female*
ANDI, *female*

Other Characters

MANAGER
EDIT KASS, *female, dance critic, forty years old*
STRANGER, *in clerical dress*
JEWELLER
GAMBLER
PARTNERS

Suburb

The stage is dark. HORVATH *strikes a match. He watches the match burn.*

BARON. Have you any cigarettes left?

HORVATH. Brother, has everything come to a snivelling end!

He turns the lighted match round in his fingers keeping it alight.

Scrape together what you can get – and run!

HORVATH *uses the matchstick to draw on the back of his hand.* BARON *gazes at him.*

I promised the moon and stars to myself. If the sky were a clean sheet of paper I'd write across it swearing deathless loyalty to anyone at all. Anyone at all.

HORVATH *turns his gaze to* BARON.

Give's that stone. Glass rattling, the night jingling!

BARON (*calmly*). Will you keep quiet.

HORVATH. Isn't your back cold against that wall? I'll lie down. If you saw an unwashed tramp standing right here, in your shirt, in your shoes, in your coat . . . wearing that face you're wearing so badly . . . you'd be amazed to be lookin' at yourself.

In a Drinking Den

HORVATH. If you could hear how my heart's beating! Like a cavalry brigade . . . Only pure hearts beat like this.

He listens. He removes his hand from his chest and gazes at it for quite a while.

BARON. We should clear out of this town before we all go mad. What story are you giving Rita?

HORVATH. I'm not glued to her! Anyway, she might clear off, too. Once, you and me were answerable only to that lousy cheat. Do you still believe in him?

BARON. Look, I'll get you some coffee. God, this is a filthy hole. I'm really afraid that in a few weeks we'll be resident here. Sometimes you just can't imagine yourself anywhere else but the place you just happened to have fallen into.

HORVATH. Can you hear it? People running in the street. Who are they? Why the hell are they running? Have they somewhere to go! I feel as if I live my life in a goldfish bowl. Oh, I no longer understand how everything has changed in this country!

Thinking.

Rita too . . .

BARON. Some great villainy should be done. Just to be seen to be done. Ha! How the bastards would shit their pants!

HORVATH. Maybe we should turn Catholic. At least they've got a destination to look forward to. Do you know the story?

BARON. The gospel?

In a Flat

HORVATH *leans on the sill of an open window throwing pebbles down a tin roof.*

HORVATH. Look, how the pebbles roll on the tin. I wish my memories would roll away like that. Adieu! Goodbye! That's what I'd say. Goodbye! Goodbye!

RITA *enters.*

RITA. Who are you saying goodbye to?

HORVATH. Has Baron gone?

RITA. You're always watching the street.

HORVATH. Is there any grub?

RITA. Where have you been? (*More to herself.*) You were looking for him, weren't you?

HORVATH. Looking for whom?

RITA. Who could we be talking about, eh?

HORVATH. How often did Erika stand waiting for him at the railway station? While he dropped Andi a note saying when he'd be dropping by.

RITA. He lied to us all.

HORVATH. If he lied, I lied, too.

RITA. Not so loud, Jutka is asleep.

HORVATH. One finally finds one's way back to one's own abode and what does one find?

RITA. This is not your home.

HORVATH. What is it then?

RITA. Have you forgotten where we're living?

HORVATH. The seasons have gone mad. One moment it rains, the next the sun shines . . . if I didn't know what month it was I wouldn't believe it.

RITA. What are you laughing at?

HORVATH. If Baron were here he'd ask: well, what month is it? That couldn't happen to you, of course: you keep track of the days, the weeks, the months and even the money. Every second and every penny, don't you, lovely angel of my heart?

RITA. You can laugh.

HORVATH. Thanks. How beautiful you are today! Like an icon. If I were a painter . . . (*Sneering wickedly.*) I would paint you as a sleepy Madonna with a long, sunless-pale, neck. Your hands would be elongated and your gaze fixed on a charming little void on the other side of the canvas. You could throw away your mascara. Gothic Virgin Mary with green eyes from the age of decline. Do you like Greco?

RITA. Sadly, it's you I like.

HORVATH (*doesn't pay attention*). Can you hear that? What is that music?

RITA. I dreamt about us last night.

HORVATH. What's that? What is that! I can hardly hear it. They torture you.

RITA (*suffering*). You hit me. What a dream!

HORVATH. What a neighbourhood!

RITA. I should go and meet the postman. He's scared of you and avoids our cosy little nest like the plague.

HORVATH. He's got nothing for us.

RITA. Let's get away from here. Let's get out. I realised days ago that Müller had left us for good and wouldn't be sending for us.

HORVATH. How do you know?

RITA. I feel it!

HORVATH. That's not enough! He has just got to pull us out of this hole.

RITA. The two chaps will leave soon.

HORVATH. Do you feel that?

RITA. Well, isn't it obvious?

HORVATH. It's obvious they have nowhere to go.

RITA. We should go with them. Please.

HORVATH. What production could we do? What would we live on?

RITA. The rent on this flat runs out in a week and Müller won't be
sending a rent cheque. So far he hasn't sent us *one* penny!
(*Thinking.*) He must be in West-Berlin by now . . .

HORVATH. There is no West-Berlin any more.

RITA. Our problem is . . .

HORVATH. What is our problem?

RITA *does not pay attention.* EDIT *enters.*

EDIT. Hello.

HORVATH. Hello. Is that you, Edit? Welcome to the condemned cell.

RITA. Hello.

EDIT. How beautiful you are, girl.

RITA. You won't write any more reviews about us, Edit. Our group's
split.

EDIT. Smashed? (*Thinking.*) Sorry, can't help. Brave new world and
all that. I'm powerless.

HORVATH. Never mind, Edit, it's none of your business. You're a
critic and you'll thrive in the worst of all situations. You'll
probably review this little tragedy, too.

EDIT. I'm hurt that you feel a need to make fun of me. I'm very sorry
for you all.

HORVATH. Thanks, but it doesn't help. Now, if you could see your
way to paying our debts – the seriously urgent ones at least.

EDIT. Perhaps you should all go and live in the country?

HORVATH. Why? It's good to live like this, so close together that we
can't possibly feel lonely or depressed. Rotting away like so many
fancy animals a bankrupt zoo can't afford to feed. I speak like a
poet, don't you think? I mean, I talk nonsense, don't I? Well, how
should a dancer speak, eh? What do you think? I swear I'd write
my memoirs if anyone were interested.

EDIT. You are so naive that I almost like it. Surely, there are levels of
innocence.

HORVATH. You smoke too much and it sounds like it. How old are
you anyway? You must be near forty, You still look good in
twilight. But your voice!

EDIT. You're very rude indeed.

HORVATH. Indeed I am. Did you know that your smile makes me nervous? Kindness doesn't suit you at all.

EDIT. You are angry with me.

HORVATH. Oh, God forbid!

EDIT. Of course you are. And you have reason enough, I suppose.

HORVATH. Don't smile like that – if you don't want me to stick a knife in your breast.

RITA. Please, stop it. I have a terrible headache.

HORVATH. Oh, suffer.

HORVATH *exits.*

RITA. I'll make coffee.

RITA *exits.* ERIKA *enters. They later engage in sex-play.*

ERIKA. Is that you?

EDIT. Hello, Erika.

ERIKA. Is it me you wanted to see?

EDIT. The atmosphere in here is deeper than depressing.

ERIKA. You don't feel uneasy, do you? Just relax.

EDIT. They talk about me.

ERIKA (*scornfully*). That's right.

EDIT. They talk your head off. How dare they open their mouths. Vultures!

ERIKA. You're insane.

EDIT. When they open their mouths you really do see right down to their bowels. They want to consume everything – don't they. Oh, love . . . They're disgusting.

ERIKA. Love? I won't be having a baby by you, that's for certain.

EDIT (*sadly*). You know too well how important you are to me.

ERIKA. Am I beautiful?

EDIT. I just ask myself . . . Of course I come here. What else can I do?

ERIKA. Are you stuttering?

EDIT. Don't laugh at me.

ERIKA. I'm fed up with you.

EDIT. Please!

ERIKA. I've had enough.

EDIT. How can you be so . . .

ERIKA. Want to make love to me?

EDIT. . . . vulgar?

ERIKA. Why vulgar? It's why you're in love with me, isn't it!

EDIT. Could you please stop laughing.

ERIKA. You go into a nervous pant at the thought of it. Don't you? You're whimpering like a beaten dog. D'you want me to caress you? Shall I wash before we get down to it?

EDIT *brushes her tears away.*

(*Smiling.*) Do you love me?

EDIT. You little villain. You forget what you owe me.

ERIKA *exits to the bathroom, laughing. She slams the door.*

She closed it.

We hear the shower.

Oh my God, and I'm peeping through the keyhole. Open it, please, open it . . . Oh my God, does she hear my voice at all? I've lost my voice . . . my throat is dry, as if . . . it's hot in here! Open it, I beg you. I'm going to explain everything.

EDIT, *sobbing, fixes her make-up and exits. JUTKA, sleepy, enters. ERIKA enters from the bathroom.*

ERIKA. Has she gone?

JUTKA. I heard her scrabbling at the door like a cat.

ERIKA. I don't give a shit what anybody thinks.

ERIKA *makes up her face at a large mirror.*

Did you get enough sleep?

JUTKA. When I've been fast asleep I often get frightened when I wake. How vulnerable we are when we're asleep. You've got no thoughts at all . . . perhaps you can't return. You lose your sensibility . . .

ERIKA. You know I'm leaving this place. You may not have been interested enough to ask, but I'm sure you know. Living here is like being left behind in life. Something just isn't happening to you. I'm not seventeen any more . . . If I were your aunt I wouldn't let you sleep so much. Why don't you go back to her? You're still so young. She brought you up, so she'll give you money like she used to if you just pretend nothing has happened.

JUTKA (*as if she were still dreaming*). When I was a child I often thought she was some horrible bird bending over me at night . . .

ERIKA. Well, how do I look?

JUTKA (*dreamily*). Perhaps I should kill her.

ERIKA. You're still a child.

JUTKA (*lies back on the sofa and closes her eyes*). I'm packing my bags, too.

ERIKA. I do look great, don't I. My sister had a baby two years ago and now look at her breasts. Thank God my body is still so . . . neat. Goodness, what would I do without it. Oh, dear. You only feel real when you look in a mirror.

JUTKA. You're a believer, aren't you?

ERIKA. I didn't know you were interested in that stuff.

JUTKA. Let me sleep.

> ERIKA *shrugs and exits*. BARON *enters. He opens the drawers, searches coats. He sits beside* JUTKA *and kisses her.*

(*Opens her eyes.*) Müller . . .

BARON. You were sleeping?

JUTKA. I was thinking.

> *They kiss.*

I'll be famous in ten years' time. Living here is little better than living in a box. We've only got enough space for thought.

BARON. Do you want to get out, too?

JUTKA. I don't know. I don't know anything. My feelings are so, I don't know, like a cat chasing after pigeons. Who on earth knows what is going to happen tomorrow? Maybe we'll all get out . . .

> *There's a silence.*

BARON. I think of Müller all the time, just him. What is he doing? What is he thinking? I wonder . . .

> RITA *and* HORVATH *enter from the kitchen. They have been arguing.*

RITA. I went to make coffee and I forgot to light the gas.

BARON. You look tired.

RITA. I didn't sleep at all last night. I was . . . oh, forget it. Has Edit Kass left?

BARON. Was she here?

HORVATH. When isn't she?

JUTKA. Can you hear the bells? There must be a church in the neighbourhood.

HORVATH. My watch is slow.

BARON. Ringing a bell is a sort of moral thing. (*Thinking.*) When we were children we used to climb up the tower. Do you remember, Jutka? You felt drunk. That pealing! As if the air itself was drunk!

Everything trembling. Bell! Vocal chord in God's throat. You feel as if you're evaporating into pure air!

RITA. There's some coffee left. Do you want some?

JUTKA. What the fuck will happen to us?

HORVATH. I can't walk on water and I can't dole out bread! The man who could has gone! I'm not sure I can do anything.

JUTKA. That's right.

HORVATH. I've made a decision. A final one. We flog everything that's left, truck, costumes, everything. Then we all start a new life on our own. You can even get some money. Just a little bit; then it's adieu.

ERIKA (*leaning to the door beside* ANDI). That's not what you said yesterday.

HORVATH. We all lie, don't we. No more talk of yesterday. Fuck them all. I gave my soul and my heart to this group, it was beating under your nose, but I've had enough. We had our last performance three weeks ago, but nobody cared a shit. Not even you. I think that's it really.

A storm has begun to blow.

ANDI. And now? What comes now?

HORVATH. Everybody loved him. Nobody loved me. Jutka, too. Who could believe that such a girl was able to love and disdain so much? Who would have imagined we'd all love that con man so much? He failed in his attempt to save the world with us. It crushes the heart to become so disillusioned. Sparrows put to flight. We all . . . search for someone . . . who can take a hold of us . . .

ANDI. I don't want to leave. Everything will settle down. I feel it, I feel it. It's all I can think of.

HORVATH. Yes, if only I could see him now. He humiliated us. If only I could see him, just for a minute . . .

HORVATH *massages his temple.*

ANDI (*to herself*). I don't want to have an ulcer.

HORVATH. The family . . . the family is a dark thing, a night thing. Corpses disintegrate in darkness too. Everybody trembles with hatred. Where do you get the strength to tremble like that? Just a little money . . . a little money . . . that's what you'll get. And nothing will settle down.

BARON. What a windstorm has blown up! We have a guest, our dear father, the wind! He wanders round the house like a watchdog! Ding-dong, do you hear brother? Why weren't our bodies made with doors and windows so that the wind can sweep through!

HORVATH. What else do you want of me?

RITA. Baron!

BARON. This is the time wandering souls start off: it is time we set off on our tour!

ERIKA. You, Horvath – you, too – and all of you, should be ashamed!

ANDI. I can't hear my own voice! What a crack of thunder!

RITA. Baron, the window!

ANDI. Where's Rabbit?

HORVATH. What choices have we been given?

ERIKA. I shall make a career – and you'll all be fucked!

JUTKA (*to* HORVATH). Why, who did you think you were?

ANDI. If he stayed out he's got wet through.

JUTKA. Do you know what you are?

HORVATH. Watch your mouth, you toad.

RITA. Let me go; the wind takes everything!

BARON (*guffaws*). Look there! Here he comes!

JUTKA. An empty-headed, high-handed, nobody. Got it?

RITA. Let me go, you idiot.

ERIKA. Money? What money are you talking about. You fool! Or do you expect us to do a runner from our creditors?

BARON. Do you want to close the window, eh?

BARON *laughs.* RABBIT *tumbles in, soaking wet.*

RABBIT. Gentlemen! The storm has arrived!

Andi and Horvath together

ANDI. Rita and you?

HORVATH. We'll get married. Yes. I've decided to be happy no matter what it takes. My only aspiration is to go to work every morning. Where? It doesn't matter. (*Enthusiastically.*) I'll be an average citizen. Grey suit and three children. Solvent. No debts. I'll watch soap operas. Phew, how wretched it'll be. Thank God! I'll be happy!

ANDI. What are you laughing at?

HORVATH. Well, don't you think it's nonsense?

ANDI. Oh, you . . . Do you love Rita?

HORVATH. I do indeed. She's the woman of my life. Believe me. What's the matter?

ANDI. Nothing. Am I pale?

HORVATH. A little bit.

ANDI (*in the mirror*). Yes, I think some mountain air would help.

She puts some blusher on her face.

HORVATH (*does not pay attention*). Oh fucking life, how happy I shall be!

ANDI. Is it better now?

HORVATH. They say I'm too full of myself! Proud. Yes! I am repulsively proud! Damn it, after all, I'm better than everybody else. Who'd say different?

ANDI. Listen.

HORVATH. You maybe, eh?

ANDI. Do you like my hair cut?

HORVATH. And who would be . . . well, who would be worthy to be by my side!

ANDI. You never listen to me.

HORVATH. Yet, can it be possible that such a man couldn't care a *shit* for others? No matter how pathetic their situation may be?

ANDI (*gazing at the window*). Are they all gone?

HORVATH. Is it possible, do you think?

ANDI (*turns back*). I don't understand you.

HORVATH. Fucking life! I was asking you a question!

ANDI (*innocently*). Don't you like me then?

HORVATH. By the time Maupassant was my age the syphilis he had inherited erupted. (*Mutters.*) He thought he would go blind. He was crucified by the most terrible fits. He cut his throat, but was saved and put into a mad house. He scrambled round on his hands and knees eating his own shit. The last words he wrote were: M. Maupassant became an animal, see.

ANDI *kisses him.*

(*Mutters confusedly.*) We can't do anything without punishment.

ANDI. And Rita?

HORVATH (*on being surprised*). But I am in love with her! Where are they all?

Kissing each other.

Same Place, Another Tête-à-Tête

BARON *and* RABBIT.

BARON. I smell a woman!

RABBIT. Do you know where Erika has been working for the last couple of weeks?

BARON. While we're stuck here wallowing in shit.

RABBIT. Do you know that place on Herceg Street? Well there.

BARON. That is something. I should never have thought her capable of it!

RABBIT. Well, there you are.

BARON. Boy, I like that. I'm hungry.

RABBIT. You can't eat in peace in this flat. You're always bumping into someone in this flat.

BARON. And to eat is to steal. Since we've been going Dutch I've been ready to die of hunger.

RABBIT. But what a capacious flat.

BARON. Sadly my last few pennies went a long time ago.

RABBIT. They were *my* pennies, but let's not argue about it.

BARON. Shut up you miserable tongue-tied stut . . . stut . . . stutterer.

RABBIT. You can't hear it any more.

BARON. The human body has been created quite marvellously! Whenever the stomach feels hunger the whole body is hungry.

RABBIT. Here's some bread.

BARON. I wonder why it's like that?

RABBIT. And some biscuits . . .

BARON (*in disgust*). Well, he does stuff his face with great ease. He's tucking in mightily. You idiot! You eat biscuits with ketchup?

RABBIT. Ach, you talk like a cop.

He clutches his belly.

Damn it!

BARON. Now the man's sick. It's not possible to appear in public with you. I make a fool of myself walking down the street with you! Hey, what have we here? Has there been a break-in? Who's thrown these books across the floor?

RABBIT. I just dip in and out. I can't choose.

BARON. Interesting habit. Look, don't make a further mess. Especially not with Horvath's books, or Rita will have your head off.

BARON *lies on the bed with his shoes on, staring at the ceiling*.

RABBIT. Baron, did you know that the joke telling record was made in America? Do you? Forty fucking hours!

BARON. It wasn't me.

RABBIT. What a lot of books they have! I do believe we should take some of these down to the second-hand bookshop. Rita will be gratified to find more space on her shelves for the others.

BARON (*doesn't pay attention*). That's for certain.

RABBIT. These two here are definitely not needed. Nor this blue one.

BARON. What is it about?

RABBIT. Some complete edition. Nothing special. And let's take this one, too. Books with pictures are always popular in second-hand bookshops. Perhaps we should go. (*Not knowing what to do*.) We need a shopping bag.

Andi and Rita Together

ANDI. You use *Lil-lets*? Perhaps I should try these.

RITA (*packing*). You smoke too much.

ANDI. Who cares. It might be worthwhile to give up if I could walk the streets in a gas mask.

RITA. Aren't you packing?

ANDI. I am not.

RITA. You rely on serendipity too much. We're leaving this place.

ANDI. You and Feri?

RITA. Yes, even Horvath. Though the two boys might rent it from now on. It's all the same to me.

ANDI. You and Feri . . .

RITA. I can't understand you.

ANDI. Be careful with that boy.

RITA. It's not really your business.

ANDI. Well, just be careful with him.

Horvath and Rita Together

HORVATH. Are you packing already?

RITA. Only what's absolutely not needed. You know how much I hate to be in a hurry.

HORVATH. You're the very spirit of order.

RITA. Go ahead, mock.

HORVATH. I'm off to the bathroom to get the toothbrushes in line!

RITA. It's high time you did just that!

HORVATH. And since you're so forgetful and still haven't put labels on my shoes to let me know which is my left and which my right I can only owe it to good fortune that I correctly found my legs this morning! How quickly hurt she is. It looks as if I'm going to get it in the neck.

RITA (*laughing*). Get away from me, you idiot!

HORVATH. And tell me, Grandma, why do you have such beautiful breasts?

RITA. They're about what they should be.

HORVATH. And tell me, grandma, I hope your teeth aren't sharp?

He kisses her.

RITA. But I am the wolf hidden in Grandma's skin!

She frightens him.

Unfortunately the wolf has to go and do the dishes.

HORVATH. I looked into your gorgeous eyes, young lady. You mesmerised me!

RITA (*sighs*). I wish I'd never looked into yours.

Andi and Erika Together

ANDI. I don't really understand what it is you do.

ERIKA. Why? We're in the same position. You won't be a ballet dancer either, not any more. Dig yourself out of the shit any way you can; fuck everyone else.

ANDI. And the money you earn?

ERIKA. It goes. It's not much. It's a simple topless bar. Why are you so surprised? They can't see any more of my body than they see at the swimming-pool.

ANDI. Did they appreciate that you can dance?

ERIKA *laughs.*

Am I naive?

On the Street

GAMBLER (*gabbles*). Have I put it here or there? Just tell me now! Three matchboxes, there's no trickery about it; here's the marble, there's the marble, where's the marble? No. It's not here, but there! Just watch my hands, no wizardry.

RABBIT. Damn it, that boy has fast hands!

GAMBLER. Please, place a bet. Or you! Sir, you can't lose on this.

PARTNER 1 (*from the crowd*). You're lying. You're a cheat.

GAMBLER. I'd sooner die! There's no magic. No swindle. Here's the marble, there's the marble, where's the marble. Again. Here it is! Have you seen it? Haven't you seen it? It's here. Isn't it? Sir, have you never played with me?

PARTNER 2. The hangman should play with you. How much do you pay?

GAMBLER. Three for one. Sir, and you? Three to one is the easiest way to get money – all you need is sharp eyes. Place a bet! Place a bet! Why are you hesitating? Your luck will change! Three for one when you win. If your eyes are good then I lose. Here's the marble. Upsadaisy! Here it is! Come on, ladies and gentlemen, make your fortune!

RABBIT. I won't. I don't have any money.

GAMBLER. Then it's high time you tripled it. Upsadaisy! Here it is!

BARON. His hands are agile, that's for sure.

RABBIT. And he doesn't get tired, eh?

PARTNER 2. Is it in that one? No, it isn't.

GAMBLER. Well, you decide.

PARTNER 2. I say it's that one.

GAMBLER. Sir, you win. Congratulations. Three thousand. Take it.

PARTNER 2. You need sharp eyes for it!

GAMBLER. Upsadaisy! Where's the marble? Here's the marble. Here, here; not here! Where is it rolling? Here it's rolling. Did you catch sight of it at all? Place a bet sir. Upsadaisy, which one is it?

He turns away. PARTNER 1 *steps out of the crowd and lifts up one of the match-boxes and the marble is beneath. He replaces the match box and steps back into the crowd.*

You don't dare to gamble, sir? Your luck will change.

PASSER-BY. Well . . . it's in that one.

GAMBLER. You lost. Upsadaisy? The marble is rolling, rolling again – here it's rolling, there it's rolling. Place a bet, you will be luckier next time! Upsadaisy! Gents, place a bet!

BARON (*grinning*). Well, I'll make a bet.

GAMBLER. Which one is it?

BARON. I'll buy all your boxes, brother – all the three.

GAMBLER. That's not possible, sir.

The PARTNERS *step forward.*

BARON. I'm afraid it is.

He knocks over the table.

(*To* RABBIT.) Take the money!

BARON *and* RABBIT *fight with the* GAMBLER *and his* PARTNERS. BARON *and* RABBIT *run off.*

Edit and Erika Together

EDIT. I'm here to say goodbye.

ERIKA. That's nice. And you brought flowers.

EDIT. I can't stand things with you any more.

ERIKA. Flower to the flower, isn't it?

EDIT. I got crazy, I got mad. I don't know what will happen now.

ERIKA. You're a nice girl, Edit.

EDIT. It's over. I feel it.

ERIKA. Surely you're not going to cry, here?

EDIT. It's over, it's over. I don't love you any more.

ERIKA (*whispers*). Anyway, you won't leave.

EDIT can hardly breathe, sits speechless.

Baron and Rabbit Together

BARON. Bloody gipsy, peasant! Fuck your swindler mother. I haven't run so much in ages. Now, pal, count the takings. How much?

RABBIT. Ten grand.

BARON. My share?

RABBIT. All of it.

BARON. Damn! Dirty pigs. Is that what they call a day's wage?

RABBIT. And now they don't even have this.

BARON. They'll be getting something soon! You feel sorry for them, eh? Tribe of thieves!

RABBIT (*guffaws*). What an idiot you are! What about us then?

BARON. Those guys are mere gypsies. Don't you understand? They should have dispersed long ago.

RABBIT. If you want to get rich by doing this you won't get far. They'll put your bowels in your hands before you've had enough time to get to gaol.

BARON. What do you mean, idiot? Nothing is dangerous. The word has lost its meaning. Don't tell me you can't protect yourself! And the nick? None of us has a flat and we won't be getting one. What the fuck are you waiting for?

BARON *steals the money from* RABBIT's *pocket.*

RABBIT (*guffaws*). You're overdoing it.

BARON. I'm a citizen of the Republic of Hungary, my friend. Policemen salute me.

RABBIT. Suburban baron . . .

BARON. Let's get a drink somewhere.

RABBIT. Look, all those stars! Everybody has a star . . .

BARON. Ours is falling.

RABBIT. That one there is mine. Hardly twinkling at all. Little brat . . .

BARON. I took your money. It's best to keep it together.

RABBIT. You know who will succeed in life? Andi will. She has no scruples . . . I went with her once.

BARON. You screwed her? Ah, you're just shouting your mouth off.

RABBIT. Not so long ago. As I said, she has no scruples.

BARON. I went with her, too. That's the way she is when she drinks. Women are all the same.

RABBIT (*doesn't pay attention*). We should be forty years old. Or look at those from 1956! At least they could go to America.

BARON. But men, too, are all alike.

RABBIT. I won't be forty years old. No way. My mother says I'll earn piles! Great barrels of money! I want to be rich. (*Whispering to a bank note as if it were his lover.*) What is your worth, you dirty one?

He crumbles up the note and throws it away.

BARON. Don't shout.

He picks up the note and flattens it out before putting it in RABBIT's *pocket. He's in a bad mood.*

Let's go. Why, they might have found a place where we can swing our hips. Let's go and practice . . .

RABBIT *does the splits on the pavement. He looks up.*

RABBIT. I no longer want to dance, don't you understand?

Empty Square, Neon Light Far Away.

The STRANGER *is dressed in a priestly manner.*

STRANGER. Excuse me, do you work in the bar?

ERIKA. That's none of your business.

STRANGER. My daughter, you dance in the night club showing your breasts . . . do you not feel sorrow in your heart?

ERIKA. Leave me alone; stay out of my sight.

STRANGER. His heart is sad, waiting for the stray lamb. Be the white lamb of God, my daughter.

He opens his bag.

His Grace be on us.

ERIKA. Please don't, I beg you. Please . . .

STRANGER (*with a razor blade*). It must happen, my daughter, it must happen. You have to understand that this is the way it has to be.

Flat: Baron, Horvath and Andi

HORVATH *and* ANDI *in bed.* BARON *enters.*

BARON. Gentlemen.

HORVATH. He's drunk.

BARON. Yes indeed, it's only natural. I'm such a mess because I've been working far too hard trying to find out what the others think. Though looking at you I'd say the easiest thing to think about is women. They love us, they love everybody, am I right sweetheart? One always imagines having an affair with a queen, a sad Scandinavian queen, who just happens to prefer stable-boys.

HORVATH. Aren't you a little bit . . . ?

BARON. Of course you sort of loose your self-confidence when talking about queens . . . And see what happens behind the back of kings? It quite puts me to the blush.

HORVATH. Get dressed you frog while I try to get rid of this animal.

BARON. Shall we drink a parting-cup, comrades? Let's drink to the ladies, to the queen!

ANDI (*to* HORVATH). You can boss your trollops about, but not me.

HORVATH. This is a spiteful thing to do, Baron. Spiteful. Syphilitic bastards shouldn't run after girls, my little Baron. Your soul has venereal disease, you shitface. The only thing you're good at is fucking everything up.

ANDI (*dressing hastily*). Not so loud. God, what will happen? Everybody will come in.

HORVATH. How much I detest you, you rat. You shit! How many times have you spoiled our work and then pulled faces when Müller walked in!

BARON (*with hatred*). What are you talking about?

HORVATH. Listen you scum: if you don't get out of here for good in two seconds I'll smash your face in.

BARON. You hate me, don't you? (*Laughs.*) Rita waits up every night for you just in there, with only a wall between you, thinking you spend the whole day running after our business. (*Obscene.*) Shall I go into her so that her wait shall not be in vain?

They fight.

ANDI. Jesus Christ, they'll kill each other!

BARON. I'll certainly kill you, you asshole.

RITA *enters.*

RITA. What's this madness?

ANDI. I just . . .

RITA *screams.*

RITA. What the hell is going on here?

HORVATH. Oh, nothing . . . Baron made a try for Andika and I happened to walk in at the wrong time. Jutka wasn't enough for this lecher.

BARON (*laugh*). Is that right Andika? Did you enjoy it, my little fairy? Your Ferike is plastered with lipstick, or haven't you noticed?

HORVATH. That's enough! Yes, I cheated you, you idiot. Did you really expect anything else? But you know it perfectly well. You've known it for weeks, haven't you? You rotten slut, why didn't you say something; why have you let me suffer so much? You knew exactly where I was. You've always known how to torture me! You can't blame anyone but yourself. Why did you stay with me? You miserable little idiot.

ANDI (*trembles*). Can't you let her alone, can't you . . . How pale she's gone.

HORVATH. Oh, the whole wretched business! And you blame me! Why don't you look in a mirror just once, you'd see the prettiest heap of shit in the world. How many times have I told myself that I should pull up sticks just like Müller! How many times have I felt sick of you . . . (*To* RITA.) And especially of you, you blonde Venus! What are you doing in this world, eh? Just look at yourself, a haggard suburban chicken! Six more years and you'll be old, thirty years old; having done nothing with your life.

BARON. You shout yourself hoarse, Horvath!

HORVATH (*delightfully*). You don't even have a child. This little brat can't have a child, did you know that? (*Laughs.*) She can't! Well just think about that!

HORVATH *exits*.

BARON (*to* RITA). Now, look, you don't want to faint away, hey!

At the Funeral. An Optional Scene.

RABBIT. Damn it, I can't stand this bloody rain.

HORVATH *stands holding* ANDI*'s hand*.

HORVATH (*irritated*). What the fuck, the priest is late.

BARON (*softly*). Look, stop crying . . .

ANDI *stops crying, but continues to snivel*.

RABBIT. Bloody November, don't we all hate it? I don't even have a winter coat . . . I must be ill.

HORVATH. Why didn't someone tell me not to curse in the cemetery?

RABBIT. Baron, did you know Erika was a Calvinist? I've never been to a Calvinist funeral before.

RITA. Lutheran. Though it's all the same.

RABBIT. Is it? What is the difference?

BARON (*softly*). Shut up, shitface. You're in a cemetery.

HORVATH. The difference is that Erika was a Swab and they aren't Calvinists. She wanted to emigrate to West-Germany, but there is no West-Germany any more.

RABBIT. Did she really want to get out? Did you know she was German, Baron?

ANDI. Maybe she could've even got herself a job.

RITA (*softly*). The priest's here. If any of you don't behave like decent human beings I'll spit in your face.

HORVATH. Did anyone tell Edit?

BARON (*mutters*). Who should've told her?

ANDI. They broke it off, didn't you know that?

RITA. Here, take this handkerchief.

ANDI. Thanks.

Everybody is looking at ANDI *and* RITA *for a moment.*

RABBIT. Edit? What will come out of that?

RITA. The pastor's giving us a sign.

ANDI *is sobbing.*

RABBIT *looks at the sky and turns up the collar of his jeans jacket.*

RABBIT. This bloody rain.

They start off.

Flat: Rita and Andi

RITA. At least it will be easier to finish moving.

ANDI (*standing*). Actually . . . I think I should beg your pardon. Perhaps, if I told you how it happened . . .

RITA. You really think I want to know?

ANDI. He wanted it. He loves me, you have to realise that. I really can't break it to you any more gently. We were just talking, several times . . . at the beginning there was nothing . . . no . . . just . . . (*Indulges in day-dreams.*) He'd be late any time we had a date, that's awful of him, but . . . He loves me. He told me, only me.

RITA (*sadly*). And you believe him?

ANDI. I know how to keep him.

RITA. You'll see.

ANDI. I needed someone.

RITA. Everybody does.

ANDI. For such a long time . . . I haven't really lived.

RITA. Come on, why are you so embarrassed?

ANDI (*bursts out crying*). Oh, my God, I want children, family . . . Why are you so . . . ? Stop playing this game with me, please.

RITA. You want me to be nice to you?

ANDI (*hardly breathing. Looking into the corner*). I know it sounds stupid, but I wish everybody loved me. I'm so tired. Somehow, everything's gone wrong.

They remain silent. RITA *is standing with her head down.*

Shall I help you with your luggage?

RITA (*shakes her head*). Well, goodbye. You won't see me again.

ANDI *strokes her undecidedly.*

At the Jewellers. Optional Scene.

JEWELLER. Have you anything in particular in mind, sir?

BARON. I've been particularly thinking about making love, but show me an attractive gold watch.

JEWELLER. Here we are, sir. Or that one. Or I can recommend this one, here.

BARON. Can I pay in German Marks?

JEWELLER. Of course, please do.

BARON. A thousand, here you are. I hope you have change.

JEWELLER. But man, this is a scrap of squared paper, with 'hundred marks' written on it.

BARON. I beg your pardon.

BARON *writes on the piece of paper.*

Another zero, it's perfect now.

JEWELLER. Now go to hell, my sweet boy.

BARON. Can't you change it? You are obviously instructed by your superego, the agent of the State . . .

JEWELLER. Get out of here before I call the police.

BARON (*grins, rests his elbows on the glass counter, plays with the watch*). Or do you know what? Don't you want to simply give it to me as a gift? (*His face is an inch from the jeweller's face.*) It would be nice of you. Who knows, otherwise I might get angry . . .

JEWELLER *is afraid.* BARON *has a good laugh. He drops the watch on the counter.*

In the Flat

ANDI *and* HORVATH *are practising dance movements, persistently, for a long time. The room is enveloped slowly in semi-darkness, they stop dancing, in a sweat. The ballet music goes on.*

HORVATH (*opposite the mirror,* ANDI *is in his arms*). I want you to be a queen. I don't want an everyday person. Crowned pair . . .

They face their reflection in the mirror seriously, shadows cast on the room.

The Flat, Sunny

HORVATH *croons a Bob Dylan song, sleepily.* ANDI *is in the kitchen.*

ANDI (*off*). What's that?

HORVATH. What?

ANDI (*off*). What you're singing?

HORVATH. Bob Dylan, I think.

ANDI (*off*). I didn't know you liked him . . .

ANDI *enters from the kitchen.*

HORVATH (*hardly pays attention*). I'd just started nursery about the time he wrote this. How could I like him?

ANDI. Do you think he's still alive? Do you know what was in the crossword puzzle this week? Whether I could list all the Beatles . . .

HORVATH (*bored. Once more he touches a chord on the guitar then he lays on his back. he is watching* ANDI). I don't know why women are more attractive when they do the housework.

He wants to get to his feet.

ANDI (*laughing*). Now, leave me alone. I want to finish this.

HORVATH *stands.* ANDI *brings the food from the kitchen and hands* HORVATH *his plate. He eats. He spits out the food.*

HORVATH. Phew, what's this?

ANDI *stiffens.*

When are you going to learn to cook? I'm twenty-five years old, but I still haven't met a girl who could cook an ordinary meal . . . (*Wickedly.*) Except Rita, of course . . . You should sign-up for a cookery course from her.

He goes to the windows and stares out. Angry. Someone rings the doorbell, they look at each other.

ANDI. Is that you, Rabbit? Come in . . .

RABBIT *enters.*

RABBIT. Why are you looking at me like that? What's up? Who did you expect, George Bush? He sends his apologies, but he won't be coming today; he's playing chess in the square with some other people.

RABBIT *sits, feeling at home.*

And then he's off to a football match. So I came in his stead.

ANDI. Sorry, I'm like Pavlov's dog . . . If somebody rings the doorbell . . .

RABBIT. Are you expecting someone?

ANDI. No; I really don't know. You know . . . I asked an agent to come along and have a look at us, but he won't be here before midnight if he comes at all.

RABBIT (*he scans her from head to foot*). Are you pregnant?

ANDI. No, of course not. That's all I need. (*Slightly blushingly.*) No, believe me. There's no place here for a child right now . . .

RABBIT. But, really . . .

ANDI. I would know, wouldn't I. It looks to me as if I've put on a bit of weight, Rabbit. It's impertinent of you to notice.

RABBIT. So you won't be having a little 'un.

HORVATH. Shut your mouth for God's sake! Can't you jabber about something else? He just turns up and talks drivel. How could she be pregnant when she's on the pill? Anyway, what would I do with a brat?

RABBIT. You make it sound as if it were a crime. At our age our fathers would have already . . .

HORVATH (*very irritably articulated*). To tell the truth I've never met such a tedious idiot. Right now, when we have started all over again . . . Andika knows quite well what I'd do if she wanted to become pregnant. She knows very well. So it's nothing of the sort, do you hear me, Rabbit? I won't end up in a basement flat changing shitty nappies all day . . . This bloody idiot comes here and announces, grinning his head off, that he has good news . . . Thank you, but no thank you; am I clear, chum? And everybody should accept it. I won't let Andi deliver a baby into a washbasin.

ANDI (*unexpectedly, darkly*). We won't ever have anything more.

They stop talking. HORVATH *goes to the window again, it can't be known what he is thinking.* ANDI *exits.*

HORVATH (*wondering, in a strange mood*). One remains alone, you see, Rabbit. Rita wanted the same thing, but she couldn't win, because I wouldn't let her. Women yearn to give birth to three kilograms of pink meat, only to abandon you after it . . . Humanity is lonely . . . (*With a dark smile.*) We can only rely on the government.

RABBIT *is laughing and eating the unwanted supper with a good appetite.*

(*He picks his nails.*) Maybe I should be a politician. Every fucking thing is the same. These guys are the same old exhibitionists. Shall I be an MP?

RABBIT (*contentedly*). I voted for the Liberal Democratic exhibitionists. Though the communists are very nice too, the red colour on the walls did a lot of good for the townscape, don't you think.

HORVATH. Do you know what your problem is, my dear old Rabbit? You don't believe in a thing.

RABBIT. Ha ha, that's true, that's why I could live without air.

HORVATH. Let's try it out.

He pushes down the other boy's head, they wrestle, laughing. He grimaces.

Damn it! I'm hungry now! Maybe I should marry someone after all. Yes, maybe . . . But as soon as I shake hands with them women start scrutinizing my life-line. Strange . . .

RABBIT. Your life-line runs off your hand, it's not hard to trace it. You have a simply obscene life-line, a perverted one. You will live for one hundred and fifty years, you swine. Oh, how jealous I am of you!

HORVATH (*doesn't pay attention*). The question is what good is all this?

RABBIT (*doesn't pay attention*). When I joined the Company I tried to be your carbon copy. But why on earth was this tiny dance group so all-important for me? And for all of us? Why? Of course you'll say it's just empty talk again . . .

HORVATH (*doesn't pay attention*). The only way to justify your life is if you have done something with it. Only success vindicates your life. I will achieve something . . . Shall I fill your glass?

RABBIT. Excuse me, I wasn't listening.

ANDI *enters, realising they are going to drink.*

ANDI. Don't you want to go out and have a beer somewhere? The truth is that I'm not feeling very well.

She smiles.

HORVATH (*he is irritated*). Andika feels sick . . . well, well . . . not too sick, just a little bit . . . She does everything just a little bit, with grace (*His face is distorted.*) and so smartly . . . Doesn't she? Great, bravo! So terribly carefully! So that nothing gets confused, mixed up. Not too much struggle, no effort, please. We've got the plebs for that . . . That's how you've lived all your life. A person who hasn't ever slogged like a dog doesn't deserve to . . . Well, what could happen to you anyway? Mummy pampers you, Daddy pampers you and, oh, those wonderful, baby-powder soft, love affairs . . . Everybody would bleed for Andika to see her laughing. (*Laughs.*) Shall I open up my veins to amuse you, my love? Would you please take my blood as a mundane gift? How honoured I am. I had once hoped to see you as a normal person . . . the sort who might not want to get out of bed in the morning . . . Oh, this smile and that early morning whimper . . . drive me mad . . . (*Hissing.*) I want . . . to see you suffering.

ANDI. Why do you talk to me like this?

HORVATH. At last Andika has gone pale. Feeling something at last. Some spark has ignited in that permanent darkness. I wish that sometimes you could at least hate me. Why the hell do you love me so much!

ANDI. What I am waiting for . . . is . . . the day . . . you will fall in love with me. (*Screams.*) So that I can take my revenge, you bastard. Sometimes . . . sometimes I feel like lashing my leg into you. Sometimes . . .

HORVATH. Go on! Bravo! Bravo! Who could have imagined that the laziest reptilian heart in the world is able to pump blood?

ANDI. You completely . . . kill me. All right. There's nothing else . . . nothing else I've been waiting for . . . these months than for you to fall in love with me. I would have liked so much to take care of you.

HORVATH. She is about to cry again.

ANDI. Can't you see? I don't want to leave you.

HORVATH. And if . . . I declared my love?

They are silent.

Not even then? Really, what would happen then?

He laughs.

What would happen?

ANDI. I'm not well . . .

HORVATH. Because you don't eat. Why don't you eat? (*Bawls.*) Why don't you eat? Who said you could go hungry? (*Amorously.*) Andika, I beg you, I love you, just eat, eat a little of this . . . it's very nice . . . shall I propose?

HORVATH *pushes food into her mouth and she eats.*

I shall propose since that's what you've been waiting for . . . First, just eat . . . ham, fried in oil; you made it for me just like a real wife . . . How much I love you! My darling, you will be my dear little wifey, won't you? Just take it easy, everything is for you so that you feel nice and comfy.

ANDI (*weakly*). I feel sick.

HORVATH. Just take it slowly. You haven't eaten for days, my dear little vegetarian. Or perhaps you don't like this any more? Though you'd devour loving caresses by the bucketful . . .

We realise for the first time that he is actually laughing.

Andika doesn't like it. It's not to her taste at all. Far too heavy. But life is an onerous burden too and this is only a little ham. You've got no appetite?

ANDI, *on the verge of bursting into tears, eats.*

(*Softly whispering.*) A soft fluffy pillow, that's what our life is; Mummy is so caressing as she brings us up. How much she loves us. How much everybody loves us. Andika is such a charming fairy, who would not love her? She becomes affectionate towards everybody. Life is but a smile. Gentlemen are agreeable and ladies nice. We get everything we can possibly need and Andika stuffs herself quite effortlessly . . .

The food turns bitter in ANDI's *mouth. She rushes into the bathroom. Convulsions of vomiting. Crying. Water flushing. When she returns her features are more settled.*

RABBIT (*meanwhile*). God, how she cries . . . My heart's in my mouth. Did you really not notice she was pregnant?

HORVATH (*cool*). It's none of your business!

ANDI *re-enters.*

(*To* ANDI.) I told you that you could count on my benevolence if you ate it, not if you vomited it.

ANDI *stands stiffly.*

Jutka and Baron, Together

JUTKA *is unsteady on her feet. She lolls and rolls about the floor, a bottle of vodka in her hand.*

JUTKA (*cheerfully*). If you drink enough, you forget everything. What a mercy! Why weren't we told this in good enough time? One day I shall certainly teach my own daughter, if I ever have a daughter, this lesson so that she doesn't have to wait so long before knowing everything that's worth knowing. You wake up in the morning in a miserable state, you look in the mirror . . . What is there to give you strength? Happiness circulates in my blood vessels, spirituous happiness, yes, happiness to be flamed, distilled . . .

BARON (*looking at his notebook*). Do you know whether or not Edit Kass has a 'phone?

JUTKA. Telephone? Have I forgotten to tell you that your mother 'phoned . . . I think she'll be here soon. She said she'd just hop on a broom and glide over, perhaps circling round to call in on some dear old friends to invite them to tea. They'll darken the sky . . . and can be expected from the east . . . with the snow-heavy clouds of November . . . Good heavens, how much I love them! Your mother is my best friend, we discuss how we should change her son's nappies . . . you dirty pig. How did I get here?

Bursts out crying.

BARON. I found it.

JUTKA (*throws her hair back*). I'm drunk? So what? You cheat, how dare you to speak to me like that?

She is about to throw a bottle at him.

BARON (*looks at her attentively*). I'm counting your brain cells going pop.

JUTKA (*doesn't pay attention*). I'm bloody talented. I can still be anything! Several agents have seen me.

BARON. Dial that number.

JUTKA (*drunk, shakes her head*). How did I get here?

BARON. Pooh, I'll do it.

JUTKA (*terrified*). I'm already twenty. Twenty-one quite soon. Surely . . .

She falls silent.

BARON. It's Edit Kass. Speak.

JUTKA. What?

BARON. You are going to be very nice to her, understood? Invite her here. Say you're alone. That you've dropped me.

JUTKA. You are dropped.

BARON (*hissing*). Speak, damn it!

JUTKA. Edit? Hello. Very well. I've kicked this stupid bastard out. (*To* BARON.) What's your name? Baron.

BARON. You're alone. You feel very lonely.

JUTKA (*bursts out crying*). Editke, I'm so lonely. I'm really being hit from all sides. How many agents have seen me and none of them want to use me. What will happen to me?

BARON. That's it, you're doing very well.

JUTKA (*sobbing*). Why don't I have someone? I did get on well with Erika . . . but she left me too.

BARON. Invite her.

JUTKA. I was brought up by my aunt. She hated me, because she was ugly and old. (*Sobbing.*) My real mum . . .

Her speech has become increasingly hard to understand.

BARON. Invite her here, you idiot!

JUTKA. . . . died from uterine cancer.

BARON (*simultaneously with her*). That's enough, you wretched thing, or you'll overdo it. Tell her you're waiting for her.

JUTKA (*becomes sober*). I'm waiting for you. (*Puts down the receiver. Mutters.*) They told me she'd be coming back. I was three years old.

BARON. How stupid you are. People don't remember a thing before the age of four. And that's enough of the vodka for now.

BARON *exits.*

JUTKA (*lights a cigarette*). Of course, how could she come back? Unless . . . (*Blows out the smoke and stares at it. Speaking to herself.*) There is nothing you can do, of course. There are probably very few things in the world worth anything at all. But what are they? We spend all our lives trying to find out. (*Blows out smoke.*) Who was it who made us swear never to exchange kind words with each other? I try to find ways to torture you and you do the same to me. Little Baron, you just go and make a mistake and I shall bite you! Then you can shout. How many times have we deceived each other? Though do you know how long we've actually been together?

EDIT *enters.*

EDIT. Sorry, the door was open.

JUTKA (*doesn't look at her*). So soon? You were very quick.

EDIT. We're almost neighbours . . . It was me who told your friend that this flat was up for rent. Didn't he tell you? It's very nice to be here . . .

Silence.

Of course I think it's frightfully expensive.

Silence.

Is there anything wrong? You were so strange on the 'phone . . . My poor little thing, how dishevelled you look! You aren't ill, are you?

JUTKA (*indifferently*). No, I'm drunk.

Smiles a little at her as she, just visibly, recoils.

EDIT (*hesitating*). Shall I make coffee?

JUTKA (*shrugs*). I don't drink that stuff.

EDIT. You're dripping with sweat.

JUTKA. How on earth could people living before our time fail to be frightened as night fell?

EDIT. Your voice is very hoarse. Well, you're ill.

JUTKA (*indifferently*). You must've been in a hurry if you got here so quickly.

EDIT. I was in a hurry. I felt something was wrong.

JUTKA. Is there a mirror in your flat? I mean a big one. How come nobody is ever interested in what *you* see when you look into one? We've got a mirror like that here.

EDIT *begins to stroke* JUTKA's *hair*.

EDIT. My dear girl . . .

JUTKA. Did you say this flat was nice? Not even the furniture is ours. What you praised belongs to someone else.

EDIT. You'll tell me everything won't you? Do you trust me?

JUTKA. This bloody big mirror!

EDIT. You should sleep; you should have a rest . . . Who else would take care of you?

JUTKA. I should smash it.

EDIT. I have known it for a long time! For a very long time.

JUTKA. Still, if you look into it you become frightened. Or you hate yourself.

EDIT. How filthy everything is here . . . all these bottles. This is horrible.

JUTKA (*into the mirror*). Am I really so drunk? Am I not dreaming it all? (*Laughs.*) Is it me doing all this and all that's to come? Is it me? (*Pulling her eyelids.*) No, I'm sober.

EDIT. Into the bath, my dear girl. Then you'll have a sleep.

JUTKA. To hell with beating round the bush! I've become tired to death with it all. (*Flatters.*) Let's go to your . . . I hate it so much here . . .

EDIT'*s body is trembling*.

Edit Kass's Flat.

BARON *is robbing the flat. A neon sign flashes just outside the window as he moves round the room.*

BARON. I knew this bitch had plenty of jewellery . . . She even blabbed where she kept it. Idiot! Idiot to keep so much cash at home behind a poxy lock! She deserves robbing . . . (*Rests, lights a cigarette.*) Let's see what the dyke smokes. She smokes shit. Light as a butterfly's wing and fucking expensive. And sweet, too, ugh! (*Smokes it with pleasure.*) What shit! And let's see what the dyke drinks. She drinks piss . . . Well let this stuff be sweet since her life's so bitter. Well, really, I can't drink this. (*Drinks it.*) Wish I could switch the light on . . . I'm lucky they've got this neon sign right here or I'd've pricked my balls on the jemmy. And tomorrow at the surgery? 'Scuse me, dear lady Doctor, but I seemed to've pricked my balls with a crowbar.

BARON *works. Squats down, the cigarette is in the corner of his mouth. Puffing.*

Is it really settled that all I am to be is a rotten little thief?

Scratches his head, rattles a necklace in his hand.

Well, who was it told me there was nothing more to me? Well, am I nothing more? Pooh.

Wondering. Working.

A door slams on a lower floor and BARON *listens as* EDIT *and* JUTKA *come up the stairs.*

EDIT (*off*). This way, this way . . . leave your shoes in the bathroom . . . towel and everything. This way . . .

JUTKA (*off*). Wouldn't it be better to . . .

BARON. Fucking hell! How right I was to re-lock the door!

BARON *jumps behind the curtain with the loot. A knife sparkles in his hand, the one with which he opened the door.* EDIT, *enters, turning on the light. She drinks, trembles.* JUTKA *enters.*

JUTKA. Well, what's up? Don't I get a drink too?

EDIT *pours* JUTKA *some drink.*

Why are your hands shaking?

EDIT. Just a little. I'm tired.

JUTKA. And why is there a tremor in your voice?

EDIT. Because . . . Sore throat.

JUTKA. And why are you so pale?

EDIT. The neon light.

JUTKA. And why are you looking at me like that?

EDIT. It's so hot in here!

EDIT *steps towards the curtain.*

BARON (*murmuring like a prayer*). Just pull it away and you'll die. Just pull it away, what are you waiting for, pull it away.

EDIT. I don't really know what to say to you now . . .

BARON (*suggests to* EDIT). Pull the curtain, just pull the curtain.

JUTKA. Nothing.

EDIT. I've never been in such a situation as this . . .

EDIT *moves away from the curtain.*

JUTKA. I don't trust you.

EDIT. What do you mean?

JUTKA. Why do you lie?

EDIT (*trembles*). How dare you suggest such a thing?

JUTKA. Why do you lie to everybody?

EDIT. Now you're talking nonsense.

EDIT *moves towards the curtain.*

You've got a temperature. You're ill.

BARON. Pull it away. At last, pull it away.

JUTKA. And you're a dyke.

BARON. Here I am.

EDIT (*screams*). Enough! That's enough! Enough!

BARON (*whispers*). I'm waiting for you, my angel. I'm waiting for you, darlin'. Waiting for you right here.

EDIT (*sobbing*). I can't stand it! Can't you see how much I can't stand it? Why are you all like this?

JUTKA. Like what?

BARON. What's your life worth, eh? Take the edge of that curtain.

EDIT. You're all hateful!

BARON. Take it. That's it. And now pull it away!

EDIT. Hateful. Indifferent. You don't think at all! You don't desire anything at all. You've got nothing inside.

Walks away from the curtain. Strokes the girl.

JUTKA (*bursts out*). Take your filthy hands off me, you scum! I hate you! I detest you! I hate everything so much I could happily die. And it's because of people like you. You scum . . .

EDIT (*screams*). Enough!

Wanting to open a window to get some fresh air she tears the curtain open.

BARON (*smiles*). Welcome.

> BARON *stabs* EDIT *in a blind rage.* JUTKA *picks up the crowbar and beats* EDIT *in a blind rage, almost not noticing the boy, out of her mind.*

JUTKA. Oh, just die! I want you to die! Everything is your fault! Devil! You're all devils! All, all, all!

BARON. How can there be so much blood in someone? So much, so much . . .

JUTKA. I kill her . . . I kill her. Did I kill her all right?

BARON. You're insane. Come on, let's do a bunk.

JUTKA. No!

> BARON *takes the girl away.*

Rabbit and Manager, Together: an Optional/Complimentary Scene

RABBIT. I know why you want to talk to me. You want me to take Feri Horvath's place in this new group. You're looking to give Horvath the boot.

MANAGER (*laughs tunefully*). If you know everything . . . You're a clever boy, Rabbit.

RABBIT (*greatly bored*). I'm afraid you don't have the power to do it.

MANAGER (*smiles*). I'll have all the opportunities I need for it. Actually, Rabbit, why are you called . . . Rabbit?

RABBIT (*greatly bored*). I had a harelip as a baby and my brothers thought I looked like the pet rabbit. Actually, I still have a bit of a speech defect.

MANAGER. You wouldn't notice it.

RABBIT. Or rather . . . I'm over it, more or less, since Müller left. Although . . .

MANAGER. The group split six months ago . . .

RABBIT. . . . I'm not seeing anyone about it.

MANAGER. . . . and I have decided to set things right.

RABBIT. To tell you the truth I never saw anyone about it. I was ashamed.

MANAGER. To tell you the truth, I can see a decent chance of success for this . . . enterprise.

RABBIT. But I don't care about my speech defect any more.

MANAGER. . . . but not as it is now. Who knows what comes tomorrow!

RABBIT. Who knows what I actually care about, really?

MANAGER. You have to understand: the Horvath group is not fit to survive.

RABBIT. But what are we talking about?

MANAGER. We are talking about the same thing, my friend. About the future.

RABBIT. Thank you for your offer; thank you but no thank you.

MANAGER. Boy! But why?

RABBIT. I know the reason.

MANAGER. You do not take the time to think, my dear young fellow. You guys never, ever, think. Though, of course, I do not need you for thinking but for dancing.

RABBIT. I don't suppose you really want to know, but I can tell you.

MANAGER (*sadly*). I had your welfare at heart. You are quite crazy, my boy. You will not amount to very much at all.

RABBIT. I won't take Horvath's place because he is much more talented than me. More precisely: he is a *talent*. Keep him, he could be of great value one day.

MANAGER (*sadly*). I am very sorry for you. I can see you are far too determined. I'm afraid . . . you will regret it, but I shan't be at hand to help.

RABBIT (*politely*). I don't need your help. (*Turns back for a second.*) You are a good man. You were a pleasant surprise.

RABBIT *goes.*

A Rehearsal Room

The three girls are in costume practising the cancan in the room with the large mirrors. HORVATH *is instructing them fiercely. The girls, coupled by their reflections, are lifting up their legs; sometimes we can see little of them except for their black stockinged legs, encircled by foam skirts, spreading like the birth of Venus. From the spray of blood-red skirts and snow-white foam a row of ballet shoes occasionally springs up like popped champagne corks, smartly and temptingly. The ankles turn circles, Ariadne unwinding her thread, the way out of the labyrinth. Beneath the music the muffled stamping of feet is a distant murmur, the warning of the body – that it is temptingly heavy in spite of it being cork-light. The ankles are in the air, milk-white eggs dancing on black water-jets. And finally three splits are sliding side by side for three beats; the three girls keep their heads erect, they are sweating and afraid of* HORVATH'*s suggestive look. Half a year has passed.*

HORVATH (*gesturing madly. Shouting, not pleased*). Rubbish, it was rubbish! It's not to caress them, (*Bangs his hand down.*) but to drive them wild! Offenbach, this is a crazy poultry-run; the cocks are blinking out there and their minds have already been addled. (*To* JUTKA.) Not to skate, my sweetheart, but to fly. To fly!

The record is on again. HORVATH *is really flying, almost in ecstasy, he shows what he meant: the crazy poultry-run. The girls have no strength even to look at each other, they are just watching him, the beads of perspiration glittering on their foreheads.*

HORVATH (*gasps*). The cancan is a storm of the body . . . the clouds have darkened the sky, the air has cooled, the trees bowed . . . I have to tremble!

He stops. Someone rings the doorbell.

All right, have a rest. Somebody is coming. (*Roars.*) Damn it! Can't one of you move your ass to answer the door?

ANDI (*cool*). Like this? I don't go out like this. It was you who wanted us to rehearse in costume.

HORVATH'*s lips are narrowing like a blade, he goes out, slamming the door. The* MANAGER *enters, seems at home.*

MANAGER. Kiss your hand, dear ladies.

HORVATH *enters.*

How's the production, maestro? I can see you don't save on energy . . .

HORVATH (*annoyed*). The 'production' is ready. I hope it's already sold.

MANAGER. Of course, of course. Or to be a little more precise, interest has been expressed in many places. (*Ironic.*) I shall work for my percentage.

RITA *and* HORVATH *avoid eye contact 'til the end of the act.*

RITA. I'm going. We're finished for today I suppose. Are you coming, Jutka?

JUTKA (*to* HORVATH). Look at this!

She executes a high kick and almost splits in the air. JUTKA *and* RITA *go to change.*

MANAGER. I envy you, Mr Horvath. You keep a whole harem.

HORVATH. I'm glad you have such a breathtaking sense of humour. I'm going to get myself a cup of coffee before my head splits open. (*Looks back from the door.*) Why don't you take a seat?

HORVATH *goes out.*

MANAGER. Well, Andi, dear? Everybody seems to have left us . . . Now you may be . . . confidential with your impresario, if you would like.

ANDI. Leave me alone, will you.

MANAGER. Miss, your shapely bottom will catch cold. Let me help you to stand up. If you honour me with this . . .

ANDI. Your incessant attempts are quite boring.

MANAGER (*muffled voice*). You sound as if you have given up on life for *ever*. Do you think you fool me? You are empty, your head is empty; your baby is confusing your brain! Why did you get together with that pushy turd? Do you think he'll achieve anything? (*Hissing.*) No, don't be a fool, he will not. You will die in a slum if you stay together. Your work is good and the others are good too, no doubt . . . I will get you a first class choreographer. If the master is good and the girls are good . . . well, I smell a success like an Arabian smells a sand storm. I bow down, I taste the sand, it is on my tongue . . . and I feel . . .

ANDI (*looks at him with eyes opened wide*). My baby . . . is confusing me? Oh, how much I have wished to have one! Blessed Virgin, why do you torture me so much? (*Tears are soiling her make-up.*) My baby . . . I won't be innocent any more. Oh filthy life, how beautiful you seemed to be. (*Sitting up she kicks the air, mutters.*) Foams and laces, the birth of Venus . . . do you see? I think I'm a little flushed. (*Exchanges glances with her own reflection in the mirror.*) Yes . . . I can't be pregnant any longer.

MANAGER. That's what the doctor said?

ANDI. No, on the contrary. (*With deep horror.*) But I . . . know.

MANAGER. (*Sincerely*). Your legs are wonderful.

ANDI. Ah, but what difference does it make?

Kisses him for a long while.

MANAGER (*steps back*). You are a strange girl. I don't want to . . .

ANDI *is unsteady as the* MANAGER *steps away.*

ANDI. What do you not want?

MANAGER. You are strange. I don't want that boy to catch us doing something. You really shocked me . . . You seemed quite agitated . . . You want it, then you don't want it . . . I'll drop in tomorrow again.

MANAGER *exits.* HORVATH *is standing by the door with an evil smile on his face. He stirs his coffee.*

ANDI (*exhausted, she can hardly speak*). I won't have it . . . understand? I won't have you leaving me with that man again. Please . . .

HORVATH (*mock innocence*). Why, anything happened?

ANDI. You want to sell me . . . you want to sell us all – the whole company. (*She can hardly breathe.*) Do you really think I couldn't see why you needed that bloody coffee so badly? (*Sobbing.*) You absolute bloody shit.

There's a silence.

Murderer.

HORVATH (*whispering*). You hate me now, don't you.

ANDI. You told me once that life is wretched, like a suburban strip-tease bar, where greying women fear that nobody will want to see them any more . . . You sell my baby . . . you sell me. Poxy little striptease bar where women are ugly . . . It's you who makes life ugly. Müller laughed at you . . . Oh, I hate you.

HORVATH (*his face is twisted*). It doesn't matter, it doesn't matter my love; the only important thing is that you let yourself be sold.

He turns and goes out. RITA re-enters in day-wear. The two girls look at each other for a moment.

ANDI (*her throat parched, whispers*). What's become of us? What's our life coming to?

They are silent.

RITA (*lights a cigarette and sits down*). I'm miserable now that I'm back.

She gazes at the smoke indifferently.

Eating humble pie. (*Smiles at her.*) Don't you think so? I've watched you struggle and I remembered the months, the years . . .

ANDI. Why are you here? Why are you here?

RITA. Things are always the same. Everything occurs again. Every-thing is the same. Nothing will ever change, *they* rule – not us. You didn't know it? You scold Feri so that he'll shave before every performance . . . and it was me who scolded him before. He tortures you, and you're like a caged squirrel in a wheel – it was me before. Why do we all tolerate this? Oh, who knows?

ANDI. One day . . . I'll leave him. I'll leave you all, everything. One day I'll be far away from here and I'll marry . . . a stranger. What will be his name? He won't have a name. I will never know his name. He will say: *'You won't see me any more if you spy on me.'* He will be a stranger, a complete stranger.

RITA (*laughs*). None of us will ever marry.

ANDI. I get proposals every day. You, too. On small torn pieces of paper. Sixteen-year-old boys, rich Arabs and people from Vienna, watching me at every turn.

RITA. You will be left alone in time. (*Looks at her.*) Only Erika, only she . . . She must have driven somebody insane to take her away from us.

They shudder.

ANDI. The Devil.

The smoke swirls before the mirror. HORVATH *returns and* JUTKA *appears in the doorway, leaning against the doorpost.*

HORVATH. Lovely ladies, well? Lessons in decorum after dance lessons. The lesson for today?

ANDI. The storm of the body, sir. The clouds have already dulled the sky and the air is cooling. It seems that I shiver.

She bows as if on stage. JUTKA *laughs.* RITA *smiles slowly.*

Horvath and Andi, Together

HORVATH (*squats beside the girl*). It's been six months since we stayed a foursome. I think it's mere necessity that keeps us together; although, perhaps, there is something else. Baron is waiting for a reprieve or his Day of Judgment. And Rabbit? He disappeared, vanished, and will never come back. And what about us? What a career! I see myself as a guilty bishop who sells immortality for cash.

ANDI. You used to be Müller's favourite . . .

HORVATH (*smirks bitterly*). We all used to be Müller's favourites.

ANDI (*looking at him for a long time*). Don't you have this strange feeling that once we were very happy.

HORVATH *laughs.*

Going from town to town, dancing in small clubs and big halls. When I think about it I feel like someone who has been slapped across the face . . . Our past sates me and arouses me as well. (*Stuttering.*) Or maybe I will finish as Erika did . . . What beast could have done it to her? If only he'd merely killed her . . . But . . . He won't be caught, ever. Jutka didn't dare look at her, though she was her best friend. That's why I had to do the identification. How often I've dreamt about her!

ANDI *sits, curling herself up like an embryo. She convulses.* HORVATH *is smoking, watching the girl, meditating. After a silence.*

HORVATH. You still have spasms?

ANDI. Why do you want to know? You never wanted to know. You told me that if I've got any problems I should solve them for myself. You always laughed at me. You told me I was a misery . . . (*Whispering.*) You don't tolerate anyone who is not perfect.

HORVATH. That's not true. I'm not perfect either. Nobody is. But I think everyone must strive for it. (*A flash of annoyance.*) You can't understand that, of course. The words mean something else to you . . . To be honest they mean nothing to you. Nothing that would make sense. You're stubborn, you're frightened. It's possible to be frightened throughout one's life, but fear must be subdued. You must cut loose from everything trying to hold you back and find a way to conquer.

ANDI. You're talking about my baby.

HORVATH (*patiently*). Don't be ridiculous. (*Pause.*) I'm not talking about it, no. But you don't understand what I am talking about.

ANDI. How uncomprehending you are. Uncomprehending as a . . . You can't see anything that is really important.

HORVATH. You're worn out. Is that really so important? *You* are really important to me. I see you sinking into that swamp: Oh, how much sorrow you feel for yourself. (*Softly.*) We mustn't feel so much sorrow for ourselves. Didn't you know that, Andika? The past is a load of shit. There is no past at all. Don't think about it.

ANDI. You idiot. (*Looks into his eyes.*) Sometimes I really hate you.

HORVATH (*smokes meditating*). Where does your way lead to, Andika?

ANDI. And yours?

On the Streets

JUTKA. I wish I knew what keeps you here . . .

RITA. That's simple, the work. I don't feel anything towards them any more, they both have their own problems. (*Hesitating.*) I even feel some sympathy for Andi, you know.

JUTKA. I was very surprised when you came back.

RITA. You were stupefied, I remember.

JUTKA. The door just opened and there you were. I thought there was about to be an uproar. I don't like that sort of scene.

RITA. What can I do? I must work. (*Low voice, after a long time.*) The door just opened and I was there . . . if you knew how hard my heart was beating.

In the FLat

ANDI. You're watching them from the window, aren't you? I can hear their voices. The problem is that you lie to me. Oh, you just rest your elbows on the sill, smoke and lie, nobody knows what thoughts pass through your head. Now I know, of course, that I was nothing to you, but in fact I think nobody was ever anything to you. But there was a time when I struggled to find out what you were thinking about. What or whom . . .

HORVATH. Oh, this is very moving. Just go on, I might even fall in love with you. But do take care I don't find myself bored.

ANDI *is searching for something in her handbag.*

Are you crying? Is she really crying? She is still definitely attractive in this light. But the life! That is quite another story, my darling. What could we say to each other?

ANDI (*in a low voice*). It's over . . . isn't it? (*Takes his hand, but doesn't look at him.*) I've known it since the day of my abortion. This bloody flat killed everything in me and this bloody year.

She looks into the mirror.

What's changed? I don't understand, I don't understand. I wanted to be your wife, I wanted to take care of you . . . for the first time in my life. How many times did I 'phone my mother before you came home so that at least I would have someone who'd be nice to me that day. Or sometimes just for advice on how to cook. (*Impatient gesture.*) I wasn't good at anything, of course, but it didn't bother you, just me. And sometimes . . . you acted like . . . (*Uncomprehending.*) What a bloody year this has been. I don't even know why I did it.

Long silence, the room is plunged slowly into semi-darkness, the only spot is the girl in the short red skirt, lying on her back watching the ceiling, trying to gather her thoughts. HORVATH *at the window, with his back to her.*

Sometimes I don't know, perhaps we should start all over again. In a totally different way.

HORVATH *bursts out laughing.*

On the Street

RABBIT. Did you mind me coming to see you?

She laughs.

RITA. No, not at all. I haven't seen you for ages. Had you something to do in the neighbourhood?

RABBIT. I heard the group was together again and I thought I might see what you were up to.

RITA. You haven't been in this part of the world for a long time. Meanwhile we've said goodbye to the ballet. Horvath's recently been investigating the cancan.

RABBIT. Will anything come of it?

RITA (*after a moment's hesitation*). Of course.

RABBIT (*seems agitated*). And what is it like?

RITA. Dancing again? (*Smiles kindly.*). It's marvellous.

RABBIT (*suddenly*). You know what? Let's go to the amusement park. It's not far.

RITA. No, I don't feel like it. I'm tired.

RABBIT (*pulling her by the hand*). Please . . .

The Amusement park. A Bench.

Distant Noises. A Hot Dog in their hands.

RABBIT. How was it?

RITA. The big dipper? Wonderful, at least it made me wonderfully sick.

RABBIT. The hot dog will do you good. (*Eating.*) I love it here. If you knew how crappy my work place is. You had no idea I'd got a job, eh? Of course it'll come to an end someday. My boss is such an asshole that – I'm serious – he drives me insane! He spells 'potatoes' without the 'e'! Like, he's a man with about three hours schooling in his life. No, two hours and he was good at sports. One morning he walked in with a face covered in scratches and I knew immediately that he'd tried to eat with a knife and fork.

Eats messily. RITA laughs. RABBIT makes a suffering face. RITA tries to clean his clothes.

RITA. Rabbit, I missed your clackety-clack. I really mean it. You've got mustard all over you.

RABBIT. And I ordered it with ketchup, too.

She has another good laugh, leans on him, and then her laugh turns to a cough.

RITA. The bloody hot dog went down the wrong way.

RABBIT (*watching her suspiciously*). The big dipper . . . I had a friend who, when he was a boy, knocked his head on a cupboard. The crack in his skull was so fine that nobody ever noticed it.

Then . . . several years later . . . he took a ride on the big dipper and when he got off he started to cough, really, really terribly. He was coughing so much that I knew there and then it was the end of him. *Fini.*

RITA. Christ, what happened to him?

RABBIT (*embarrassed*). I didn't tell this story to allow him to survive, though in fact he did.

He clamps her head.

Perhaps it won't be fatal to you either. I'm serious. It's more than possible.

RITA. Jesus Christ! I can feel it. I have a case of the hairline crack.

RABBIT. Well now! I told you so. Here at the back . . . No, at the front, on your forehead. That's the dangerous one. There is hope, my dear.

RITA. Is there? You're not joking, are you? Really?

RABBIT. There is, I swear. Let me see. A doctor used to live next door to us on the outside corridor, so I'm an expert in this.

Embraces her.

RITA. So I'll survive. Thank the gods.

Slowly she takes his hand and twists his arm back.

It's interesting, I feel much better now. Don't you? What's the matter?

RABBIT (*groans*). I'm afraid that in your condition such displays can be seriously harmful. You might even get spasms.

RITA. Spasms. That's interesting. I don't feel any pain.

She twists his arm again and RABBIT *cries out. An elderly lady passes by.*

RABBIT. Mam, I've fallen into the hands of a very brutal woman. If you see a telephone kiosk on your way please call the police.

WOMAN (*disdainfully*). You youngsters think you're allowed do anything you like.

She shuffles off. RABBIT *puts his hand on* RITA's *shoulder and looks into her eyes, boyishly.* RITA *casts her gaze down to the ground; confused. She steps away.*

RABBIT (*drinks, sipping. Turns the coke can over and over*). These bastards will outlast us. (*Throws the can away wildly.*) Fucking life. I haven't become successful, what shall I do? Everybody makes it somehow. My cheeks are burning. The most successful thing in the world is success itself. I'll break the bank at roulette. I'll buy the Hawaiian islands. Or I'll be a doctor. Those guys are rich.

RITA. But they get woken up at night.

RABBIT. I'll be a plastic surgeon then. Women don't come in a wailing ambulance to get their breasts pumped up. (*Meditates.*) Or who knows . . .

RITA. I think our band of three might become a success. Maybe I should leave it. I should go away. But where?

RABBIT. You're fooling yourself. But you're right. Who wouldn't?

RITA (*sadly*). How could you understand that, Rabbit?

RABBIT. Those three pigeons, you see? On the bar. They're watching my hot dog. (*Jealously hiding it.*) Bugger off!

RITA. Perhaps you're right. Perhaps I should decamp. I'm fed up with everybody. Oh, how much I'm fed up with everybody. Oh, Jesus, damned hell.

RITA *lies back on the bench.*

RABBIT. They're watching me . . . They're watching me. They're already four. Look at that, scratching about in the dust and thinking that . . . (*Anxiously.*) Tell me, have you seen Hitchcock's *Birds*?

RITA. To leave this place for good. To follow those clouds. No matter where.

RABBIT. I feel miserable. Listen . . . let's give them the hot dog of our own volition and get out of here.

RITA. My life will end badly.

RABBIT. Huh, they're gone. What did you say?

RITA. Nothing. Never mind.

RABBIT (*embraces her.* RITA *lets him. In a low voice*). Don't you feel a little pressure on your temple now? Your hairline crack, you know . . .

RITA. You shit.

RITA, *laughing, pummels him.*

RABBIT. You don't know what I feel. When you want to get things off your chest very much . . . . . . It's good to be with you. Good . . . but more than that needs to be said.

RITA (*smiles at him*). Rabbit, you talk too much.

RABBIT. Once I was by myself in a very rundown cinema and I was sitting in the first row, you know? And I saw . . . some smoke in front of me. 'What could this be', I said to myself. Somebody had thrown a cigarette or a match on the floor and there were all sorts of papers and everything lying there, you know. So that's where the smoke was coming from. And there were flames too. I jumped up, wanting to shout, because I was the only one who saw it, but all I could shout was f-f-f-f . . . And everybody was yelling at me to sit down and shut up. I stood there and felt myself to be a complete idiot.

RITA. It must have been terrible.

RABBIT. Everybody hissing.

RITA. I would've been hissing too.

RABBIT. But the worst thing was that they thought I was crackers. The truth is that similar things had happened before. I had a date with a girl after the film. I turned out of the cinema feeling quite dizzy and bought her flowers. (*He is already shouting.*) And then I felt that I wouldn't be able to say to her, 'I brought you flowers', so I was only going to say 'flower' and give it to her. But then she came, and I was standing there like an idiot, and I couldn't utter a damned word, I was just standing there, fucking life, and she started yelling at me, and then I told myself I should shout now, at the top of my voice, 'flowers' and then I opened my mouth and (*Yells.*) what I shouted was: fire, fire, fire!

Guffaws, his face buried in his hands.

RITA (*she has a good laugh. Demandingly*). Take me to the Ferris-wheel!

RABBIT (*wickedly*). All right. With pleasure. Yet let me tell you that in earlier days I worked at a place like this and I saw that the guys who fix those dangling swingy things get terribly drunk every day and mix the cog wheels up. Well then it turns out only when . . .

RITA enjoys it very much, pays attention to him. RABBIT wants to kiss her unexpectedly.

RITA. No, please don't Rabbit. No.

They go. After a moment of embarrassment RABBIT starts to play the clown again. The wheels are turning, the swing-boats are dangling, the barkers are shouting, the hubbub is going on. Lights, neon-ads, Mickey Mice, stepping Marlboro-boxes, madness of a market, slowly calming down.

Evening Silence

RITA. It wasn't worth it . . . It wasn't worth it . . .

The STRANGER enters.

STRANGER. There are few things that are worthwhile, although you don't know that yet.

RITA. You've scared me. You quite scared me, seriously.

STRANGER(*with a nice smile*). Pardon me. I didn't mean to; I don't like frightening people. May I sit down?

RITA. Sure, I'm alone, totally alone . . .

STRANGER. We are never alone. There is always someone who will be interested to see our ups and downs.

RITA. Do you think so? No, I don't think so. I guess you're a priest. It's your clothes, that's why I thought it was . . . (*Laughs.*) Otherwise I wouldn't be sitting here with you. This place has a bad reputation. A priest walking through here, it is so unusual, if only you knew that! One can imagine, we're at peace again; you see, I am nearly crying, excuse me. You know, my childhood came into my head . . . my mother. It is quite strange that I'm talking to you like this, but . . . How many times I fell asleep on my mother's knee at Christmas mass, but it all seems so far away. Of course I must feel ashamed if I'm so affected. You see how and why I unburden my heart to a stranger . . .

STRANGER (*listens to her attentively*). The soul. The only thing that is of worth. (*Smiles.*) I hope you understand that we mustn't let it be lost.

RITA. It is my soul! You have nothing to do with it. Forget it. Why are you sitting here with me? Surely your lambs wait on you already.

STRANGER (*hesitates*). Lonely lamb, lives threatened . . . in a strange place, a bad place. The soul shines clearly through, it's impossible to dirty it.

RITA. What are you talking about, for God sake! Oh, how many people are anxious for me – too many! Everybody wants something from me – what do you want? Salvation, is this the right word? Your efforts are hopeless. I'm afraid it has already been lost for ever.

STRANGER (*his throat dry*). You are a dancer, aren't you?

RITA (*indifferently*). How do you know that?

STRANGER (*laughs tunefully*). I've been watching you for a long time. If you knew my dear child what a long time! I have walked in your footsteps . . .

RITA. Mine? That's pointless. You would feel as if you were dreaming. You would have nightmares. And how much flattery you'd use. You'd want everything . . . even you. You'd be tortured by unease – the most terrible sickness. And how much you would love money! You'd learn tricks like a magician – on a grand scale. And you would have a horde of hangers-on. Deceitful days. And you'd enjoy it so much, Father! What we have here is just a worthless imitation.

STRANGER. You make me sad, my child. Your immortal soul is ill.

RITA. And most likely not immortal. (*Bursts out crying*.) Oh, Father why is there no way out? Please, help me, can't you see I am crying, please. Perhaps you are the last innocent man, otherwise you would have realised what I am and run away. I am a worthless little nobody. I have humiliated myself, I am a coward. Why can't I draw the conclusion? Perhaps my feelings are too deep, or too shallow. I won't ever see what is in the depth.

STRANGER. A whirlpool swirls in the depth, the one who looks into it will become light-headed. Its image would shock you . . . It must be eradicated without mercy, eradicated. Do you understand? How does it read? Call it up yourself, I beg you. If it shocks you, you should get rid of it, regardless of what it is, a part of your body or a thought.

RITA (*madly hoping*). Does immortal life exist, I wonder?

STRANGER. There is an immortal, immaculate life. (*After some hesitation*.) And 'til then? Everything that is immaculate . . . a busy life, rearing children, fear from what comes. The threshold all of us have to cross . . . (*Day-dreaming*.) What shall we be given at the final reckoning?

RITA (*madly*). Busy life, and to bring up a child . . . Father, I have had three abortions. Who wanted that? Who humiliates us?

STRANGER. I know.

RITA. Why is it that I can no longer have a child? And why are we all alone?

STRANGER. His heart is sad, waiting for those who have fallen into sin. Get rid of what's outraging you, my little child. (*Awfully sadly*.) Whiteness, do you know anything about it? The whiteness of snow, of bed-clothes, of pure linen, of the foam of running stream. We have to be purified, I am sorry for you, my child! My heart's breaking.

RITA (*sobbing*). My dear God.

STRANGER. If I could shed a tear drop, I would cry with you my child.

He takes his bag and opens it.

His Grace be on us.

HORVATH *enters.*

HORVATH. Rita! You here?

STRANGER *disappears.*

RITA. Feri! Feri!

RITA *runs up to* HORVATH.

Visiting Hours in the Convict Prison, the Three of Them.

JUTKA *and* HORVATH *arrive.*

JUTKA. Hello.

BARON. Hello.

HORVATH. Hello. How are you?

They feel embarrassed.

JUTKA (*through the wire net*). The yard screw told us we have 'til one o'clock.

BARON. Don't use that word.

JUTKA. It's all the same. Well, 'til one. 'Til one . . .

HORVATH (*sitting beside* JUTKA, *remains silent*). Jutka brought you something. We left it in the room outside.

JUTKA. I brought you . . .

BARON. I don't need anything, thanks.

JUTKA. A parcel. Things that you like. It had to be left outside. We'll stay 'til one.

BARON. Don't bring me anything next time.

JUTKA. They said you'll get it.

BARON. I told you the last time, too.

JUTKA. I dreamt about you last night, you know.

BARON (*spiritlessly*). And what was it about?

JUTKA. That everything takes a turn for the better. That you aren't . . . here . . .

BARON. I heard you're going to marry, Horvath. You're doing the right thing.

JUTKA. It's great . . .

BARON. You will be lucky with Rita, believe me.

JUTKA. Why on earth do I come here all the time?

HORVATH. I'm not so sure. She wants it very much.

BARON. You should want it, too; anyway, try it at least once.

HORVATH. Let's leave it for now.

BARON. At last, someone who can stand you.

JUTKA. I'm absolutely sure everything will take a turn for the better.

BARON. Jutka, they take you for a fool because you come here so often. You spend all your time here.

HORVATH (*embarrassed*). Will you two stop it. What will happen to you? Sometimes I have a feeling that you have been brainwashed.

BARON. The bill has to be paid, once, Horvath. I can't be a rascal for ever. (*Walking up and down.*) The charge is prepared, I am waiting for the sentence. I killed a woman and . . . I made a mess in her flat . . . and I took her things . . . and still the blag was no great success. Pooh. Does anything else matter? I can't sit here for ever, I have to know the truth in my case.

JUTKA (*whispers*). The judges won't accept anything . . .

BARON. We cannot always escape the things to come. (*Walks up and down.*) I rode on such a high horse – although I was a nobody, a rogue. It's time I really understood *everything*. I wanted to be a boss, a big crook and failed in that enormous fraud . . . I will be stuffed by it and shall pay the bill.

JUTKA. Baron . . . I would like to wait for you. I would like to . . . I don't know whether I can do it or not. Baron . . . will you hate me?

BARON. How happy I'd've been! Children by the dozen! I would have gone into the delivery room with you. This thing, this place doesn't matter. Criminals, crazies, villains, forget it; get out of here, forget me! I can do at least this much. I am a miserable rogue, a worm, a worm with good taste, I am disgusted by myself. My hair is drenched with sweat, my lips tremble, yet in my dreams I do it again, I do everything myself. I am annoyed with those who remain decent. Even you. What do you know about me? Fragments . . . if I told the story of my life I'd pollute everyone with it. What trace, what mark, will I leave behind? Wouldn't it be better to disappear for ever, right now? What am I waiting for? I count my steps. I write endless comments to my life. Well, farewell fantasy, amiable magician! Let's bury it, put earth over it, quickly.

JUTKA. If only you could get out of here at least!

BARON. Nothing, nobody, will wait for me; life goes on. Am I really at this point? I feel cheated, I couldn't even become a real crook. I take a deep breath, that represses the shame.

Laughs unnaturally.

JUTKA. I'm sorry, but I can't bear this any more. I can't bear you torturing me. I swear I've done everything for you, of course you may do anything you like, but what else do you expect from me?

BARON. You won't come here again, will you?

JUTKA. Well, you want it to be that way, nobody else but you.

BARON (*laughs at her*). Oh, really, how stupid you are. Yet if this thing is seen through to the end it will be harder for you. But you can't see that yet.

JUTKA. You told me it would count for nothing.

BARON (*calmly*) It will never add up to anything. Go away!

JUTKA (*brokenheartedly*). Excuse me, I can't come here any more. I am not guilty of anything. I know that. I don't want to think about this any more.

JUTKA *leaves*.

BARON. Well, can't you be surprised by anything? Anything at all?

HORVATH. The noose is round your neck, you'd better be quiet. This is not a joke any more. Everything has been considered. (*Offers him a cigarette.*) Tell me, what will survive of you, man?

BARON *smokes*.

All the animals run for dear life; remember it. Solace can always be found. You must try and find it.

BARON. All the animals run for dear life . . . They cry under the knife. And what is it that distinguishes a human being from the dirt, from animal life? Is our skin made of gold? Is it worth so much? Who can foresee what's waiting for us beyond all this? Is it good, or is it total madness? The rope's lying on my neck, I'd rather be quiet.

HORVATH. Cry, soak the shoes of the judges – the three good-hearted souls who can hardly wait for you to malign yourself. Their hearts are melting butter and they can put up nothing to hold the rope. Tremble 'til you have flesh on your bones. Stutter to find words 'til you have a tongue. Beg to whoever you believe in to be merciful. Otherwise what will remain of you? (*Lights a cigarette.*) Windblown sand.

BARON. I have been sitting in my cell for half a year and I will be sitting here for another half a year waiting for mercy, that will, of course, come. I have thought over my life and I will tell my only visitor, that's you, what I have found out by myself. What rights and what duties I have had. What could I have done? I examined the case and justice with her scales teetered. Let's measure this earthy piece of business, line for line, weight for weight. What did I leave behind? My sin is accidental, my life is accidental, I was the axe of Raskholnikov. I have to understand for what purpose I have lived twenty-four years. I suppose I did not understand too much of all this, but it doesn't matter at all.

HORVATH (*stands on his tip-toes at the window with wire-net*). The prisoners are eating, do you see? The guard is in the middle. You'll be eating like that for twenty years. How strange that whole thing is over there. (*Grins.*) Listen, Müller would like it!

BARON. To work with Müller . . . was of course awful. He hated artificial light but hated it when the sun was blazing down, too. It was my duty to rent the hall and I felt sometimes that I would go mad. Only filtered light was good enough, only the clouds, the clouds . . . or dusk. You felt you were fighting with God. Suffer, suffer and who says you'll succeed? Of course it was horrible the way he instructed us – did I tell you that? Horvath, are you listening? If you instruct someone they will begin to hate you. Or they will be afraid of you. You have to give them orders. Make sketches, draw them on paper; if you draw somebody, you have got them in your power. Understand? This way leads to hell, of course.

HORVATH (*watching the prisoners*). It is like a Baroque German nightmare. The supper of the Saint George marksmen to the prince. Who painted it?

BARON. Holbein, yes, a brave villain, I like him. Every day he got drunk and beat his wife. Tried to find the way to salvation.

BARON *stands on tip-toes and watches.*

HORVATH. It's like a painting. Well, don't you see?

Laughs, drums on the net with his fingers.

They are grey, aren't they. Damn it, they are grey!

Complementary Scene

Can be placed in the middle of the play. Two figures are bending down to a body in a square late night.

POLICEMAN 1. What are you made of, man? I am not able to look at it . . .

POLICEMAN 2. Does it turn your stomach?

POLICEMAN 1. You can't get used to it.

POLICEMAN 2 (*examines the body*). The bloody cross is on her belly. The 'monk' has been working.

POLICEMAN 1. But why does he cut them up like that? (*Feeling sick.*) Everything is all over . . .

POLICEMAN 2. And now?

POLICEMAN 1. Yes, yes lieutenant, the lesson has been given.

Turns away.

EVERYWOMAN

a mordant comedy by

Péter Kárpáti

English version by Jack Bradley
with verse passages by Tony Curtis
from a translation by Ágnes Gál

Péter Kárpáti was born in Budapest in 1961. He studied dramaturgy at the Academy of Dramatic Arts, graduating in 1983. Since then he's worked as dramaturg in different theatres, and, at the time of writing, is dramaturg/literary manager at *Új* (New) Theatre, Budapest. His first play, *Singapore, Terminus*, was produced in 1988. He's written four others since his début (and adapted a few works for puppet theatres), and is known for anxiously revising his plays before, during, and after the rehearsal periods. His second play, *The Unknown Soldier* (rewritten as *Immortal War*) premiered in 1990. *The River at the End of the Road* (1990) was conceived when he spent some months of sociological research in a small village of gipsies. That play, and its production, won several prizes, as did *The Golden Orb* (1995), a more playful expression of his affection for gipsy culture. This later piece, based on witty and poetic gipsy folk-tales, mingles different forms of comedy, puppet theatre, fairy tales, and gipsy folk-music.

Everywoman was first performed by the Katona József company on 11 February 1993 in Dunaújváros, and the production returned to the company's Budapest venue a few days later. The play is a free adaptation of the medieval Everyman story. Set in today's Budapest, this tragi-comedy tells of the last day in the life of a middle-aged woman, who learns she has cancer. Facing death, her attempts to arrange everything before she passes away reveal her whole history, all her missed or ruined opportunities, in a novel way. Kárpáti's tender irony and subtle poetry enthused his actors and audiences alike, winning for the play and its theatrical presentation many accolades.

Today Kárpáti lives in a small house with his wife and three children (plus dogs, cats and parrots): he has commented that 'although theatre consumes my days I try and spend the remaining time as far from the theatre as possible, so the world will not only remind me of the stage, and people will not only seem to me to be actors and actresses'.

Translator's Note

As the title suggests, the play has as an influence the English Medieval Mystery play *Everyman;* indeed, the playwright has actually interpolated passages from the original into his play. However, despite the explicit religious references to God and redemption, Heaven and Hell, and the presence of Death as a character, *Everywoman* should not be viewed as intrinsically Christian in its moral intention. The inclusion of these passages serves rather to stress, by contrast, the very secular existence that the protagonist, Emma, has in contemporary Budapest.

To fully understand the world of the play one must grasp two very specific features of Hungarian life: firstly, the chronic housing shortage and, secondly, the difficulties people have in making ends meet. The world of the play is one informed by a quiet desperation as individuals go to ludicrous lengths to secure a living. So we find Aranka, Emma's mother, sub-lets her daughter's bedroom whilst at the same time offers makeshift home tuition in whatever subject she can think of to whomever she can persuade to participate. Meanwhile Emma moonlights as a freelance estate agent brokering hair-brained tenancy deals for the destitute and dying.

If the play is not religious in the strictest sense of the word, it is nevertheless a spiritual play in so much as it begs the question: what am I doing with my life? And implicitly asks: why are our lives the way they are? In essence, the social fabric of life in Budapest causes Emma's spiritual crisis. Quite simply, she is so busy trying to earn a living she has no time to take stock of her life. It is only when she attempts to adjust to the knowledge that she may be terminally ill that Emma rather belatedly begins to put her affairs in order in readiness for her death.

Given the very specific social circumstances that pertain in this play, I have not tried to re-locate it. Names of people and places remain unanglicised. Whilst *Everywoman*'s themes are quite universal, it seems to me that the play's aesthetic is profoundly Hungarian and should be unequivocally set in Budapest. One liberty that has been taken has been to modernise slightly the excerpts from *Everyman*. This has been done for the sake of clarity. There has been no attempt to secularize these passages by removing references to Our Maker etc. It strikes me that these excerpts work as a bold theatrical device but should not be taken literally to mean that Emma is actually undergoing a pilgrim's journey towards redemption and forgiveness.

Characters in Order of Appearance

EMMA
MRS KOVESI
MR KOVESI
A GIRL WITH A SMALL BABY
A LADY
THE OLD WOMAN
DOCTOR
THE TUBERCULAR YOUTH
MAN/DEATH
A DRUNK
TOTH GYULA
ARANKA – Emma's Mother
TODOR
MARI – Emma's Friend
PETER – Emma's Ex-Husband
ERIKA – Peter's New Wife
VERA – Emma's Daughter
A POLICEMAN

NB. *The characters in this play may be doubled using 11 actors:
6 women and 5 men.*

ACT ONE

Scene One

A white wall separates the downstage area from the main stage.

The only set: a desk and a few chairs, downstage centre. At the outset, the house lights remain on. The audience should be admitted and left to wait. Nothing happens. A long silence.

Finally, EMMA, *a woman in her forties, overworked and dishevelled, enters hurriedly from the rear of the auditorium.*

EMMA (*to the audience*). Sorry, sorry, sorry, sorry, sorry! Good morning, everyone. Apologies for the delay but we can now get started. Here we are . . . Now, one at a time . . . Mrs Kovesi, would you like to step up, please?

MRS KOVESI (*standing up*). Come on, Kovesi, come on, love.

They make their way from their seats. EMMA *and the* OLD WOMAN *help the doddery* OLD MAN *up.* EMMA *sits them both down, then she sits down herself at the desk, takes out a pile of documents from the drawer and starts to go through them briskly, looking for something. She finds it . . .*

EMMA (*reading*). A basement flat in a period house on Mathias Hill – is that the one?

The OLD WOMAN *nods.*

(*Still reading.*) Two adjoining bedrooms, original features, including an antique heating system, north east facing. In need of some work . . .

MRS KOVESI. Well, I suppose some might say that . . .

EMMA. Available for viewing on Wednesday afternoons? Garden?

MRS KOVESI. Naturally.

EMMA (*writes this on the form, then looks at the audience.*). Now who did I have in mind for this?

GIRL WITH A BABY. You spoke to me about it . . .

EMMA (*to the* OLD WOMAN). And you'd have no problems about the baby?

MRS KOVESI. The baby? Of course not. A baby teaches you the importance of routine. And my husband is very particular about his routines. Come here, my dear . . .

The GIRL *goes up onto the stage.*

His begins at eight. Every morning. Straight to the table. He's always at his best in the mornings – so his newspapers must be ready for him very first thing . . .

GIRL. I see. (*The baby starts to whimper. The* GIRL *comforts it.*) I'm sorry about this.

MRS KOVESI. Don't mention it. For breakfast, he has milky coffee – but without sugar. He can have sugar in cookies or cakes but in his coffee . . .

GIRL. No sugar.

MRS KOVESI. No, never! We always have sweetener on the table, he can add that himself. I'll make a note of where you can get it; in fact, I'll tell the shopkeeper to expect you, my dear . . .

GIRL. Thank you.

MRS KOVESI. He likes a roll, toasted, with his coffee. But mind you don't ruin it . . .

GIRL. I know. You want them to have just that hint of colour . . . they shouldn't be either dried to a crisp but not too doughy either . . .

MRS KOVESI. Exactly.

GIRL. What shall I . . . (*The baby is now crying, she rocks it.*) What do you like him to have on his roll?

MRS KOVESI. Nothing. He dips it in his coffee . . . Sometimes he might have a spot of jam, if you think he needs a change . . . Is it hungry?

GIRL. Yeah.

MRS KOVESI. Well come on, do something then! Children should always come first. For lunch we usually have soup, hot soup with noodles or with dumplings. We never miss our soup.

The GIRL *nods her head. She is now breastfeeding the baby.*

Now, he takes a long walk before lunch. Five times round the flat. That's why we find it so useful to have the rooms adjoining each other. You have to follow him and count his laps. After the second one, he may well start to shout: 'Stop it Hannibal!'

The GIRL *nods her head.*

That means you are Hannibal chasing your elephant – 'Evil Hannibal!' – he will shout . . .

The GIRL *stares at her.*

But that's just his little joke.

The GIRL *gives a smile.*

Make sure he does all five laps. Don't upset him tho'. Chivy him gently, so that he won't lose his temper. He always ends up so breathless if he has to raise his voice . . .

The GIRL *is quietly breast-feeding the baby.* MRS KOVESI *sits watching her.*

See if you can't gently spur him on. First, you can try saying. 'Gee-up elephant, down to the Plains of Po' and then, when his five laps are finished, say: 'Hannibal ante portas'. On that, he will collapse into the armchair, and on 'veni, vidi, vici' – you'll see him groan and close his eyes. But don't let that worry you, he always does that.

GIRL. I understand.

Silence.

EMMA (*to* MRS KOVESI). So, what do you think?

Silence.

MRS KOVESI (*she eyes up the* GIRL). She'll do.

EMMA (*to the* GIRL). Well, when can you move in?

The GIRL *looks at* MRS KOVESI.

When would you like her to start?

MRS KOVESI. How should I know? God above might know but I'm sure I have no idea when it might happen.

EMMA. I don't understand. What's the problem? Why can't we simply fix a date?

MR KOVESI (*tearfully*). Marishka! Marishka!

MRS KOVESI. It's alright, honey, I haven't gone yet. Don't worry . . .

MR KOVESI. Marishka! Marishka!

MRS KOVESI. Don't cry, Hannibal. You never know, I might never have to leave you.

GIRL. I thought you said I'd do, Ma'am?

EMMA. Would you like to see someone else, Mrs Kovesi?

MRS KOVESI. Oh no, you'll do just fine, my dear. You are exactly what I wanted . . .

EMMA. Good. Then, perhaps we could agree on an approximate start date. I'll need to have put something down here in my records . . .

MRS KOVESI. I'm sorry, but you want me to be able to tell you when exactly I'm going to die?

GIRL (*quietly*). I don't want anyone to die . . .

MRS KOVESI. Nor, may I assure you, do I!

EMMA. You've completely misunderstood me. I just wanted to know when the girl could move in ...

MRS KOVESI. Move in where?

EMMA. To your flat ...

MRS KOVESI. You can't possibly think that I am going to let a stranger into my flat.

EMMA. But Mrs Kovesi ...

MRS KOVESI. I was offering the property on an understanding: I need to feel sure that there will be somebody who will look after my man, my little Hannibal, when I am gone, someone who will want to have him buried decently. I think that's a reasonable offer ...

EMMA. Yes, but ...

MRS KOVESI. We all know there are those who'd expect an annual allowance paid to them until they died, whereas I am offering to let her have the house for free. In effect, she's to have a very generous tip – all the rent she'll never be asked to pay – because I want her to remember me with gratitude. That way, when I can no longer be here to look after him, she will treat him well after I'm gone.

GIRL. And where am I going to live until then?

MRS KOVESI. I really don't think that's my problem, my dear.

The GIRL *stands up.*

But do come and visit me sometime and bring that enchanting baby of yours, too. I can show you round the flat. We could have such a nice little chat ...

GIRL. But we have to have somewhere to stay! Emma, please! Where's my child to sleep?

MRS KOVESI. You should get yourself a home before you get yourself pregnant.

GIRL. Oh, drop dead!

MRS KOVESI. You what?

GIRL. You bastard!

EMMA. Alright, alright, just wait a moment. We're bound to find someone interested in your offer ...

She gestures to the GIRL *to return to her seat, but the* GIRL *doesn't budge, she just stands there.*

So, to re-cap. we have a basement flat, perfectly situated in the Buda green belt. A highly desirable residence that already comes with its very own kind old gentleman in situ, and it has a whole eighty-eight square ...

MRS KOVESI (*interrupting her*). No, no! It's my husband that is 88. The flat is 78 square metres . . .

EMMA. So, ten metres here, ten years there . . . would you know the difference, Mr Kovesi, eh?

OLD WOMAN (*stands up, with great difficulty*). I'll take it . . .

EMMA. Thank you, but, no . . . So is there really nobody prepared to take care of this old man after this nice lady's death?

OLD WOMAN. I said, I can do it . . . I'm a qualified nurse . . .

Silence.

MRS KOVESI. Sometimes, out of the blue, everything will just go black . . . then I think: that's it, I'm done for! But what do I know? It could be my heart or could be my nerves? How am I to be sure . . . ?

Silence.

EMMA. I think we'd best move on, shall we?

Silence – except for the OLD WOMAN *muttering to herself.*

MRS KOVESI. Come on, you!

She helps the OLD MAN *to his feet. She leads him to the stairs, then, to someone in the audience sitting in the front row.*

Can you help me, young man?

Together, they help the OLD MAN *off the stage.*

(*To the* HELPER.) Thank you, God bless you . . .

Silence as the old couple slowly passes through the rows of seats and leaves the auditorium by the door at the rear.

EMMA. Mrs Kovesi! Mr Kovesi! Goodbye. (*Pause.*) O.K., do we have any other town properties available for consideration?

LADY (*nods her head*). Yes, my end of balcony flat. Here you are.

She goes up onto the stage and puts a large pile of documents in front of EMMA.

EMMA. You don't want a live-in carer as well, do you?

LADY. Heavens, no! This is a property for sale with me as a sitting tenant . . . but it's not available for occupation until after my death . . . Take a look. I've had an examination done. Here are the results.

EMMA. Oh, excellent. You've had the flat surveyed and valued already . . .

LADY. Goodness, no. I always think flats are like kisses. I mean, how can you put a price on one that you like? After all, there are some flats, perfectly nice and clean, very attractive even, but they leave you cold, unkissed . . . No, it's my life expectancy I've had assessed. There as you see, is the hospital's stamp with Professor Peterfy's own signature . . .

EMMA. Oh yes, I see . . .

LADY. And believe me, I'm not selling anyone a pig in a poke here. I do have a slight congestive liver condition, coronary artery problems, inflated colon – I might live another ten or twelve years. Unfortunately, they can't be more precise in their estimation, given the pathetic clinical instruments we have here in Hungary . . . I want three and a half million for the flat, take it or leave it. But I'd also like to rent my flat for the 10 -12 years I have left, so I suggest we deduct that amount from the price. I'm willing to pay a hundred thousand a year for my flat, which means for those ten to twelve years that's a million or a million two hundred thousand. Now let's take the average and deduct that from the price, that makes three million five hundred thousand minus one million one hundred thousand – that makes two point four million: so that's the price I want for my flat. And it's a first rate one, if I say so myself. Smack in the centre of town – a real bargain.

EMMA (*takes a deep breath*). There you have it, ladies and gentlemen . . .

LADY. I would recommend it to young couples particularly: in ten to twelve years, just as the kids are growing up they'll have a nice, big, empty property to move into . . .

EMMA. I think someone, over there . . .

DOCTOR (*stands up*). When is it available for viewing?

LADY. When? Here . . . (*She points to the table.*) It's all on the table for anyone to see . . .

DOCTOR. Not that . . .

EMMA. Do come forward.

DOCTOR. Thank you.

He makes his way out of his seat, carrying a big suitcase.

EMMA. I think this gentleman would like to see the flat first . . .

LADY. He can come at the weekend.

DOCTOR (*reaches the stage*). Not before?

LADY. When, did you have in mind?

DOCTOR. Well, today?

LADY. When exactly?

DOCTOR. Tonight, perhaps.

LADY. I'm sorry, I'm not interested.

EMMA. Why ever not?

LADY. Well you can always spot a serious purchaser, people who know what they want but still need some time to think things over – and then there are the time-wasters, people who are really only looking to see a lady home . . .

EMMA; You don't just want to see the lady home, do you?

LADY. Thank you, but I've said I'm not interested.

EMMA. As you like, tho' perhaps it's best to think things over. (*To the* LADY.) Would you like to go back to your seat then, please? (*To the* DOCTOR.) I am very sorry . . . (*She looks into the documents.*) Is the young man from the Institute here?

A very slim boy stands up, coughing as if he has tuberculosis.

Ah, there you are. Can you come up?

The boy makes his way out of his seat.

LADY. Oh no! Don't move! Stay where you are. I'm not finished yet.

EMMA. I don't understand. Didn't you just say that . . .

LADY. My dear, all I want is a firm offer from a serious buyer . . . If someone would just put the money down on this table, I'd sign immediately, provided a detailed contract could be properly drawn up. (*The* DOCTOR *murmurs something to himself.*)

EMMA. Pardon?

DOCTOR. Right, so you'd like to see the money here on this table?

EMMA. I think we were speaking metaphorically . . .

DOCTOR. I see. So what would you like to see put here, metaphorically speaking?

EMMA. Are you really interested in the flat?

DOCTOR. I would rather have a look first.

LADY. I receive viewers at the weekend only.

DOCTOR. That's too late.

EMMA. I'm sorry.

DOCTOR. Then at least tell me a little about what it looks like . . .

EMMA. Could we make a rough sketch for the gentleman?

LADY (*drawing*). There's the front door, here's the pantry, that's a corridor. A bedroom. Another bedroom . . .

DOCTOR. Very good. How much did you say?

LADY. I haven't drawn the kitchen yet . . .

DOCTOR. It must be next to the pantry. (*He points his finger.*) Or opposite . . .

LADY. Exactly.

DOCTOR. Beautiful, very stylish. An excellent layout . . . how much is it then?

EMMA. We said two million four hundred thousand, didn't we?

LADY. Precisely.

The DOCTOR puts his suitcase down and opens it. He lifts out sundry belongings: his pyjamas, toothbrush, coathanger, camera, dish. He then begins to take out bundles of money and piles them on the table. Silence as they start to count the millions . . .

MAN (*in one of the back rows*). Excuse me, Madam!

EMMA. Who, me?

MAN. No, the other one. Yes, you! Tell me, what do you want to do with all that money?

LADY. It's none of your business. Believe me, I won't need any help spending it. I'll do this and that. I'll live a little. Travel perhaps.

MAN. Travel where?

LADY. To begin with? . . . I don't know, maybe Malta. Then we'll see.

MAN. What if the plane crashes?

LADY. There'll always be the unforeseen to contend with.

MAN. Do you have a family?

The LADY takes the first million in her hand and starts to count. From now on, she is counting the money . . .

I asked you a question.

LADY. That doesn't mean I have to answer, does it?

Silence.

I live alone, if that's you mean . . . Well, what?

MAN. Any heirs?

LADY. If I sell the flat there'll be no inheritance, so there'll obviously be no heirs. I would have thought that was perfectly apparent to anyone, wouldn't you?

MAN. Put it another way: do you have any loved ones?

Silence.

LADY (*quietly*). No, I don't.

MAN. And what if in ten or twelve years' time, when you're lying there on your last bed . . . and through that final enshrouding mist you see them, all those whose existence you've today denied, and they're leaning over you with their eyes full of tears, smoothing the pillows under your head, moistening your dry lips . . .

LADY. It's too late for all that now. Far too late. (*To the* MAN.) What are you staring at?

MAN. Ingrates were they? Is that it? They all left you, didn't they?

LADY. Yes, they did, if you must know. Just like that. But they still feel like a millstone round my neck. I don't have a single day to myself. They just dump their kids on me and go off out to the cinema. If they borrow my iron, I can whistle for it. I want to just be for a little while: walk about, laugh, flirt. I want to live a little for a change!

MAN. You will only live a little on two and half million.

LADY. Well, it's enough not to worry . . .

MAN. And what then?

LADY. Then nothing.

MAN. Then there you are, all alone, without two sous . . .

LADY. Then there I am, all alone, without two sous . . .

MAN (*he steps onto the stage – he is wearing a black hat, and uses a walking stick*). Looking at you a little more closely, I can't help but admire those professors . . .

LADY. Why?

MAN (*looking at her very closely*). Not a sign, not the slightest little sign, not a wrinkle, not a missing hair, not the smallest tic even, nothing . . .

LADY. Just take a look at my liver . . . (*She points her finger at the medical reports.*)

MAN. I'd rather look at that vibrant face, those fiercesome eyes. But, of course, you're right. How many times have we seen it happen . . .

LADY. What happen?

MAN. That a pretty woman, a woman oozing joi de vivre, is – without warning – blown a kiss by death . . . and in an instant that beautiful head hangs listless and lifeless. But I think you could be the kind that death does shun, as keenly as a tiger does dead meat . . .

LADY. And how would you know that? Are you a doctor?

MAN. Not exactly . . .

LADY. What are you? A gynaecologist?

MAN (*laughing*). You're getting warm . . .

DOCTOR (*he has finished counting the millions*). Do you have a bag?

The LADY *looks at her small handbag* . . .

EMMA. Let's see if we can find something, shall we? (*She jumps to her feet.*)

MAN. Not so fast . . .

The MAN *grabs* EMMA *by the wrist – a frisson ripples across the room – he looks at* EMMA's *palm, strokes it, then very gently releases it.* EMMA *runs out. The* MAN *lifts the medical documents from the table.*

How much did you say you wanted for the flat?

LADY. I'm not interested in haggling.

MAN. Neither am I. So?

LADY. Two point four. Two point four, and that's it.

MAN (*takes a note book out of his waistcoat pocket, looks into it*). Didn't you say three and a half?

LADY (*nods her head*). Minus the rent, which for ten to twelve years is one million one hundred thousand . . .

EMMA (*returns with a shopping bag*). Here it is. We found one.

MAN. Ten, maybe twelve years, how long is that? No sooner has it begun ticking away – no sooner have you started to really live again – and it's over – as brief as any honeymoon . . . (*He tears the medical documents into little pieces and throws them up in the air.*)

LADY. What do you think you're doing?

MAN. What do you think you're doing? Why for a mere ten or twelve extra years would you even contemplate exchanging your chic metropolitan apartment?

LADY. Did I mention it gets the sun?

MAN. And in return you'd accept some half-life, a shadow of your former existence for so little! What if I were to make you an offer. What if I said I'll buy your flat for the princely sum of . . . nothing, but promised you could live for another thirty-five years. Thirty-five long years on the sunny side of life in your sun-trap flat. How does that sound?

DOCTOR. We've got a bag . . . (*He waves the bag.*)

Silence.

The LADY *looks at the mountain of money on the table, then at the* MAN, *then at the money . . . It is a struggle.*

LADY (*quietly*). Yes. I think that's a very good offer . . . (*To the* MAN.) I'll take you.

EMMA. Sold! To herself! The Lady's own balcony flat. (*A beat.*) And that will be a thousand for the agency commission.

LADY (*handing over the money to* EMMA). Of course, my dear . . .

EMMA. Thank you. And Congratulations! (*To the* DOCTOR.) There's nothing to pay, after all.

DOCTOR. Oh, damn! . . . To hell with all this . . .

EMMA. Don't worry, we'll find you something . . . we find something for everyone . . .

She resumes going through the papers again.

GIRL. And what about me? Who is going to take me home? Tell me, where am I going to sleep tonight?

DRUNKEN VOICE. Hey, sweetheart! I'll take you home for four thousand. I've a lovely little room for you, darling.

GIRL. Stand up.

The DRUNKEN MAN *stands up, reeling.*

GIRL. Do I get to go and come as I please?

DRUNK. Come as you please? I'll see you do! Front and back! Every which way!

GIRL. What?

DRUNK. Only joking. (*Laughing.*) 'Scuse me.

GIRL. Four thousand?

DRUNK. Four. (*A beat.*) But no kid.

GIRL. What do you mean?

DRUNK. I mean four. Plus we share the bills.

GIRL. Five – with the kid.

DRUNK. I don't want the kid. The kid is out.

GIRL. Five and a half . . . and the kid stays.

DRUNK. Don't haggle with me. You'll only make me angry.

GIRL. Six thousand.

DRUNK. Do you really need that kid?

GIRL. Six and a half.

DRUNK. Done! . . . But the kid goes.

Silence.

GIRL. Yeah, you're right, what good's the kid to me, anyway?

She screams and throws the baby up in the air.

Darkness. A heart rending child's cry, issuing from an enormous, unearthly throat. The actors are lit, casting shadows on the white wall, as if on an ancient baroque relief. The MAN *kneels down, takes his hat off and as he does so, he rips his face off, to reveal himself as the figure of* DEATH.

DEATH. Lord, I will move over every inch of this earth
    And I will search out each one of you,
    And I will set upon those who live like beasts;
    Beyond God's laws and dread not his wrath.
    You that love riches, I will cut down.
    You that hunt beauty I will blind.
    Cold earth shall be your only friend
    Hell shall be your bed.

EMMA takes a few steps, doubles up with pain, breathes heavily, holds her stomach tightly.

See there how Everywoman walks.
An inkling whispers I come for her
Yet still she dwells on flesh and coin
But soon it's time to stand before
Our Lord, the King of Heaven.

Silence. Only EMMA's heavy breathing is heard.

Woman, be still! Where are you going?
So happy? Have you forgotten your maker?

EMMA. Is it me you've called?

DEATH. Yes, I have something for you:
    I am sent to you post haste,
    From God, in all his majesty.

EMMA. What, sent to me?

DEATH. Yes, most certainly.
    Though you may have forgotten him,
    He, in his heaven, thinks of you!

EMMA. What desires God of me?

Silence.

So you've come. Yes, I've had you on my mind!
It lies in your power to save me;
If you are kind to me, I could be kind to you.
I could give you money, a thousand . . .

She holds out the money she was given earlier by the LADY.

Silence.

EMMA (*searching through her purse*). Two!

Silence.

EMMA. Look! (*Emptying her pockets.*) Three thousand and sixty-two fifty!

DEATH. Put away your money.
    No one will I save:
    But to their heart suddenly will I strike.

EMMA. Come on, strike! What are you waiting for? Strike then! Strike! (EMMA *collapses*.)

A figure appears, leaning over EMMA. *It is the* DOCTOR. *A hypodermic needle glistens in the dark.* EMMA *cries out.*

DOCTOR. It's alright, relax. Don't be frightened. Hold onto my arm. That's it. It didn't hurt, did it? Who's Vera?

EMMA. Vera . . . she's my daughter.

DOCTOR. Should we call her?

EMMA. Oh no! For Christ's sake, please don't!

DOCTOR. All right.

EMMA. Was I calling out for Vera?

DOCTOR. Can you stand up? Hang on to me, there's no rush, take your time, that's it . . . gently does it . . .

EMMA. Who are you? Leave me alone. What do you want?

DOCTOR. One step . . . slowly does it . . . It's O.K., I've a hold of you.

EMMA. Where are we going?

DOCTOR. Keep moving . . . relax . . . You'll soon be feeling better.

The two figures, clinging together, move slowly away.

DEATH. I thought you were gone to meet your maker,
Your excuses to offer in his presence.
But you are still, I see, on that cruel journey,
A path from which there is no turning.
And though you cannot see it
You carry with you your book of stains
From which you'll make your reckoning.
For all of your bad deeds, and your few good,
You will have to answer before the Lord of Paradise.

(*A beat.*) Next one, please.

He sits down to the table. With his hollowed eye sockets, he surveys the audience, as if awaiting his next customer.

Act One, Scene Two

The rear wall is removed to reveal: an X-ray room. Intermittent neon lights flash blindingly. The DOCTOR *is now wearing a white coat.* EMMA *lies on a trolley bed.*

DOCTOR. Name?

EMMA. Oh, anybody.

DOCTOR. Address?

EMMA. Put down Thirty-three Isabella Street.

DOCTOR. What do you mean, anybody?

EMMA. Oh, write whatever name you want. I won't be on any of your records. I haven't paid any health insurance. So you can call me whatever you like . . .

DOCTOR. Alright. Let me think . . . I know . . . Roza Kovatsh . . . (*Pause, then realising.*) Oh, no . . . perhaps not her . . . Ilona . . . Ilona Kovatsh – does that sound O.K.?

EMMA. Perfect.

DOCTOR (*writes it down*). I hope this won't lead to complications.

EMMA. It won't for you.

DOCTOR. We usually ask for some kind of identification . . .

EMMA. Say that I've lost it.

DOCTOR. So, how long have you had these symptoms?

EMMA. Well . . . I've never collapsed before . . . that is, I haven't had to be picked up off the street . . .

DOCTOR. When did they first start?

Silence.

A month ago?

EMMA. More or less.

DOCTOR. How long exactly? Two months? Three?

EMMA. O.K., say three.

DOCTOR. Three. (*Writes it down.*) Have you ever had any need for an operation in the abdominal region?

EMMA. Not up until now . . .

DOCTOR. Or been internally examined?

EMMA. What kind of a girl do you think I am?

DOCTOR. I meant an X-ray?

EMMA. I'm not that easily seen through!

The DOCTOR looks at her. A beat.

EMMA. No, I can't remember anyone giving me that kind of treatment, ever trying to look inside me.

DOCTOR (*goes to her*). Where can you feel it? Does it hurt anywhere in particular. What does it feel like exactly?

EMMA. I don't know.

DOCTOR. You don't know?

EMMA. It burns. I drink a glass of milk and it goes away.

DOCTOR. So, if you take milk it goes away . . .

EMMA. No. But sooner or later it does. Well, it always has done, so far . . .

DOCTOR. Any nausea?

EMMA. Yes.

DOCTOR. Do you feel bloated?

EMMA. Awfully.

DOCTOR. Any constipation or diarrhoea?

EMMA. Not really.

DOCTOR. How's your appetite?

EMMA. Appetite! I don't have one.

DOCTOR. Then how do you eat?

EMMA. I chew then I swallow.

DOCTOR. How regularly would you eat . . . I mean, how many times a day . . . ?

EMMA. When I get round to it. Particularly if I'm on edge. I tend to just grab something. Look, I eat. O.K.? Why, when do you eat?

DOCTOR (*completing form*). Eats irregularly . . .

EMMA. Well, I am on edge quite irregularly. Although of late, I'm managing to be on edge on a more regular basis.

DOCTOR. Do you work a lot?

EMMA. As much as you.

DOCTOR. Wouldn't you say you overdo it a little?

EMMA. Of course I do.

DOCTOR. Do you like your job?

EMMA. Do you like yours?

DOCTOR. What do you do about relaxation, fun, recreation . . .

EMMA. It's hardly top of the agenda . . .

DOCTOR. You should try and switch off more often . . .

EMMA. I know. But whenever I switch off I become so nervy that I spend all day eating only to throw up, and my stomach it just burns, burns, burns. I would almost say it is unbearable if . . .

DOCTOR. If?

EMMA. If I wasn't able to bear it. (*She gives a smile.*)

DOCTOR. Why didn't you go see a doctor? Is there no one around to tell you should. No one to scold you if you don't go?

Silence.

Why don't you look after yourself?

EMMA. I'm too busy. Anyway, I thought that was God's job.

DOCTOR. Have you lost any weight?

EMMA. Quite the reverse.

DOCTOR. How much exactly?

EMMA. A lot.

DOCTOR. In kilos?

EMMA. I don't watch my weight.

DOCTOR. Impossible . . . (*Tense.*) There isn't a woman in the world that doesn't step on a set of scales now and again. There just isn't . . .

EMMA. Well, here's one.

DOCTOR. What shall I put down? Ten kilos?

EMMA. Alright.

DOCTOR. Undress, please.

EMMA. Why? Don't you believe me? (*She starts to take her clothes off.*)

DOCTOR. Not here . . . can you get up? (*He helps* EMMA *down from the bed.*)

The DOCTOR *opens a door leading to a dark dressing room. A man,* TOTH GYULA, *wearing only his underpants, jumps up. He is unbelievably thin, his ribs show and his Adam's apple moves up and down . . .*

Come in, please, that's it, come straight through. (*He puts his lead apron on.*)

TOTH GYULA *passes by* EMMA – *for a moment, they gaze into each other's eyes – they could be Adam and Eve met once more, this time in an X-ray room . . . The* DOCTOR *closes the door after* EMMA.

(*To* TOTH GYULA.) Have you ever had gypsum before? You have? Oh, good. Well, we can always add something to it. There's vanilla, that's very popular. But it's not really that unpleasant. We've even been known to try it ourselves from time to time . . . perhaps you'd prefer it neat . . . (*Hands him the glass.*) Stand there, if you will . . . (*He helps* TOTH GYULA *into the X-Ray machine.* EMMA *opens the door.*)

Now, when I say so, take a gulp. I may have to make a few adjustments. I might even have to turn you upside down. You won't mind standing on your head, will you?

The DOCTOR *switches the machine on and the lights off – on the screen we can see the outline of his spine, his ribs, his pumping heart.*

Don't move! Now, deep breath!

EMMA. I don't understand. How can someone get to be so condescending?

DOCTOR. That's it. Now take a spoonful in your mouth, don't swallow it immediately – chew it for a moment . . .

EMMA. You get to look into this poor creature's stomach – there, where, by rights, only God should be able to see – only God and now you. You peer right in, thanks to your bloody machines! Is that what gives you the right to make these, stupid tasteless jokes?

DOCTOR. Now gently does it, you can swallow now, good . . . another gulp . . . (*To* EMMA.) Actually, it gives only an impression of it . . .

EMMA. I beg your pardon?

DOCTOR. Unfortunately, it's not his stomach as such . . . only a representation of the stomach-wall, a relief, as it were . . . Can you go and take your clothes off . . .

EMMA. Ugh! What is that horrible splashing there? (*She points to the spuming on screen.*)

DOCTOR. That's his diaphragm, my dear . . . (*To* TOTH GYULA.) Swallow some more, come on. (*To* EMMA.) Watch, that's it trickling down. There's his gullet . . . Then we agitate it until we've completely lined the stomach wall, and then any nasty little lesions will all show up . . .

The figure on the screen moves – EMMA *steps back frightened.*

Stand still! Swallow some more! Come on, now! Chin up!

EMMA. Listen, patients ask you all the time, don't they? Don't say they don't.

DOCTOR. Now, turn round! To the right!

EMMA; They beg you to tell them the truth, the whole truth and nothing but the truth, even if it drives them crazy, don't they?

DOCTOR (*to* TOTH). Try not to retch – swallow! Swallow it back!

EMMA. And what do you do? Do you lie to their face and leave truth to come as a nasty surprise?

DOCTOR. Will you undress please. Do hurry up. I don't see what you
want . . .

EMMA. Look doctor, even when I was expecting with my daughter,
even then I was always running here and there, always rushing
about like a blue-arsed fly – but, then again, I suppose, who
doesn't.

DOCTOR (*to* TOTH). A half turn to the left . . . not that much . . . a
half turn!

EMMA. When my time had come, all the warning bells rang for me
and I knew I was finally due – How I love that expression!

DOCTOR. Half turn to the right . . .

EMMA. But somehow I couldn't . . . take it in . . . couldn't quite feel
that a whole new life was forming inside me. And again, now, I
know but still find it so very hard to grasp that this . . . that there's
something (*She points at the skeleton on screen.*) again kicking
inside, growing inside my body.

DOCTOR. On your stomach . . . to the right . . .

EMMA. In the end I nearly gave birth on a river boat. In those days I
worked as a tourist guide – with my stomach out like this! It could
very well be that the Korean group's most enduring memory of the
Danube will be my water's bursting. The whole group came with
me to the hospital. Imagine the midwife's face as she brought out
the new born baby to thirty cheering little Koreans, every one
identical in their steel rim glasses and their executive suits. Good
thing I didn't give birth on the boat. My God! I just don't want to
be unprepared again. I suppose, if a brick lands on your head, or
you're hit by a truck, then there's no 'I must just pop into the
launderette first'. No, those dirty clothes stay dirty forever. But for
anyone to be lying in a hospital waiting to die and to be worrying
about things like: the plumber hasn't called, the bath is blocked,
my daughter's Sunday best is still in the laundry . . . Can you see
what I'm saying?

DOCTOR. Just take off your clothes.

EMMA. I want an honest answer! I don't mind going to hospital if it's
really worth it . . .

DOCTOR. That's very good of you.

EMMA. But I won't go for the sake of it, just because there's nobody
who'll tell me to my face – I don't have the patience for that, my
dear Doctor. To be quite frank, I don't have the time or the money.

DOCTOR. Well, there are certain attractions to a spell in hospital –
but there's no need for us to dissect them here . . .

EMMA. But I want you to dissect them. Try to convince me.

DOCTOR. Look . . . illness is a very complicated business, so I do understand your anxiety but that distress can be alleviated. Whether it's peace with God, a relaxed state of mind, an acceptance of reality or some other psychological readiness, whatever it is that calms you – perhaps, simply a supportive home atmosphere . . . all of these things can have a very positive influence on the process. But . . . But you also have to agree there is another side to all this.

EMMA. Such as?

DOCTOR. Tell me, why should a patient, some poor defenceless creature who's dying, why would he want to do without the services of a well-equipped hospital? After all, that's why they are there. Why not use them as long as you are alive?

EMMA. You mean, why miss the opportunity of being cut up and hacked about?

DOCTOR. It's there. Free of charge. The health service has budgetted for you.

EMMA. How very thrilling. I've never been a budget item before. But it comes to us all eventually, I suppose.

DOCTOR. There's no need to be tasteless . . .

EMMA. Like your gypsum stuff, you mean . . .

DOCTOR. Are you willing to undress or not?

EMMA. I should be grateful to you really. I was sinking and you reached down for me . . . You were good enough to lift me out of the mire – why?

DOCTOR. That's my job . . .

EMMA. Does that mean you'll be good enough to tell me to my face?

DOCTOR. What?

EMMA. If I'm finished. That it's all over; that I'm for the knackers' yard. Destination: six feet under!

DOCTOR. Such a delightful turn of phrase!

EMMA. Well you can tell me in Latin then, if you'd prefer.

DOCTOR. And if I did? That doesn't mean you'll definitely die . . . I'm not God, you know.

EMMA. So? What can you say then?

DOCTOR. Only what my expertise deems to be true.

EMMA. And where does that leave your humanity in the meantime? Locked in your suitcase? (*She lifts the* DOCTOR's *suitcase.*)

DOCTOR. Put that down!

EMMA. Why? What's in the bag? The sum of your compassion!

DOCTOR. Put that down! Do you hear me?

EMMA. See you, old chap . . . (*She waves goodbye to the skeleton on the screen – hurries out with the suitcase.*)

DOCTOR (*frightened*). Wait! What are you doing?

EMMA. Come on, I'll show you something . . . an apartment . . . It'd suit you down to the ground . . . (*She runs out.*)

DOCTOR. Wait, Come back! Wait for meee! (*Runs after her.*)

A moment of eerie, echoing silence. In the steel-coloured penumbra, the figure on the screen moves, TOTH GYULA, *like some uncomprehending ancient, looks out from the X-ray machine.*

Act One, Scene Three

Darkness.

The sound of a key in a lock. Two figures enter. They are moving about in the dark . . .

EMMA. No, noooo! I don't believe it! Seventeen long years I've had to put up with this flat, and I still can't find the bloody switch.

DOCTOR. Is this where you live then?

EMMA. God, no! But where . . . where's it gone . . . help me . . . Perhaps there isn't a switch after all. Who knows, maybe I've been living in the dark for all these years and never ever noticed.

A horrible bang – something has fallen down.

DOCTOR. I'm so sorry . . .

EMMA. It's alright . . . The old dear is a bit deaf, but that's quite handy. It really is. Here it can sometimes feel like you're the only one left in all the world. You can take a bath at any time, day or night, listen to the radio or even scream and shout all night long if you want to. (*A beat.*) Can you hear something?

From somewhere else in the flat, from behind a door, French children's songs can be heard.

EMMA. What can she be thinking of? French, French – that must be her latest fad. Does she think she can speak French now? What my poor Dad had to put up with . . .

Lights up – The DOCTOR *has found the switch.*

You see, it's like you've lived here all your life. That's a good sign . . .

DOCTOR (*looks round horrified*). Hmm . . . what is this? A store-room?

EMMA (*nods her head*). A closet. And a hallway. And a corridor, as well. I like to think of it as multi-functional, three uses in one, as it were . . .

DOCTOR (*looking around*). So this leads to the bathroom . . . and this to the bedrooms . . .

EMMA. Precisely!

DOCTOR. It's comfortable enough as hallways go, quite roomy even . . .

EMMA. Big enough not to be always bumping into one other, I like to think. And then there's the bench which I just love. It's a favourite of mine. Try it . . .

DOCTOR (*sits down*). It's . . . nice.

EMMA. It is, isn't it? Though it's made of a hard wood. (*Sits down next to the* DOCTOR.) But somehow it's so well made . . . Traditional furniture has a history, don't you think . . . Just lean back against it . . .

The DOCTOR *leans back against it. Silence. They sit on the bench.* EMMA *nervously lights up a cigarette.*

DOCTOR. Look . . . why exactly do you want to die?

EMMA (*looks at him*). Is that what you think I want . . . ?

Silence.

Would I, if I really wanted?

DOCTOR. Of course.

EMMA. As if I could really want to . . . give up life. You don't just give up life. It's not something you stub out like you would a cigarette.

DOCTOR. Tell me what you like most: the thing you like best of all.

Silence.

EMMA. Ice cream. Pistachio, nocciola, fragola . . .

DOCTOR. Seriously . . .

EMMA. Seriously, I love it. Really. It will be difficult to give that up . . . And this. I like to sit down like this . . . to light up over a coffee or with a man . . . that's when the whole world becomes so clear . . . And yes, that too, the other thing, the thing you're thinking about right now . . . Yes, those moments of utter naked abandonment, when you found yourself crying and moaning and clinging to a man's neck as if it was life itself, I used to like all that – well, as far as I can remember, I liked it. What must it be like to really live a little?

DOCTOR (*he shrugs his shoulders*). Nothing special. Sometimes shit.

EMMA. Maybe so. Still, to live, to be alive – that must be what I'll miss most. Though, it's not as if it was that good to me . . . Perhaps life's like nicotine, your body just gets used to it. So you only miss it when you cut it out . . . After all, what does it really do: it makes us sick, makes us fat, it burns like acid in our stomach, generally it just mistreats us – in fact, I think life should carry a government health warning . . . No . . . when I think about it, I ought not to mind my death coming at all. But, all the same, somehow it does hurt, it tears at my insides, something will die with me . . .

DOCTOR. What?

EMMA. Well, that's it . . . If only I knew . . . If only I knew, I might have the strength to fight . . . Something . . . what life might have been . . . is clutching at me, holding on to me, and I'm like some sad one-legged dog, dragging it to the grave . . .

Silence.

Do you know what I mean?

DOCTOR. Of course.

EMMA. Because it'll be far too late to discuss it up there. Only down here on Earth could dying be such an awful business . . .

DOCTOR. Well, I'm sure it's no easier for Martians!

EMMA. Or on Venus! And it's probably even worse on the corner of Rumbach Sebastian Street . . . where they've lost so many to so many other heavens!

DOCTOR. Don't dwell on it. Simply strip off and take the test.

EMMA *takes her jumper off.*

I don't mean now! Tomorrow morning at eight. And remember: don't eat beforehand!

EMMA. Tomorrow then . . . (*She gestures resignedly.*)

DOCTOR. What's there to face but stepping into one of my blasted X-Ray machines?

EMMA. And if I do? Will you tell me my results to my face?

DOCTOR. Of course.

EMMA. And can I believe them?

DOCTOR. Oh, you'll believe them alright. Unless they leave you needing to clutch at straws. Then, like everyone else, you too 'll reach out for them, desperate.

EMMA. You know I feel sorry for you.

The DOCTOR *murmurs something to himself.*

Call this a profession? How can you bear to do this job?

DOCTOR (*nods*). It's a living. Well, for me it is!

EMMA. Everyone nags you, torments you, damns you to hell a thousand times – they give you abuse, when it's God's face that needs slapping . . . As if you weren't a person just like them.

DOCTOR. Good of you to notice.

EMMA. With your pathetic looking goggles and your protective apron, and with your battered old suitcase . . . That suitcase. Thereby hangs a tale, I bet . . .

DOCTOR. I couldn't begin to explain . . .

EMMA (*indicating the suitcase*). What is that anyway: the end of one chapter, or the start of a new one?

DOCTOR (*stands up and opening a door looks into a room*). Lovely tiling . . .

EMMA. Do you really think so? We had hoped to change them . . . but we never quite got round to it . . . Now that you say it, though . . . you're right, really lovely. Come on through to the lounge. Do, please.

She opens a door, ushering the DOCTOR in first. He enters the semi-darkness and screams in horror. Deafeningly loud French children's songs can be heard. Beneath a red lampshade is an unkempt, grey-haired woman. Lying at her feet on the floor are people all wearing black eye shades.

ARANKA (*switches off the tape recorder*). Thank you darlings. That's all for today. (*Claps her hands.*) Up you get, come on! We'll make up for it tomorrow. Thank you all for now.

The people get up muttering complaint.

C'mon, chop chop! Leave the eye shades there on the table, please. Not like yesterday . . . Karol, dear, it's your turn tomorrow. So will you choose a discussion topic? Au revoir, ma classe. A bientôt, mes chéries!

STUDENTS. Au revoir, madame . . .

ARANKA. Au revoir . . . (*To* EMMA.) Well done, you've ruined that now, haven't you?

One man remains lying on the floor. Concerned, EMMA *leans over him.*

It's O.K., don't bother about him . . .

EMMA. What's going on here, Mum?

ARANKA (*she collects the dictionaries and throws them into a corner*). Well what do you think of it. My Learn and Lounge Language School. It's the latest thing: a six week intensive course in French as well as in relaxation technique. I call it my Karma Crammer.

EMMA. Well, it seems to be pretty exhausting . . . (*Looking at the man on the floor.*)

ARANKA. Leave him to me, my dear . . .

DOCTOR (*to* EMMA *whispering*). She doesn't appear to be deaf . . .

EMMA. Sorry?

ARANKA. Of course I am not deaf, my friend. Emma so nice of you to have introduced me to Mr . . . Do sit down, please. Fancy a beer?

EMMA. Beer! Since when did you drink beer, Mother?

ARANKA (*to the* DOCTOR). Make yourself comfortable . . . (*Pushes him onto a chair and opens the beer bottle on the door-post.*) Emma, you can't have any. You already have a beer-gut as bad as poor old Vilmos. You'll probably end up looking just like him. Well, bottoms up . . . (*Drinks from the bottle then passes it to the* DOCTOR. *He looks down. Beneath his chair the* OLD MAN *lies stretched out.*)

(*Looking down too.*) A hopeless case. French nanny, French kinder-garten, French grandmother. His whole life he was immersed. he grew up listening to the beautiful, soothing tones of the French language. So, it's not surprising that he developed this Pavlovian response: whenever he hears a French word, he curls up like a dog and his eyelids close . . .

EMMA. Why a dog?

ARANKA. Don't ask me, ask a vet . . . Do French dogs sleep more than others? Todor suffers from insomnia. You know, to be honest, I don't really know whether he's here to learn French with his money, or has just come for a rest. I'll give him a prod. (*She kicks him.*) If we leave him alone for a moment, you'll see, in a few minutes he'll wake up refreshed and rejuvenated.

EMMA (*whispering*). Mum . . .

ARANKA. Yes, my dear. You see there's no need to whisper . . .

EMMA. You're not deaf, Mum?

ARANKA. I never was. That was just a notion you developed . . . (*To the* DOCTOR.) Let me show you something . . . (*Hurries out of the kitchen.*)

Silence.

EMMA. Well? (*She points to the flat.*)

The DOCTOR *attempts a smile.*

How do you like it?

DOCTOR (*looking around, estimating the room size*). Four and a half by four and a half . . .

EMMA. Oh, it's at least four and a half by five . . . it's never square . . .

DOCTOR. How high is it?

EMMA (*looks up at the ceiling*). As airy as an apse!

DOCTOR. It's very pleasant.

EMMA. I said you'd like it. I always know what people want. Somehow I can sense it.

DOCTOR (*motions towards the kitchen*). And that's your mother?

EMMA. You'll get on with each other really well. My mother is a smashing woman, really young at heart – sometimes she seems even younger than me. (*She jumps up.*) Did I show you the bedroom?

DOCTOR. There's no hurry.

EMMA. And of course, it'd be nice if you brought back a bird from time to time.

DOCTOR. Well, if no one would have any objections . . .

EMMA. On Tuesdays.

DOCTOR. Why Tuesdays?

EMMA. And Bank Holidays. We'd like that. It'd be good for you both. And maybe you could bring the papers up sometimes, as well . . . Come, this is a very nice room . . . Hang on, what's all this? (*Reading a sign on the door.*) CA-NA-LI-ZO . . . ?

ARANKA (*returning*). Emma, do sit down.

EMMA. I just want the Doctor to have a peek at my room.

ARANKA. He's not peeking anywhere. Sit!

EMMA *sits back in a huff.*

(*To the* DOCTOR.) Her room, hah . . . (*Nodding towards* EMMA.) I think I'll have it sealed up. Emma . . . One morning she gets up, dashes off to school . . . that evening she phoned home and said. 'Mum, don't bother to wait up for me tonight.'

EMMA. Did I mention we have a telephone?

DOCTOR. Oh yes? Very handy.

ARANKA. And I've been waiting for her ever since . . . to come back and tidy it up . . . just once . . . even just to sweep the floor would have been nice. Everything is still as it always was . . . Records, knickers, boxes, sea-shells, even her bubble pipe is still lying where she left them. It's like a gallery installation. You could call it: Pubescence, a Still Life . . . But I swear today I'm throwing them all out!

EMMA. I'll do it, Mum . . .

ARANKA. Of course you'll do it . . .

> EMMA *moves towards the room.*

> Come here, will you!

EMMA. Oh, Mum . . . (*Her hand is on the door handle.*)

ARANKA (*shouting*). Heel, I said!!

> EMMA *returns to her seat.*

> Look . . . (*She shows what she has brought in, wrapped in greaseproof paper.*)

EMMA. What is that hammering?

ARANKA. Well, what do you think? (*She unwraps a piece of bone and shows it to the* DOCTOR.) Is it real?

DOCTOR (*takes it in his hand, examines it thoughtfully*). The sacrum.

ARANKA. From which animal?

DOCTOR. It's a woman's . . . hip-bone . . .

> TODOR, *still half-asleep, gets up from the floor* . . .

ARANKA. Voilà, j'ai le vérité encore, Todor. Ce n'est pas un mouton, n'est-ce pas?

TODOR. C'est une génisse donc, ma chérie.

DOCTOR (*examining the bone*). Gracilis, quite delicate, very fine . . . could be from a monkey.

TODOR. How would a monkey get into the park?

ARANKA. How would a bull?

TODOR. Heifer, my dear. Heifer.

ARANKA. An ape perhaps? Half woman, half ape. What does your professional eye tell you . . . ?

DOCTOR. What do I think?

ARANKA. But my daughter said that you were studying these kind of apes . . .

DOCTOR. Really?

EMMA. Did I say that?

ARANKA. You did.

> *An awkward, confused silence.*

> So, whereabouts is your latest dig?

DOCTOR. Where is my what?

ARANKA. Do you dig abroad, too?

DOCTOR. Well, I can't say I do, no . . .

TODOR. Why would he dig at all? That's no longer the fashion, my dear. They wouldn't lift a spade nowadays . . . It's all done by the push of a button – am I right?

DOCTOR. Well . . . (*He looks at* EMMA *for help.*)

But EMMA *has not been listening, she is staring at* ARANKA . . .

EMMA (*with difficulty*). Mum . . . I won't be able to bring you up the papers any more . . .

ARANKA. That's fine.

EMMA. You could get them delivered . . .

ARANKA. Where's the need? After all, I have given up so many things over the years . . . and never really missed them. But see, what I did manage to get: French Playboy magazines, all second hand, but still worth getting them photocopied somewhere . . .

EMMA. Whatever for?

ARANKA. For them to take home, of course. For their homework. (*To the* DOCTOR.) Do you have a photocopier, by any chance?

DOCTOR. Unfortunately not . . .

ARANKA. Never mind. Emma, my dear, you take them. Don't worry, I'll pay for it . . .

EMMA. I can't take them, Mum . . .

ARANKA. Well, thank you very much.

Silence.

EMMA. But you are O.K. for money?

ARANKA. Yes.

EMMA. How is all this going?

ARANKA. I'm turning them away . . . (*Glancing at* TODOR.) I ought to be more selective . . .

EMMA. Do you have enough washing powder?

ARANKA. No idea . . .

EMMA. I can't bring you washing powder any more either, Mum.

ARANKA. Alright.

EMMA. And we'll not be buying chicken any more either . . .

ARANKA. I don't want chicken, or turkey, or sausages, nothing of that sort.

EMMA (*pointing at the* DOCTOR). But, it's O.K., he'll bring a bird every Tuesday . . . he promised . . .

ARANKA. No matter.

EMMA. Whatever do you mean?

ARANKA. We like having pulses now.

EMMA. Pulses? Who does?

ARANKA. Irma and I. We have poker and pulse evenings.

EMMA. The two of you sit, eat pulses and play poker?

ARANKA. That's right. Is that O.K. by you?

EMMA. Yes . . . I suppose.

Silence.

(*A coffee-maker whistles somewhere.*) Mum, are you making coffee?

ARANKA. You're hearing things . . .

EMMA (*looks into the kitchen*). But I can smell it. I swear to God I can smell coffee.

Sits down. Lights up a cigarette.

(*With difficulty.*) The thing is, Mum . . .

ARANKA. Throw that smelly cigarette away!

EMMA. Couldn't you put up with it just this once!

ARANKA. No. You always say; next time you'll have . . .

EMMA. There isn't going to be a next time, Mum . . .

ARANKA. How many times have I heard you promise! How many times heard you swear? I'm fed up!

EMMA (*puts out the cigarette*). An opportunity has come up . . . it might sound a bit weird at first, you might even get angry, but let me just explain . . .

ARANKA. Do stop beating about the bush . . . just spit it out!

EMMA. Don't interrupt!!

Silence.

(*To the* DOCTOR *whispering.*) Get it out . . .

DOCTOR. What?

EMMA. What do you think? The thing that makes the world go round: the money!

The DOCTOR *does not reach for his suitcase . . .*

EMMA *watches him . . .*

Silence.

Mum! Here's this man, and you know what? He wants to buy your flat! (*She screams.*) Don't say a word!

ARANKA *is silent.*

Don't try and interrupt! Just listen! He buys it, right . . . but you stay in it. and you get an allowance – like a pension – until you die. All he needs is a bedroom. He can move into mine. You share the bills and the bathroom. You can come to an agreement, Mum. You'll get a lot of money. You can go to . . . I don't know . . . Malta.

Silence.

He's a nice man, and he loves the flat. What's more he is a doctor, you see. So if you have any problems . . .

ARANKA. He's not an archaeologist? My dear, I thought you said . . .

EMMA. No, Mum, the archaeologist . . . he's in Cairo . . .

ARANKA. So, you're a doctor?

EMMA. She'll be like putty in your hands now . . .

ARANKA. He's not lying, is he? Are you sure he's not an archaeologist?

EMMA. Oh, Mum.

ARANKA. Her first husband – she had him well trained. All the time I thought he was studying to become a doctor then suddenly one day he turns up with a doctorate.

EMMA. I didn't train him to do anything. What are you talking about?

ARANKA. 'Doctor'! He had the gall to call himself a Doctor!

EMMA. What has that to do with anything?

ARANKA. A lot. What kind of doctor are you? Are you a specialist?

EMMA *(whispers).* Say you're a surgeon . . .

ARANKA. Don't tell me, you're a surgeon. Am I right?

EMMA. Agh! *(Runs into the hall.)* Mum, I've got to go. I may be back later, bye!

DOCTOR. Madam! *(Runs after her.)*

EMMA. Stay . . .

DOCTOR. Madam, please . . .

EMMA. But, you're getting on famously. What is it?

DOCTOR. Don't leave me here . . .

EMMA. What are you afraid of? It'd be easier if I wasn't here, just tell her for me. Don't be afraid – at least she won't drop dead on you . . .

DOCTOR. It's not my job to tell her, is it?

EMMA. But of course it is! Who else is there to do it?

DOCTOR (*pleading*). Why are you doing this to me? Stop torturing me, please Madam . . .

EMMA. Oh, pull yourself together! What have you to worry about? Look, examine her, estimate her life-expectancy and all that, then do the necessary calculations and agree on a price. What an opportunity! It'd be a sin to pass this up. (*Seizing him.*) Try to understand. I need you to be here!

Silence.

ARANKA *and* TODOR *have been following all this very closely.* EMMA *spots a large plunger on the floor.*

And what's this? What is this doing here? Mum, whose plunger is this?

ARANKA (*whispers to* TODOR). Say it's yours . . .

EMMA (*drags it in from the hallway*). Mum, what is this?

TODOR. Oh, that's mine. What's it doing there?

EMMA. I suppose it fell out of your pocket . . . Well, alright (*She pauses, looks around, preoccupied, as if for the last time.*) Mum . . . you've taken to drinking beer . . . you don't seem to be deaf anymore . . . you have your poker and pulse evenings . . . and this Frère Jacques mullarkey . . .

There's our curious Mr Todor and his plunger . . . What does all this mean, Mum?

TODOR. Rajczi.

EMMA. Sorry?

TODOR. The name's Todor Rajczi.

EMMA. Listen Mum . . . You do realise that I am going to die?

DOCTOR. There's no need to be so melodramatic . . . we'll all going to . . . at some stage . . .

EMMA. Mum! I am going to die!

ARANKA. Todor, time and again you've said . . . You'd get this fixed . . . (*She takes her hearing aid from her ear.*) It definitely needs mending . . . (*Hands it to* TODOR.)

EMMA (*shouting into* ARANKA'*s ears*). Your daughter is going to die, Mum!

ARANKA. But make sure you bring it back by eight. Dallas is on.

EMMA (*to* TODOR). Does she know?

TODOR. She knows. Of course she knows . . .

ARANKA. What did he say?

Silence.

I don't know . . . I don't know anything about anything . . . Nobody ever tells me anything.

Silence .

We don't die, don't try and upset me . . .

Silence.

(*To* TODOR.) Quel grand taureau, mon ami!

Crying, suddenly overcome, she tries to wave them away.

TODOR. Why do you have to take it all so seriously? We all have to snuff it sometime.

ARANKA. Todor!

TODOR. Even you, my dear Aranka, will meet your maker one day.

ARANKA. Must we talk about this now?

TODOR. It's no big deal. (*To the* DOCTOR.) None of us live forever, do we?

DOCTOR. How can I put it . . .

TODOR. You must've learnt that in the University, surely. Our days are numbered. And when they're up, that's it. You just line up the bucket and kick it. That's the way it is. Or have you managed to find yourselves your own stairway to heaven, eh, clever-clogs?

ARANKA. What?

TODOR. Well, where is it then, this heaven you've found?

ARANKA. Who said there was? Did I say that?

TODOR. So, why make such a big fuss about it. Heaven? Hell? Hahaha!

ARANKA. This is getting tiresome. Will someone just please change the record? (*Runs out to the kitchen.*)

TODOR (*shouting after her*). I bet I'll get to heaven before you! She'd love to get up there for a good look round . . . Wouldn't you, Aranka? You know, I think that woman thinks that heaven will be some kind of huge exotic department store . . . Heaven? Idiots! They put you into the ground and that's it. Finished. If there is a heaven, it's children. But they're hell, too hahaha . . .

EMMA. So, this has proved a great visit. (*She makes to leave – to the* DOCTOR.) Where do you think you're going? Just sit down you, will you Mr Surgeon! Look, you'll be like a pair of dove-birds in no time. Before you know it, you'll be in the park playing rounders with my shin-bone. (*She stops.*) What's that knocking?

Silence. Then more knocking . . .

ARANKA *looks in from the kitchen.*

Who's knocking?

ARANKA. It's just a bit of spot welding that they're doing . . .

EMMA. Who is? . . . (*She slowly approaches her bedroom.*)

ARANKA. Emma!

She opens the door to find: desks, mountains of paper, coffee-maker, a secretary at a typewriter. The boss is dictating, walking up and down . . .

EMMA. What is this, Mum?

ARANKA. That? (*She shrugs her shoulders.*) Oh, that's the bedroom.

EMMA. Wrong. That's my bedroom. And you've sold it?

ARANKA. Excuse me. I rented out.

EMMA (*she pushes the door back, and spells out the sign on the door*). CA-NA-LI-ZO . . . And what exactly are they doing?

ARANKA. Them? Oh, they're very nice people. They do drains, sewers, taps, waste-pipes . . .

EMMA. Do they unblock baths?

ARANKA (*nodding*). Oh, blockage-removal: a speciality.

Silence.

EMMA (*shouting*). But why didn't you tell me, Mum?! (*She rushes into the room.*)

ARANKA (*going in after her*). Darlings! Let me introduce my daughter . . . (*She shuts the door.*)

Loud sounds of talking and laughing.

TODOR *takes a very loud, deep breath. He watches the* DOCTOR.

TODOR. Life is hard.

Silence.

DOCTOR. What?

TODOR. Hard.

DOCTOR. You think so?

TODOR. I think so.

DOCTOR. Whatever you say.

Silence.

TODOR. Why on earth did we climb down from that tree?

Silence.

Am I right?

DOCTOR. Absolutely.

TODOR. So? Do you know why we climbed down?

DOCTOR. Not yet.

TODOR. You don't.

DOCTOR. I'm afraid I . . .

TODOR. I'll tell you why: for the stones. To have something to hit each other on the head with. That's the long and short of it.

Slowly he leans back. He lets his chin fall to his chest. He watches the DOCTOR finish his beer, get up, nod and leave the flat. The DOCTOR comes back, takes his hat, nods again and leaves. He comes back again, takes his suitcase, nods once more and leaves. Finally, he is gone.

EMMA (*bursting out of the bedroom, to the absent DOCTOR*). So the thing is that it's completely free from six to six in the morning. You work in the morning, anyway. Agota here is so nice, she could lend us a camp-bed . . .

She realises that the DOCTOR has gone. She looks into the hallway. Silence. She glances at TODOR. Behind the door ARANKA is still chatting. EMMA goes to the cupboard, switches on the tape-recorder, hurries out to the hall and lifts her coat. Suddenly she sits down on the bench. TODOR puts a pair of eyeshades back on and folds his hands across his stomach. From the loudspeakers, the recording of Frère Jacques resumes playing very loudly.

Frère Jacques!
Frère Jacques!
Dormez-vous? dormez-vous?
Sonnez les matines
Sonnez les matines
Ding, dang, dong!
Ding, dang, dong!

End of Act One.

ACT TWO

Scene One

A Clothes Department Store. MARI, *the shop assistant, is behind a counter.*

EMMA (*hurries in and goes straight up to her*). Listen, I need someone to go to GELKA . . . Are you listening to me?

MARI (*to an unseen customer*). . . . Sorry, Madam, no, you can't. But you can always pay for one now and leave the other here until later . . .

EMMA. GELKA. You know, the washing machine place. And I've lost the repair warranty . . .

MARI. No, I can't put it to aside for you . . . And I'm afraid, we're right out of catalogues as well. Sorry about that!

EMMA. I must have it somewhere . . .

MARI. What?

EMMA. The warranty. But it's no use looking for it . . . so just go into the shop, take Vera with you and tell them, 'See this girl, here? She's lost her mother, and now her washing machine's packed up . . . ' They'll come and repair it then surely?

MARI. Have you managed to decide yet, Madam? How nice! Then would you please pay at the cash desk . . .

EMMA. Listen, when your mother died, did you get any help from here, was there a grant or any insurance money or anything?

MARI. Six thousand. Hardly worth it. (*To customer.*) There you are, Madam, thank you . . .

EMMA. And if there was, I suppose they only pay up if you have a receipt to prove you spent it all on the burial . . .

MARI (*to a customer*). I'm so sorry, we don't refund without a receipt . . .

EMMA. You could speak to the cemetery: with Vera still a minor, maybe they'd be a bit lenient about quite how it is all spent . . . you never know . . . when they are doing the paperwork. They might turn a bit of a blind eye . . .

MARI (*to a customer*). Receipt, I said! Is that clear?

EMMA. I could try and pop out to the cemetery to soften them up . . .
I just don't know if I'll have enough time. I'm scared. There's
so many other things still to . . . There's Vera's sailor-blouse in
the dry-cleaners, and the ticket for that is lost as well, of course.
But Vera'll manage to get it back somehow – she's very good at
that sort of thing – she just needs to be told everything ten times
a day . . .

MARI. No, we don't sell hair-nets . . . Well, they may do, I don't
know, but I know we don't . . .

EMMA. Let's make a list.

MARI. Washing machine, cemetery, laundry . . .

EMMA. But there's so many other . . . I just can't keep track . . .
I mean, I even forget memorable things, like . . . my memories.
Tell me something from my life! A memory. Anything.

MARI. No, not in four or five . . . I'm afraid . . . only three or six . . .

EMMA. Nothing except a white wall . . .

MARI. What wall?

EMMA. But, that's it . . . a mud wall . . . And white goats and cows . . .
And I see myself in a white shirt chasing white chickens in a white
yard – which didn't exactly happen very often down our street. We
didn't even have a garden. Let alone a dog. But I see still myself
jumping about on the white verandah, and in the distance mother
walking on a blossoming hillside. I run outside in my white shirt
and call 'mamenyika priyahala'.

MARI. Mummy has come . . .

EMMA. 'MAMENYIKA PRIYAHALA!'

MARI. Sh! There's no need to shout!

EMMA. Yes. Mum has arrived. Mamenyika priyahala. But, don't you
see, that wasn't my mother who'd come back. Not even my memories are my own. It's from that old film. The one we saw with the
crackly old soundtrack read by that gravel-voiced old codger who
did the narration. Remember? Mummy has arrived, ugh!

MARI. Don't you want to sit down?

EMMA (*walking up and down among the dress stands*). It is so good
to be able to walk . . . to stroll about . . . jump even . . . (*She tries to
jump.*) To feel the wind blowing about my feet . . . (*She turns
around.*) Oh, but the flat needs attention. our door-frames need
a wipe!

MARI. Whatever for?

EMMA. Snow-white door-frames – I mustn't forget them! It's always
so disappointing . . . to be always meaning to do something about

a thing . . . it's always next time, next Spring! But the blocked drain – that's the biggest headache . . .

MARI. And Vera? What will happen to her?

EMMA. Vera? She'll do something. I'm not worried about her. Her head's screwed on the right way – which is more than you can say for that blocked drain, not to mention the poor old washing machine . . . (*She ducks under the dress stand.*)

MARI (*to a customer*). But we don't sell belts. Try the Leather Department . . . excuse me . . . (*She goes after* EMMA.)

EMMA. Vera. I wonder how her life'll turn out. Who'll she find to love? Who'll she find to love her?

MARI. Don't worry she's not the kind to rush into things, to just jump into bed with the first . . .

EMMA. But she should do. Well, into a few, at least. I want my little angel to try and enjoy life a little . . . unlike . . . It's so strange, in the past when I've thought about things, when I've thought of her, of Vera, I'd cry. And now I have this feeling, it's like when your husband leaves you . . .

MARI. What? You have feelings about Peter?

EMMA. No. For Vera. It is pathetic I know, but I do cry, and yet it's . . . now it's so fantastic to think of Vera like that – growing up to be an independent, modern experienced single woman, it's so exciting . . .

MARI. She's growing up. It's not that special? The revelation is hardly worth dying for . . .

EMMA. You don't think so? But perhaps that is what makes it all worthwhile . . . not dying as such . . . but how you come to see things . . . (*She holds a purple evening dress in front of her.*) What do you think?

MARI. Pretty.

EMMA. Where's the changing room?

MARI. Are you crazy?

EMMA. Do you say that to all your customers?

MARI. It doesn't suit you.

EMMA. And this? (*Pointing to her own dress.*) This does?

MARI. Have you looked at the price?

EMMA (*laughing*). I wouldn't dare . . .

MARI. You'd better not . . .

EMMA (*to one of the changing cubicles*). Could you hurry up, please. There are other people waiting to try things on too. (*A fat woman runs out of one of the cubicles.*)

MARI. Sh! You're frightening my customers away . . .

EMMA. Even though I'm not a ghost . . . quite yet. (EMMA *goes inside*.)

The changing rooms. A bench, coathanger and full length mirror. There are two other cubicles next to EMMA's. *A typical East-European clothes department. threadbare and shapeless people are taking off their threadbare, shapeless clothes to find themselves in an haute couture fantasy world of ready-to-wear fashion. They stare at the mirror, seize the price-tag with tremulous hands, they search in their purses, at struggle with themselves. Then finally they put their old dresses back on and start the long journey either to the exit or to the cash till. Others immediately take their place in the changing room.* EMMA *quickly removes her dress, puts the evening dress on, steps in front of the mirror, turns up the collar of the dress, adjusts the hem, imagining a belt at her waist – she is trying on the dress like a professional model. Suddenly in amazement she stares at her own reflection in the mirror: a woman with uncombed hair in a purple evening dress – ridiculous, odd. But perhaps it is not that ridiculous, not so odd after all. She is still* EMMA, *but now she is elegant, pretty, desirable, almost beautiful. She fixes her hair. She holds the pose a moment, then she picks up the price-tag on the bottom of the dress, reads it, takes the dress off, and puts her own dress back on. She catches sight of herself in the mirror again. She sits down on the bench, takes her purse out, empties her hand-bag and searches through the pockets of her coat. Her hands go through the torn lining . . . then she just sits very still. She sits motionless.*

MARI (*from outside*). Hullo! Shall I have a look?

EMMA. Don't! (*Pulls the curtain further across.*)

Quickly she gets out of her dress and puts the evening dress on again. She stands half a metre away from the mirror, just stands like a statue . . . She picks up the price tag at the bottom of the dress again, starts to laugh. Bending forward she screams silently with all her might, scratching at her thighs with all ten fingers. Then she takes the evening dress off, puts it back on the coat-hanger, puts on her old clothes once more and leaves the cubicle. MARI *is still standing there next to her cubicle, close enough to have seen the whole performance.*

So then: washing machine, cemetery, laundry, Vera, door-frame – the drain, no, not that. That's being seen to . . .

MARI. Good. So now we're going to take a little walk to the hospital . . .

EMMA. See you!

MARI. Wait! I'll come with you.

EMMA. No. Mari, you've come with me far enough.

MARI. What are you so afraid of? Why are you frightened? A slightly unpleasant examination – one or two weeks of treatment and you'll be right as rain.

EMMA. Or on the coroner's slab.

MARI. Hey, none of us live forever.

EMMA. But you will, for me. (*She is on the point of leaving.*)

MARI. Emma!

EMMA *turns round.*

Silence.

Remember . . . remember, when we went to the flea-market at Ecseri.

EMMA. I would've loved to. I always dreamed I would. I'd have loved it. But it wasn't to be. The Ecseri.

MARI. Don't talk rubbish! Where do you think we bought that Venetian-looking mirror of yours then? Which reminds me, where did that mirror ever get to?

EMMA. Where? It's in Peter's bathroom . . .

MARI. But it's yours!

EMMA. So? Should I go and get it back, do you think? Yes! Add that to the list. the Venetian on the wall . . . That was a real bargain wasn't it?

MARI (*to a customer*). I'm sorry, just a moment . . . (*To* EMMA.) I don't remember how much it was.

EMMA. Nor me . . . You see, it's all forgotten . . . Haha ! Do you remember how by the time we got it home a piece of it had been broken off?

MARI. You're telling me, dear. (*She shows her palm to* EMMA.)

EMMA. This? (*She touches it.*)

MARI. Emma, where are you going?

EMMA. My Venetian mirror scarred your palm? That's bloody wonderful! Do you still feel it?

MARI. Not at all. Where are you going?

EMMA. Washing machine, cemetery, laundry, Vera, door-post, the Venetian – six things to see to! Can I trust you Mari?

MARI. Of course . . .

EMMA. Swear!

MARI. Don't be stupid.

EMMA. Swear!

MARI. I swear on . . . what . . . I know: on John Lennon no less! . . .
O.K. on the accuracy of Pythagoras' hypotenuse . . .

EMMA. Is that it?

MARI. . . . Alright! On Billy Karsai from the fourth year, so help me
Miss Ibi, amen!

EMMA. Do you really think there is a God?

MARI (*shakes her head*). No, but there is a Miss Ibi.

EMMA. Actually, Mari, there's no Miss Ibi either . . .

MARI. Of course. I'd forgotten . . .

EMMA. Funny.

MARI. What?

EMMA. That you forgot . . .

MARI. No, I didn't, just for a moment it slipped my . . . How could
anyone forget poor Miss Ibi?

EMMA. You didn't, not her – you merely forgot her death. That she's
not alive anymore – a small detail . . .

MARI. Listen . . .

EMMA. All right, it's more than a detail . . . But it's not the most
important thing about us either. Whether we're alive or not . . .
Miss Ibi doesn't cease to be the Miss Ibi we remember because she
ceases to be . . . (*She starts to leave.*) That helps, doesn't it?

MARI. Emma!

EMMA. Please forget it! This is the last thing I'll ask you.

MARI. What?

EMMA. Please, just forget my death . . . not me.

MARI. How?

EMMA. It's easy. Wipe it from your mind . . . (*She starts to leave.*)

MARI. Emma!

EMMA. Oh, sorry. (*She gives the purple dress back.*) Makes me look
fat . . . (*She leaves.*)

MARI (*to a customer*). So why did you wash it then? I'm sorry . . .
So? And what has it got to do with me . . . I am not being
condescending! Good! Go then! Talk to him! You can go to the
top, talk to God for all I care! (*To someone else – using a different
tone of voice.*) I would say, the blue . . . goes with your eyes . . .
Would you like it wrapped?

Act Two, Scene Two

A Street.

OLD WOMAN (*from the first scene*). 'Ere Lady, how'd you like a good tip? Only twenty forints.

EMMA steps over her, walks away then turns round to watch the long queue in front of the ice-cream shop: sad, tired people silently queue, patiently waiting their turn. EMMA joins them. The first in the queue chooses, pays for and gets his ice-cream, then he leaves savouring his ice-cream. Everyone else takes one step forward . . .

Hey, Mister, I've got a hot lottery tip for you. Only twenty forints.

The next in the queue chooses, pays for and gets his ice-cream. Everyone else takes one step forward . . . finally, it's EMMA's turn. She chooses, pays for and takes her ice-cream. She is about to walk off but she stops. She is licking the ice-cream, just licking it and licking it and as she does so she stares at the OLD WOMAN. She walks over to her.

EMMA. Alright then . . . Give me a good tip.

OLD WOMAN. Twenty forints . . . (*She holds out her hand – EMMA gives her the money.*) Let's see . . . four . . . fourteen – write it down . . .

EMMA. I'll remember it.

OLD WOMAN. So. . . . four . . . fourteen . . . fifteen . . . sixteen . . . and seventeen.

EMMA. Well, it won't be difficult to remember those . . . Why don't you ever try them?

OLD WOMAN. Haha. I make what I need from this . . .

EMMA. I can imagine. If you sell them to everybody, there'd be two thousand winners every week . . .

OLD WOMAN. These I kept especially for you, Lady, for just you . . . and for the little one . . .

EMMA. What did you say?! (*The OLD WOMAN laughs pointing at EMMA's stomach.*)

EMMA (*looks down*). Oh, God . . . (*She hurries off – but immediately returns and gives the OLD WOMAN the ice-cream, then hurries away.*)

OLD WOMAN (*licking the ice-cream*). Hey Mister, want a good tip. Only twenty forints . . .

Act Two, Scene Three

A bathroom. PETER *is taking toys out of the bath. The TV can be heard off.* PETER *drains and rinses the bath. The bell rings. Somebody turns the TV down. The sound of footsteps, a door opening, then a scream.* PETER *runs out of the bathroom. Tense, indistinct voices.* ERIKA *rushes in, takes a toothbrush out of a glass, fills the glass with water, wets a towel and rushes out . . .*

EMMA (*off*). It's nothing . . . leave me alone . . . oh, that's cold, don't . . . thanks . . . It must have been that ice-cream I had . . . May I use the bathroom?

ERIKA (*off*). Yes, it's through . . .

EMMA (*off*). I know the way . . .

> EMMA *enters, sits on the edge of the bath . . . stands up, shuts the door, leans against the basin. She takes the plastic bowl out of the basin and puts it on the floor. Then she washes her face, and with her face still wet, looks around.*

EMMA. Peter, have you got a second, please . . .

> PETER *comes in.*

Which towel can I use?

PETER. Any one you like . . .

EMMA (*she dries her face, holds the towel in her hand*). You'd better wash it.

PETER. Why, what have you got? Leprosy?

EMMA. No, it's just . . . there might have been salmonella in the ice-cream . . .

> *Silence.*

I don't think so tho' . . . It didn't taste odd at all. It was good. Chocolate and strawberry. (*A beat.*) Which is your favourite?

PETER. Do you really want to know?

EMMA. Yeah. (PETER *laughs.*)

EMMA. You do still eat ice-cream?

PETER. Only in the summer.

EMMA. When you're with the children I suppose . . . But what about when you're by yourself?

PETER. Pistachio, nocciola, fragola . . .

EMMA. Still? Yes, it was always con crema, wasn't it? (*Looks at him.*) Con crema, grazie. Remember?

> *Silence.*

And the children?

PETER. Sleeping.

EMMA. So Zoli sleeps on his potty?

PETER. No, he's doing a poo.

EMMA. I thought he was watching TV. How are they?

PETER. Touch wood . . .

EMMA. Can you imagine, I saw him as a grown up.

PETER. When? In a dream of yours?

EMMA. No, I was in an X-Ray Department. But you have to try
and picture little Zoli with a beard, with bony ribs, in only his
underpants . . .

PETER. The underpants I can imagine . . . Look, Emma, is there
anything wrong?

EMMA. Nothing special.

PETER. Really?

EMMA. Why should there be? What if I said I was just passing by
and . . . well, I've never really talked to Erika . . . so since I just
happened to be in the neighbourhood, and I felt like having a chat,
I thought . . .

PETER. It doesn't look that way . . .

EMMA. Do you think I've put on any weight?

PETER. It doesn't show. (EMMA *laughs*.)

   Silence.

EMMA. Should we go inside?

PETER. Not if you don't want to . . .

   Silence.

EMMA. Is this embarrassing for you?

PETER. Oh, no, not at all . . .

EMMA. Why? You never know, I might just lose it and start
screaming, maybe smash the washing machine against the wall and
end up chasing Erika around with a coathanger. Is that so
inconceivable?

   PETER *continues putting the clothes on the clothes line.* EMMA
   begins to help him . . .

EMMA. Your toothbrushes . . . I could snap your toothbrushes in half.

PETER. Stop acting the goat!

EMMA. 'Acting the goat' – How I've missed hearing that! I haven't
heard anyone use that expression for so long! . . . not since before
we . . . How's your father keeping?

PETER. He's dead.

EMMA. I'm sorry.

PETER. It's alright. I suppose I really should have . . .

EMMA. What? Sent me a telegram?

PETER. Didn't Vera tell you?

EMMA. No.

PETER. She must have forgotten to mention it . . .

EMMA. Why wasn't she at the funeral?

PETER. I told her about it, but there was that . . . what was it? . . . some school trip.

EMMA. But that was in May.

PETER. Yes, May last year.

Silence.

EMMA. It's a pity you didn't tell me. I liked your father.

PETER. He liked you too, Emma.

EMMA. Actually, it's a really shitty thing not to . . .

PETER. What?

EMMA. Oh, forget it.

PETER. O.K., O.K. Point taken.

EMMA. He was always rather sweet your father . . . silly, but sweet.

PETER. Is this why you came?

EMMA. To express my condolences? No.

Silence.

PETER. What is it? I can't work out if you're about to laugh or cry?

EMMA. Nor can I.

They are still sorting the clothes out, large and small shirts, socks of all sizes, underpants, tights. EMMA *is holding a peaked cap.*

Peter . . . when I was waiting for the lift downstairs I had this thought . . . what if we had a really big row . . .

PETER. Well, we very nearly just did . . . Are you sure you're alright?

EMMA. No, I am serious. Why did that huge argument never happen? – Have I bottled it all up? For some reason I feel unatoned. You know: mea culpa, mea maxima culpa . . . I wondered if I could somehow let it all out, you know, release it . . . without my appearing totally ridiculous . . .

PETER. I don't think so.

EMMA. If I could somehow talk about it, get it all off my chest.
   Maybe . . . what I need is to take a leaf out of Zoli's book: just sit
   there until I've dumped all the crap from my life out of me . . .
   perhaps then my digestion would return to normal. I might even
   lose a few kilos. Oh, God, I'm just babbling!

PETER. Shush! Remember the children are asleep . . .

EMMA. Listen Peter, could a seventeen-year-old girl, a student, end
   up having to pay death duty?

PETER. What is this?

EMMA. This is a question.

PETER. You're getting worse, love . . .

EMMA. Really.

PETER. Yes. Where's that famous sense of humour of yours gone?
   Where's my little Emma's legendary wit?

EMMA. Perhaps I should try again using it? . . . Listen, Pete, if I
   happen to kick the bucket, will my daughter be all washed up –
   financially speaking?

Silence.

*From the next room, footsteps are now audible. The TV volume has
been turned down.*

PETER. What's the matter?

EMMA. This is the matter.

PETER. Are you having some kind of breakdown?

EMMA. No. I am very much in control.

PETER. You've not been drinking?

EMMA. Only something called Gypsum.

PETER. Then, for Christ's sake, what the hell is this?

EMMA. I shall tell you how it is:
   I am commanded to go on a journey,
   A long, hard and dangerous journey,
   And I must go soon, to give an honest account
   Before the chief judge, Adonai (Our Lord).
   So I pray you'll keep me company
   On this journey, as you promised.

PETER. A promise is a duty! And one that bears a story.
   But I have never promised you anything.

EMMA. Why, you said on our wedding day,
   You would never forsake me, not until death,
   Even if it prove sheer hell.

PETER. I'm not sure I like where this is heading . . .

EMMA. I'm almost finished, just tell me . . .

PETER. What?

EMMA. I came because you are the only solicitor I know in this
bloody town – so tell me: is it possible that a girl who is still a
minor might have to pay death duty?

PETER. It's unimaginable.

EMMA. But such things can happen?

PETER. This can't. She won't have to pay until she comes of age . . .

EMMA. Obviously she should get some kind of state benefit. But will
she get any? That's the other question. I haven't paid a stamp for
years – could she miss out on her entitlement?

PETER. Orphans' benefits – they're paid by a completely different
department.

EMMA. Alright. But what happens in a year's time when she comes
of age? Will they withdraw her allowance, and then make her pay
the death duties?

PETER. Fifty per cent of them . . . Then again, they're not going to
ask for more than she can afford.

EMMA. Well whatever little they ask for she can't afford . . . And if
she doesn't pay it? Will they take the flat away from her?

PETER. Of course not.

EMMA. Good. So then? What do we do?

PETER. We'll have to find a property handling agency . . .

EMMA. What she needs is a proper guardian . . .

PETER. She might do. But for this an agency'll be more useful.

EMMA. But Vera is too young to draw up any contracts with them.

PETER. Then I'll arrange it.

EMMA. Would you, really?

PETER. I am her father, in case you 've forgotten . . .

EMMA. Oh, really, it'd quite slipped my mind!

PETER. What did you think I was?

EMMA. Just a very nice man who gives her dinner once or twice a
week, if she babysits his children . . .

PETER. And when she does she sleeps over in the children's room.
Little Zoli loves her. They're very close.

EMMA. I know.

PETER. Of course you don't know. You haven't got the slightest idea.
You haven't got the remotest idea what it means to Vera to be in a
supportive environment, at least once a week . . .

EMMA. Funny. We can have maybe only one conversation a year and
still it manages to get boring . . .

PETER. You're not suggesting we should talk more often?

EMMA. I don't know . . . Before, somehow, it wasn't boring. We
were never bored . . .

PETER. Yes we were. We were bored lots of times . . . But it was
alright. We didn't seem to mind being bored . . .

ERIKA (*opening the door*). Are you feeling better?

EMMA. I'd better go now. Try to find me that property handling
agency then. The flat'll need to be valued . . . Tho' somebody once
told me that the value of a flat is like a kiss, for the right one you'd
pay twice the price, but for another . . . I suppose, you can count
the bricks but you can't count the value. I guess the paint may
peel but it's still my home. I liked it. It had windows. And sometimes, when they were clean, you could look out and the sun
shone through them. Look, I'll see you. Well, actually I suppose
I won't . . . but, I will invite you, Peter . . .

ERIKA. Where to?

EMMA. And it would be nice if you could make it . . . hopefully you
won't have a prior engagement . . . like a school trip . . . to go to.
(*A beat.*) I'll just have a quick look at the children . . .

ERIKA. Zoli has just gone down. Next time . . .

PETER. Did he do a poo?

ERIKA. No.

PETER. Did you tell him off?

ERIKA. Hey, Emma, did Vera ever go through a phase when she
resisted going to bed at night. Like now, for example, Zoli says
he's frightened – do you think he really is? Or is he just saying
that knowing I'll fall for it? What would you do if . . .

EMMA. Erika, another time, O.K . . . (*She goes out.*)

ERIKA *follows her, we hear the front door closing.* PETER *takes
the lid off the dirty clothes basket, and starts to pull the clothes out.*

ERIKA (*coming back*). Ugh!

PETER (*stuffing the dirty clothes in the washing machine . . . with
difficulty*). Shit! . . . Bloody stupid washing . . . what are you
staring at? I couldn't exactly throw her out, could I!

ERIKA. I didn't say you should have . . .

Silence.

Why does she think she's going to . . . (*She suddenly stops.*)

Silence.

ERIKA. Has she started drinking, do you think?

PETER. I doubt it.

ERIKA. Why?

PETER *puts washing powder in the machine, shuts the lid.*

Ghastly, isn't it, how fat she's become . . . ghastly . . . you don't think she could tell that I was . . .

PETER. She wouldn't have noticed . . .

ERIKA. I'd hate it if she realised that I had been . . .

PETER. Just leave it!

ERIKA. Aren't you coming out?

PETER *is sitting on the edge of the bath, massaging the soles of his feet, staring at the tiles.*

Well, what did she want anyway?

PETER. Nothing.

ERIKA. Leave your feet alone. Don't do that. I wish you wouldn't do that. It's so disgusting.

PETER *puts on his socks quickly, then steps into his shoes.*

So are these little visits going to be a regular occurrence from now on then? Where are you going?

PETER. Nowhere. (*He kicks off his shoes, switches on the washing machine, and exits.*)

ERIKA (*switches off the lights*). What school trip was she going on about anyway? (*Leaves the bathroom and closes the door.*)

Darkness. The noise of the washing machine. The door bell rings.

Footsteps, a door opens. EMMA *comes in, switches on the light –* ERIKA *and* PETER *watch from the doorway as she carefully takes the Venetian mirror off the wall from above the basin and exits.*

Act Two, Scene Four

EMMA'*s home. As* EMMA *enters it is in semi-darkness and appears empty.*

EMMA (*entering*). Vera?

She puts the mirror down, goes over to the bed and lies down. From there she scans the room and its disarray: the wardrobe door lying open, the stained ceiling, the dirty plates on the table, and the clothes lying all over the floor.

Voices can be heard from behind a door.

VOICE OF A MAN. Wait, don't . . . don't touch it . . .

GIRL'S VOICE. But I'd like to . . .

MAN'S VOICE. Well, be careful . . . It might seem very easy to do, but if you've never tried it before . . . Now, that's good. But it has to go in really deep. Now, give me a hand. I want to see if I can turn it round slowly, that's it, round and round . . .

Creaking, rattling noises are more audible.

GIRL'S VOICE. Ouch!

MAN'S VOICE. Watch out, let go of it! I told you: it's much harder than doing it by yourself . . .

The door opens up, a seventeen-year-old GIRL hurries out wearing a red dressing gown. She picks up a cigarette from the table, notices the mirror, which is propped up against the wall.

VERA. Mum? (*She looks for her in the kitchen, comes back again, is caught by her reflection in the mirror. She lights a cigarette.*) Do you want a cigarette? (*As she turns back towards the bathroom, she notices EMMA.*) There you are! Wherever have you been?

EMMA *stares at her from the bed – just as she had been staring at the room moments earlier.*

Can you believe it? They finally came to fix the bath. He's ever so good with his hands. I've been helping him.

Silence.

What is it, Mum? (*Puts out the cigarette, goes to her.*) Aren't you pleased?

EMMA (*takes VERA's hand, and holds it – then, with some difficulty*). Say a woman starts to feels sick . . . to put on weight . . . has abdominal pains . . . what might it make you think, Vera?

VERA. I'm sure it isn't anything very serious.

EMMA. But imagine it wasn't me. Some woman, any woman, she's nauseous, and has been putting on weight . . .

Silence.

VERA (*realising*). But how? And whose is it?

EMMA. How? I don't know. And it could be that archaeologist, for all it matters?

VERA. Mummy!

EMMA. That's it: cheer, why don't you!

VERA. But aren't you pleased?

EMMA. Are you?

VERA. Well . . . it's better than being ill, isn't it?

EMMA. You mean it's better to be screaming in labour than screaming at death's door. Better to be feeding a baby than feeding the worms. Better to be facing nappies to wash than to be facing God with a lifetime of dirty linen to excuse.

VERA. It's got to be better, hasn't it?

EMMA. Remember, about a month ago, I said I had the flu . . .

VERA. Why? Wasn't that what was wrong with you?

EMMA. I was lying there shaking, paralysed with fear . . .

VERA. But what were you scared of, Mum?

EMMA. Then, when the bleeding stopped and I got up, and . . . and I still had this nauseous feeling and my stomach was still upset – Vera, it was such a victory!

VERA. Why didn't you say anything? Why didn't you tell me, Mum?

EMMA. I was waiting . . .

VERA. For what?

EMMA. I was waiting . . . for someone else to ask . . . I had been waiting for weeks . . . for someone to begin to notice . . . But no. Only I seemed to suspect. There was only me ask myself what it might be. And I have done. A thousand times. (*She stifles a laugh.*) Until today when an old woman . . . I gave her my ice-cream . . .

VERA. What ice-cream?

EMMA. I don't know: pistachio, fragola . . . does it matter?

VERA. What are you talking about? Are you crazy?

EMMA. Maybe, but if only someone had asked me just once, perhaps I might have realised in time? Vera, I can't be pregnant.

VERA. You can't?

EMMA. No. But I think I got a blooding of another kind earlier down at the agency office . . . Next thing I knew I was in a hospital . . .

VERA. You've been to hospital?

EMMA. Yes, and there was this doctor in a lead apron standing over me shouting. Take off all your clothes! Take off all your clothes! And I didn't know what to say, I was panicking that . . . what if I was . . . I still thought I could be . . . and if I was, I daren't expose my baby to an X-Ray!

VERA. But what did the doctor say? What's so funny? Why are you laughing? Don't laugh! Tell me!

EMMA. Why? But it's hilarious . . .

VERA. Is it?

EMMA. That I could ever think . . . Yes, I feel sick. Yes, I'm putting on weight. But my stomach is on fire. And this time, it's no cute little baby kicking and growing inside me . . .

VERA. Then what is?

EMMA *suddenly utters a horrifying scream.*

Muuum!

EMMA *continues screaming – then as abruptly stops.*

EMMA. I must get a grip or I'll be losing my voice next. Now, dear . . . (*Gets up and goes to the bathroom.*)

TOTH GYULA *is lying working on the floor, surrounded by tools, pipes and the plunger.*

Excuse me, my toothbrush . . .

TOTH. You want to brush your teeth?

EMMA. No, I'm taking it. Pass it to me.

TOTH. The red one?

EMMA. The yellow.

TOTH. Toothpaste?

EMMA. Please. Vera, I've put some in the glass for you, but buy some tomorrow . . .

VERA. O.K.

EMMA. And don't forget!

VERA. I'll buy some. O.K.?

EMMA. I know you, you'll forget, . . . ah . . . Excuse me, you can't see the cap by any chance?

TOTH. Cap, cap . . . (*He looks for it on the shelf, then under the washing basin.*)

EMMA. Leave it, it's not that important.

TOTH. Put a serviette on it.

EMMA. On what?

TOTH. On top of the tube.

EMMA. Good idea. Toothpaste, toothbrush, serviette. What else do I need? Vera, could you give me my dressing gown back?

VERA (*whining*). Do I have to?

EMMA. No, you don't have to. I'll walk up and down the hospital corridor in my overcoat. Could you at least buy me a pair of furry slippers then?

VERA. Where?

EMMA. M&S. And, Vera, lend me a nightdress?

VERA. Which one?

EMMA. An old one. I'm not asking for your favourite.

VERA. Well, alright. (*Runs out.*) Mum, what's this?

EMMA. A Venetian mirror.

VERA. From Venice?

EMMA. No, from the flea-market.

VERA. You've been to Ecseri?

EMMA. Vera, I'm in a hurry . . .

> VERA *goes out.*

> EMMA *stands there, feeling like a stranger in her own flat.* TOTH GYULA *is working in the bathroom. They look at each other. Each is on the verge of speaking. Of today? Or yesterday? Of something from their past? Perhaps even something from a previous life. They are like Adam and Eve framed in that bathroom door.* VERA *comes back with a red dressing gown and something pinkish in her hand.*

VERA. A bit frayed at the hem, but you don't mind, do you? It doesn't really matter in hospital, does it?

EMMA. Perfect.

VERA. What else?

EMMA. Nothing. (*She goes to leave.*)

VERA. Mum!

EMMA. Yes?

VERA. Why are you so . . .

EMMA. So . . . what, ill?

VERA. No, so bitter.

EMMA. I'm sorry.

VERA. Stay a little longer.

EMMA. I have to go.

VERA. Wait then, I'll come with you.

EMMA. Don't worry . . . I can find my way by myself.

VERA. But we could go together as far as the tube station.

EMMA. You're going to your father's?

VERA. Yes.

EMMA. Where are they off to this time? The cinema again?

VERA. Wait! I won't be a minute. (*Runs into her room.*)

EMMA. And what about Mister Dyno-rod here?

VERA. Oh, he can always shut the door when he leaves . . .

EMMA. Vera!

VERA. Don't, don't be like this . . .

EMMA. Grow up, Vera!

VERA. And how do I do that?

EMMA. I don't know! I don't know! That's something you'll have to find out for yourself . . . Jesus . . . Will you ever get by without me?

VERA. Yes. Look, it's O.K.

EMMA. Is it? Good. So, I am free to go then. I suppose I have organised everything.

VERA. What have you organised?

EMMA. Tho' you'll still actually have to do things by yourself, love. (*Laughing.*)

VERA. What?

EMMA. Well, there's the laundry, for one thing!

VERA. Yeah, where did that ticket go to?

EMMA. You'll have to look for it!

VERA. Where?

EMMA. Work it out! Just try being a grown up for once.

VERA. If that's what you want . . . (*She hugs her mother.*)

EMMA. That is what I want.

Silence – they hug.

What's that you've got on? (*She smells her own perfume on* VERA.)

VERA. Are you mad at me?

EMMA. Not at all. You have it . . . everything is yours now, Vera . . .

VERA. Ouch!

EMMA. What is it?

VERA. My arm . . . You've pinched me . . . See, all five fingers . . . That'll leave a mark there, now . . .

EMMA. Not for very long.

VERA. Till morning. It doesn't matter. It doesn't really hurt.

EMMA (*puts nightdress, dressing gown, toothbrush and toothpaste into a bag*). What are you doing tomorrow?

VERA. I don't know yet.

EMMA. It's O.K. I was just curious. Bye.

She is about to leave – but suddenly she stops – throws the bag down – goes into the bathroom, wets a sponge and starts to scrub the door-frame.

VERA. Mum, don't . . . What is the matter? Shall I do it? Look, tomorrow. I'll do the whole bathroom! Mum! Stop it! Leave that! Pull yourself together, for God's sake, Mum! What the hell are you doing?

EMMA *buffs it with a dry cloth. The door-frame is restored to a beautiful white sheen.*

EMMA (*picks up her bag*). One last thing. Don't leave that plumber alone in the flat . . .

VERA. He's a very nice man . . .

EMMA. I'm sure he is. All the same . . . (*She goes.*)

VERA (*shuts the door after* EMMA, *and goes into the bathroom*). Shall I help you clear up?

TOTH. Thanks . . . (*Silence.*) That your mother?

VERA. She's gone.

TOTH. Seems nervy . . .

VERA. Yeah. She's got lot on her mind . . .

Silence.

They gather up tools.

Why? Don't you ever have any worries?

TOTH. Mind yourself. I still have to put the lattice-frame on . . .

VERA. I often think that all life does is give us things to worry about – silly little things mainly – and that's how we spend it . . . (*Then, melodramatically.*) There's only one real solution to life I suppose, but that's an end not an answer . . .

TOTH. Your feet will get wet . . .

VERA. Oh, who cares! . . . You know, we're centuries apart, you and I, don't you think? Centuries apart.

TOTH. I don't look that old, do I?

VERA. No, I mean . . . hundreds of light years apart . . . In understanding. Mum was still at college when she was first expecting me. I wasn't planned, nor did I ask to be, but . . . then I think she thought I'd win her some sympathy in her finals from her professors. And it did, after all she passed – but look at her now. Where did it all get her? Now all she worries about are my results, me failing in physics and all my other subjects. Somehow her passion for life has ebbed . . . it has even made her ill . . . Just think . . . what might my mother have become if she hadn't had me! Would you believe it: my mother was a botanist. Flowers, ferns, mushrooms, mosses on the trunks of trees, they were her first love! She was a mountaineer too. An Alpinist. Whereas now all I do is drag her down to earth, to grey reality. I'll go and see her tomorrow. Tho' maybe that isn't such a good idea either . . . we only end up hurting each other . . . yet even if she was at death's door, I know all she'd be thinking about would be me . . . Oh, anyway I can't go and see her in the afternoon, I'm busy tomorrow! But then I can't just sit in school and not go and see her either . . . Oh, I don't know what I can do!

Silence.

They are now sitting together on the floor, looking at one other . . .

VERA. I must go, my little Zoli will be waiting for me . . .

TOTH. You've a date? Been seeing him long?

VERA. For the last four years . . .

TOTH. Together all that time – that's great!

VERA. No, Zoli is only four. But I'm mad about him, we even sleep together! You should meet him.

TOTH. I'd love to. Maybe one of these days . . .

VERA. No, I mean it! You'd really like him.

TOTH. Is he cute then?

VERA. Just guess who he looks like? You! Imagine yourself – but only this big! (*She shows him.*) About this tall, with sticky out ears, and with a lovely pink bum – can you picture it?

TOTH. Well . . . that's how I always imagine myself! . . . hahaha!

Silence.

So what is it that's worrying you?

VERA. Let's not go into that . . . For me, it's, ah! . . . It doesn't matter. Look, the subject is closed. Dead and buried. Finito. Let's forget it.

Silence.

Well it's just that boys don't seem to like me . . . I mean it's not really a problem . . . It's just a bit . . . you know . . . depressing.

TOTH *mutters to himself.*

Sorry?

TOTH. I said: you're not unattractive . . .

VERA. I know that. But sometimes I feel . . . and then at other times
I do manage to believe in myself. The real problem isn't that they
don't like me, or anything. I know they do because there have been
occasions when . . . I mean quite a few times when . . . there were a
few who definitely liked me. That's not the problem . . .

TOTH. Then what?

VERA. Oh, let's not go into it . . .

Silence.

Alright, we don't ever seem to be . . . on the same wave-length . . .

TOTH. Sometimes it takes a little fine-tuning . . .

VERA. Well not with you . . . with you, from the outset I felt . . .

Silence.

Boys . . . boys are like . . . say, a girl is flat-chested, she might be
blonde, and blue eyed, but they'll presume she's innocent . . . and
yet there's my friend Pepi . . . and she's gone with at least twenty
boys. Don't get me wrong, I don't want to be like her. But just
because a person happens to have big breasts then straight off they
assume all kinds of things about her. They don't – or can't – see as
far as her face or personality, or behaviour. All they can see are her
breasts, and then . . .

Silence.

I don't mean she's naked or anything. I mean even if she's fully
clothed, it's just . . .

TOTH. I see.

VERA. You understand what I'm trying to say?

TOTH. Oh, yes.

VERA. And if a girl isn't like that . . . then they think that you're just
a tease, so they dump you . . . And what I really want to know is:
why do I always get stupid little boys in horn-rims falling for me!
Oh, and you wouldn't believe the things they whisper! 'Take me to
your Pleasure Domes, Let me be your Passion Machine!' I ask you!
Agh, let's just talk about something else . . .

Silence.

Shall we tidy up these tools? Why are you looking at me like at?
Be careful, we want to watch where we put things, we don't want
to lose anything important . . .

*We hear the sound of the tool-box rattling. They are all over each
other. The door closes – but certain noises are audible: the
rustling of clothes, the movement of bodies, a gasp, then a deep
exhalation and, finally, silence.*

VERA *comes out carrying her skirt, and goes straight back with the washing powder: she runs the water.*

This'll need soaking . . . or it will never come out . . .

Noise of running water in the bathroom.

EMMA *returns, lifts the Venetian mirror – but the bag and the mirror together are too much for her. She puts down the bag, and leaves with the mirror.*

VERA (*in the bathroom*). You don't repair hair-dryers, by any chance?

TOTH *mutters a reply.*

Pity. With a hair-dryer we could dry it . . . I like this skirt . . . It's my favourite . . . (*She comes out of the bathroom, goes into her own room and returns with a pair of trousers. She is singing.*)

And so, is that it? Really?

TOTH *can be heard groaning in the bathroom.*

Sorry? . . . You did realise, didn't you? . . . I guess that now makes me a fully-fledged grown up, doesn't it?

TOTH. Definitely. (*He continues to groan.*)

VERA (*puts on her trousers*). Funny, I suppose I'll never forget you now.

TOTH. Me?

VERA. Yes, of course. Who do you think I'm talking to? I shall always remember you . . . So what's your name, then?

TOTH. Mine?

VERA. Yes! Yours!

TOTH. Mine! Toth Gyula! (*Wailing.*) Toth Gyula! I am Toth Gyula!

VERA. Listen Toth, what's wrong with you? I'm not angry with you or disappointed or anything. It's no big deal. It's something everyone has to go through, I suppose. I'm really very grateful. (*Peers into the bathroom.*) Look, is something up? Are you feeling alright?

TOTH (*quietly*). It's nothing . . . it'll pass . . .

VERA. Well, drink this!

TOTH. I'll throw up . . .

VERA. But it's only water!

TOTH. Anything . . .

VERA. Well, do you want to try hot water? That helps if you are going to throw up . . .

TOTH. Don't . . . agh!

VERA. Just, please, try not to be sick in the bath. It will only get blocked again . . . Sit down. Lean against the wall. I'll put the bowl on your lap. Is that any better?

TOTH. Yes, that's very . . . very good . . .

Silence.

Just don't look at me . . .

VERA. Has that worked? (*She leaves the bathroom, notices the bag.*) Mum? (*Looks out into the kitchen, returns, pulls the dressing gown out of the bag, takes it to the bathroom.*) How are you?

Silence.

Are you any feeling better? (*Silence.*)

Look could you just pull the door to when you leave? . . . (*She leaves the flat, leaving the front door wide open.*)

Act Two, Scene Five

An empty underground station. Late at night. A long grey marble wall. A tunnel leads to the other platforms. At the front of the stage is the platform edge, and imaginary rails run between the stage and the audience.

A few people are waiting on the platform. Others sit leaning against the wall. It is littered with rags, rucksacks, a pair of crutches, a portable radio, newspapers, bottles . . . EMMA arrives from the escalator, carrying the mirror. She walks down the platform, stops, and waits.

A humming noise in the distance. A rush of wind – the humming gets closer and closer. The wind tears at EMMA's skirt and hair, getting stronger and stronger. A few people move towards the edge of the platform – sharp headlights from the side, the deafening sound of the arriving train, brakes screech. Darkness – silence.

LOUDSPEAKER. Doors closing. Mind the doors. Next stop is . . .

We hear the doors closing. The train slowly starts up and rattles away into the tunnel. The darkness lifts. Those waiting for the train have disappeared. Those alighting the train hurry towards the escalator. EMMA is standing on the platform, holding the mirror tightly. She is alone except for the homeless propped against the wall, seemingly silent and lifeless.

The echoing sound of footsteps are heard – the DRUNKEN MAN arrives. Slowly he passes by behind EMMA. Walks back and stops by the wall, watching EMMA.

Silence.

*In the background, a new born baby cries, wailing hopelessly –
then she falls silent, her gurgles echoing, disturbing the quiet.*

EMMA *puts the mirror down noisily onto the floor. She shivers.
Somebody by the wall makes a move.* EMMA *turns round.*

OLD WOMAN. Woman, I hear you are summoned
To make account of yourself before
Our Messiah, the king of Jerusalem,
And would like for us to journey together.

EMMA. That is why I've come. My sorry tale to tell,
And to pray you'll come with me.

OLD WOMAN. I would gladly come, but I cannot even stand.

EMMA. Why, has something fallen on your feet?

OLD WOMAN. Yes, madam, I have you to thank for that.

*She points to the papers that are lying about her feet. They
resemble those from* EMMA'*s office.*

Look, the books of your dark deeds
See how they lie like chains at my feet,
Just as they hang heavy on your soul.

EMMA. Lord Jesus help me!
For one bad deed I am damned.

OLD WOMAN. There is a harsh reckoning in time of distress.

EMMA. Good Deeds, I beg of you to help me
Or else I am damned forever.

OLD WOMAN. I lie here, cold on the ground,
Your sins hath me bound so tight,
I cannot move.

EMMA. Good deeds, I am so frightened,
I pray, advise me.

OLD WOMAN. That I will do;
Though I am unable to go with you,
I have a brother who will,
Knowledge is his name,
He will stay by your side.

DOCTOR (*struggles to his feet – he has been sitting on his suitcase.
He looks shabby and unshaven.*)

Woman, I will go with you,
I will be your guide.

EMMA. Thanks be to God.

DOCTOR. Now let us go together
To that cleansing river, confession.

EMMA. I could weep with joy, oh, that we were there!
    But, I pray you, tell me
    Where dwells this holy man, Confession.

    The DOCTOR *leads* EMMA *to the rear – a* POLICEMAN *enters from the darkness.*

DOCTOR. Here is Confession. Kneel down and ask mercy,
    For he is on good terms with Almighty God.

POLICEMAN. Woman, I know your sorrow well.
    Because with Knowledge you come to me,
    I will comfort you as best I can (*He takes his rubber truncheon off.*)
    And a precious jewel I will give you:
    With it I will chastise you,
    Harsh penance you'll endure
    To remember your Saviour who also bore for you
    The sharpest thorns and scourges without complaint.

    He prods EMMA's *stomach with the rubber truncheon – as if marking it. As* EMMA *doubles up, the* POLICEMAN *disappears.*

EMMA (*clutching her stomach tightly, she whispers*).
    O eternal God, O heavenly figure,
    O way of righteousness, O goodly vision,
    Who was born to a virgin pure
    So he could redeem us all,
    Who Adam condemned by his disobedience,
    O treasured spirit, elect and high divine,
    Mirror of joy, and fountain of mercy,
    Who illuminates Heaven and Earth,
    Though much belated, hear my pleas:
    I am a dreadful sinner
    Lord, as penance, scourge me!
    My flesh for its sins must pay dear.
    So, body, take that!
    You revelled and scorned a better way
    And brought me to the path of damnation
    So now there is a punishment to be felt.

OLD WOMAN (*stands up unsteadily*).
    Your faith restored, I can walk again.
    On two bad feet I will follow,
    Woman I will go with you,
    All your good work I will help to proclaim.

EMMA. My heart is light,
    As it shall be evermore,
    Now will I strike faster than before.

OLD WOMAN. Woman, pilgrim, dear friend,
    Be blessed without end.

EMMA. Now I hear your voice,
    Welcome all good deeds.
    I cry with the sweetness of love.

OLD WOMAN. Be no more sad, but evermore rejoice,
    From his throne above God sees your life.
    Before you meet your judge
    Put on this garment, it will help you
    It is wet with your tears.

    The OLD WOMAN *lifts the purple dress that* EMMA *had tried on in* MARI's *store.*

EMMA. What is it called?

OLD WOMAN. It is a garment of sorrow,
    A garment of remorse,
    It can bring you forgiveness.
    It pleases the Lord to see it worn.

DOCTOR. Woman, wear it to heal yourself.

EMMA (*puts it on*). Then, let's go without delay.
    Will my sins be paid for?

DOCTOR. Yea, indeed, I have it here (*He lifts his suitcase.*)

EMMA. Then I trust we need not fear.

BOY WITH BAD COUGH (*struggles onto his feet from among the
        homeless*). I, Strength, tho' weakened
    Will stand by you
    Until your long voyage is done.

DRUNK (*steps away from the wall*). And I, discretion, will
        accompany you,
    No matter how hard the pilgrimage!

GIRL WITH BABY. And we, beauty and love,
    We too will stand by you.

BOY. Then we will all go together.

GIRL WITH BABY. Believe me, we mean to help and comfort.

EMMA. Sadly, I am so weak I can hardly stand,
    My legs are folding under me.
    My friends, I can go no further;
    Not for all the gold in the world.
    Into this cave I must crawl,
    Turn to earth and finally sleep.

GIRL WITH SMALL BABY. Into this dark grave? No!

EMMA. Yes, and there must we hence abide.

GIRL WITH SMALL BABY. What, must I be now hidden from
        the world?

EMMA. Yes, by my faith, I fear
 You'll never more appear.

LOUDSPEAKER. Stand clear! Mind the gap!

The GIRL *lies back down by the wall.*

EMMA. Beauty quickly slips away from me,
 Tho' she promised to stay 'til the journey was over.

BOY WITH A BAD COUGH. Woman, I too must leave.

EMMA. But you said you'd stay.

BOY. I have brought you this far enough.
 You are old enough,
 To undertake your pilgrimage alone. (*He lies back, coughing.*)
 Go, be buried if you will.

DRUNK. And I must go as well.

EMMA. Look, for pity's sake,
 This is my grave.

 EMMA *leans forward and takes a look into the grave.*

LOUDSPEAKER. Stand clear! Mind the gap!

 By the time EMMA *turns back, the* DRUNKEN MAN *has
 disappeared too . . .*

EMMA. O, Jesus, Help! They've forsaken me.

OLD WOMAN. No, Woman, I will stay with you.

EMMA. And Knowledge, will you abandon me also?

DOCTOR. Yes. when you go to God.
 But not 'til then.
 I will not leave
 Until I see what you become.

LOUDSPEAKER. Mind the gap! Stand clear! (*Shouting.*) Somebody!
 Grab her! Take her away!!!

EMMA (*steps closer to the edge*). I think I must be going,
 Remember this, all you who see and hear it.

OLD WOMAN. All earthly things are but vanity:
 Beauty, Strength, and truth all forsake us,
 Family, wise and foolish friends,
 All flee save your Good Deeds,
 And that is who I am.

EMMA. Lord have mercy on me!

 *A humming noise in the distance. The wind begins to rise once
 more.* EMMA *takes a last step towards the edge of the platform
 gripping the mirror tightly to her.*

LOUDSPEAKER. Leave the safety zone free! (*Crying out.*) Madam, step back, for God's sake, please get back. Get back!!!

A rumbling sound. The wind is tearing at EMMA's skirt and hair. Once again, bright headlights appear from the side. The loudspeaker cries its warning at full volume. DEATH rises up from below and stretches out his boney arms to EMMA. EMMA closes her eyes, and wearily leans forward. Darkness – the train's brakes screech. A shattering noise as the mirror breaks into a thousand pieces.

Long silence. Black.

The sound of a match being struck.

EMMA *lights a candle on an iron candlestick.*

On the now empty stage people stand motionless in their coats – ARANKA, PETER, TODOR, VERA, ERIKA, MARI, MRS KOVESI, MR KOVESI and the OTHERS – everybody from the play. Beside the candlestick there is a long table – we recognise it from the estate agency – EMMA sits on it, searching through her pockets. She takes a packet of cigarettes out, takes her last cigarette, crushes the empty packet and throws it away.

EMMA. Mum, this really is the very last one . . . O.K.? Can you bear it just this once? (*Lights up the cigarette with the candle and inhales deeply.*)

ARANKA doesn't say anything. She seems to be tolerating it for once – she is strangely small now – a little OLD WOMAN, supported by TODOR on one side and PETER on the other. Silence. EMMA is sitting on the table, watching them as she smokes her last cigarette.

TOTH (*entering*). Excuse me, can I have a light, please?

EMMA. 'Course you can. (*She points to the candlestick.*)

TOTH goes to the candlestick and proceeds to light one up.

(*Staring at him.*) You . . . !?

GYULA holds his head sadly.

EMMA. But – how? So unexpectedly!

TOTH. Oh, I was expecting it . . .

EMMA. For how long?

TOTH. Actually, since the day I was born.

EMMA. Well, it's different then. If you were expecting it . . . But who knows? Is it ever easy? The main thing is that we are over the most difficult part, aren't we?

TOTH. Do you think so? (*His brow is furrowed in doubt.*)

EMMA (*with concern*). How do you think you will fare? Do you think you have much to answer for?

TOTH. You know how it is . . . All your life you're careful, then when you least expect it, a banana skin.

EMMA (*nods her head*). A woman?

TOTH. Best not go into that . . .

EMMA. But you cleared her blockage?

TOTH. In the end . . .

EMMA. Would it have given her a lot of trouble?

TOTH. No, I just wish she could have had . . . (*He looks down at himself.*) . . . agh . . .

EMMA (*realises*). Never mind. How much do I owe you?

TOTH. Forget it . . .

EMMA. Thanks a lot.

TOTH. Oh, it's nothing . . .

EMMA. No, nothing goes unaccounted for . . . (*Pointing up at the sky.*)

With the candle in his hand, GYULA *exits groaning.*

Where are you going? (*Looks over to the other mortuary.*) Are those your relatives? What a fine looking old lady. And such a lovely dog!

Barking outside.

TOTH (*off*). Prince, shut up . . .

EMMA (*taking a deep breath*). Prince . . . (*Looking at the faces:* ARANKA, PETER, MARI, VERA *and all the* OTHERS.) Imagine having a dog to pine for you . . . Mum, why did I never have a little dog?

Silence.

(*To* MARI.) Why are you griselling? Pull yourself together!

But MARI *is not sniffling any more – she's wailing loudly. The crowd itself murmurs, then falls into silence . . .* EMMA *watches them. Something is not right. Somehow the whole thing is unsettling. Even her cigarette doesn't please her any longer. She throws it away . . .* VERA *and* ERIKA *are standing holding on to each other.* VERA *looks startled staring into the candlelight. Biting her nails, she leans to* ERIKA's *ear and whispers in it.* ERIKA *nods her head . . .*

What did you say? What did you say?

Silence.

I don't understand. Why do you all look so anxious? I've settled everything, haven't I? There's nothing left to worry about . . . Or did I forget something? . . . What then? . . . The washing machine, cemetery, dry-cleaning, Vera. I washed the door-frame. And what's more we even sorted Vera's blockage before we went . . . O.K., I broke the Venetian mirror. So is that the problem? Well, if it is, it's a pity. Very sad . . . But . . . And look, Peter, remember you have to go and find a property agency, you know . . .

Silence.

Mother . . . what's the matter? Sorry? Are you angry with me for something?

ARANKA, *her eyes half-closed, leans forward, breathing heavily.* PETER *and* TODOR *are supporting her* . . .

You said, you didn't need chicken, or turkey, or salami, that you have your poker and pulses . . . and now, she's angry! Mother! What's the matter? Look, I've settled everything, don't annoy me, O.K . . . Look, I've had a hard day, and now I'm tired.

She takes a black drape out of the table drawer, opens it, and covers the table with it. Then she throws a little embroidered black pillow to one end of the table. With the habitual movements of someone late at night, dead tired, she prepares for bed. She bends down, groaning, undoes her shoe-laces, takes her shoes off, and puts them at the end of the bier. Then she lies back on it and closes her eyes.

The end.